Edinburgh

P9-AEY-035

Top The Forth rail and road bridges, **centre** Canongate Tolbooth, **below** St Mary's Cathedral.

Edinburgh

The complete guide to Scotland's capital city

MERCAT
PRESS

Copyright © 1987 by
James Thin Ltd.

All rights reserved. No part of this publication may be reproduced, stored in a retrieval system,
or transmitted, in any form or by any means, electronic, mechanical, photocopying,
recording or otherwise, without prior written permission of the publisher.

First published 1981 — Revised edition 1987
ISBN 0901824 887

Published by
The Mercat Press
53-59 South Bridge
Edinburgh

MERCAT PRESS

Acknowledgements

Authors
Myrtle Ashmole
Francis Bamford
Geoffrey Baskerville
Alice Beberman
Robin Bell
Joana Blythman
Patricia Brindle
Andrew Brown
Ann Charlish
Jane Collins
Patrick Conyngham
Ank Crees
George Dalgleish
Andrew Dalmayer
Danuta Doroszenko
Allan Edwards
Richard Emerson
Dr. R. A. Fawcett
Gilly Gaskell
John Gifford
Gilly Glass
Veronica Gordon-Smith
Rory Knight-Bruce
Gordon Knott
Carolyn McAdam

Brian McAbe
Sheena McDonald
Janet McEwan
Ann McKim
Bill McLean
Julia Merrick
Glen Murray
Norman Orr
Alice Rugheimer
Ann Simpson
Anne Simpson
Betty Smith
Gill Summers
Kim Tweedie
Hilary Whyte
Andrew Williams
Conrad Wilson
Editors
Liv O'Hanlon
Hope Cohen
Ronald Thompson
Marilyn Bowering
Cartography
Cartografics (Edin) Ltd.
Illustrators
Richard Blakely

Marilyn Bruce
Terry Burton
Bob Chapman
Chris Forsey
Sheila Hadley
Elaine Keenan
Edwina Keene
Sally Launder
Brian Sayers
Rosalind Taylor
Lorna Turpin
David Weeks
Photographers
Trevor Wood
John Wyand
Picture Research
Judy Garlick
Liz Ogilvy
Design Assistants
Andrew Fenton
Simon Borrough
Paul O'Connor

The publishers would like to express sincere thanks to the following for their help with the compilation of this book:

British Tourist Authority, Dawson International, Edinburgh City Libraries (the Edinburgh Room), Herbert Coutts, Edinburgh City Museums, Edinburgh District Council, Edinburgh Zoological Park, Faculty of Advocates, The Glenlivet Distillers Ltd., The Marquis and Marchioness of Linlithgow, Lothian Regional Council, Department of Recreation and Leisure, Mrs Patricia and Miss Jean Maxwell-Scott, Mr and Mrs Peter Maxwell-Stuart, The National Museum of Antiquities, Trustees of the National Gallery of Scotland, National Library of Scotland, National Trust of Scotland, The Earl and Countess of Rosebery, Douglas Henderson, Regius Keeper the Royal Botanic Garden, Royal College of Surgeons, Royal Scottish Museum, Scottish Development Department for Ancient Monuments, Scottish Tourist Board.

Contents

Introduction

THE STORY OF EDINBURGH

SEEING EDINBURGH

SOME USEFUL INFORMATION, ADDRESSES, AND CITY MAPS

Introduction

*S*cotland's capital is one of the most
rewarding cities in the world. This guide book is purpose-
planned to enable every reader
to get the most out of everything Edinburgh has to offer.
Not only is Edinburgh
one of the most historic cities of Europe;
it is also one of the most attractive, with architectural
glories, such as the New Town
and Holyroodhouse, vying with treasures of the national
heritage, such as the vast art collections
of the Scottish National Gallery and the other great
museums of the city.
Edinburgh, however, is much more than even this.
Its Festival is world-famous. In addition, there is no city sprawl.
Within a few minutes' walk of the city centre
can be found the small village communities, oases
of quiet calm that have
existed in Edinburgh for many centuries.
This volume is *the* ultimate handbook to all this and to
much more. Not only does it include
an authoritative guide to all the city's major places
of interest, lavishly illustrated with hundreds
of specially commissioned colour photographs and drawings;
it also covers such important areas as
shopping, history, literature, folklore, statues and
momuments and stately homes.
The book also has a list of useful addresses
and a 20 page section of maps.
The Edinburgh handbook is an essential reference whether
you are
a visitor to Edinburgh or live in the city.

The Story of Edinburgh

A town born in trouble and beset by rebellion that has blossomed in maturity to become one of the most distinguished cities in the world

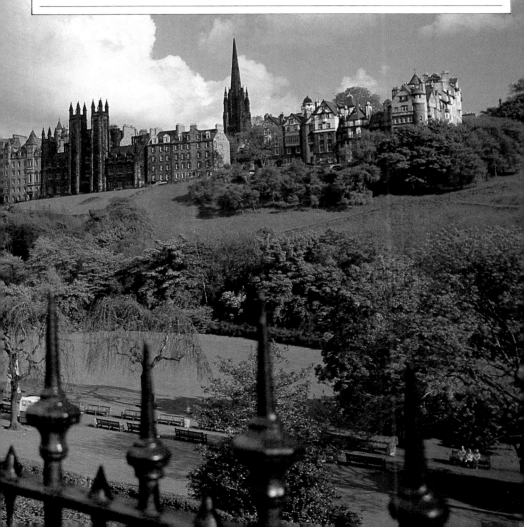

*E*dinburgh, like Rome, is built on seven hills. But, in the words of Robert Louis Stevenson, 'Edinburgh pays cruelly for her high seat in one of the vilest climates under heaven. She is liable to be beaten upon by all the winds that blow, to be drenched with rain, to be buried in cold sea fogs out of the east, and powdered with the snow as it comes flying southward from the Highland hills. The weather is raw and boisterous in winter, shifty and ungenial in summer, and a downright meteorological purgatory in the spring.'

In this turbulent climate the city's history, too, has been tumultuous. It has been the site of endless warring and argument, fighting and rebellion. But now, after centuries of history – and prehistory – the city stands as one of the most ordered and classically beautiful in Europe.

The fighting began thousands of years ago. The first people to arrive were the stone-using hunters, about 5000 years ago. They were followed by primitive farmers 2000 years later and immigrant Beaker people who brought pottery and metal-working skills from the continent.

The Celts started arriving, too, driven north by successive invasions of England by tribes from lowland Europe, and they caused more warring and battling with the natives. The long brawl of Scottish history had begun.

The Romans came north in AD 78 and defeated Calgacus 'the Swordsman', who, according to Tacitus, said, 'They made a desert, and they called it peace.' When the Romans left, in the second century, the people were faced with ceaseless invasions. There came Angles, Britons, Vikings and eventually the Scots from Western Ireland – after whom the country takes its name.

The Scots finally took possession of the Castle Rock in Edinburgh when the Northumbrians abandoned their northern border town. In 1018 Malcolm II managed to push the boundary further south and Edinburgh ceased to be a frontier stronghold.

Ironically the Southerners – or a few of them anyway – were welcomed back 50 years later after the Norman invasion of England in 1066. Among the refugees who went to the court of Malcolm III (Canmore) was Margaret, sister of Edgar Atheling, King-elect of England after Harold's death at Hastings.

Margaret and Malcolm married and produced six sons, four of whom in time were kings.

In the meantime Margaret spread her sophisticated Saxon culture and her profound religious thinking among her new people. She lived periodically at Castle Rock and died there. On the rock was built the small Norman chapel in her memory that is Edinburgh's oldest chapel and the oldest ecclesiastical building in use in Scotland.

David I founded the Abbey of Holyrood in 1128. Legend has it that after a miracle prevented his being killed by a stag, the wounded David heard voices telling him to found a house of canons devoted to the Cross. So the abbey was built – by 20 skilled men summoned from France.

In the foundation charter for the abbey, King David refers to 'my town' which suggests that Edwinesburgh was at least from that time regarded as a royal burgh. But, at least 600 years before, the town had been known as Dun Edin, hillfort of Edin.

Along with the abbey the Augustinian canons were given the right to build a burgh (later the Canongate) between the abbey and the royal burgh. Thus the future city began to grow. The burghers or 'burgesses' of this new village were given privileges to sell their wares and buy freely in the Edinburgh market.

David began establishing Anglo-Norman families in Scotland and over the next century they married into the Scottish nobility. Some, like Robert the Bruce (the elder), acquired, along with the earldoms, claims to the throne in these unions of families. The upshot was that by 1286 Scotland was under the rule of a succession of regents as there was total confusion about who was the rightful heir to the Scottish throne.

Edward I was asked to arbitrate for the regents who could come to no decision. It was a chance that the land-hungry Edward had been waiting for. He chose a puppet monarch, John Balliol, whose claim to the throne was through his mother Devorguilla, the foundress of Balliol College, Oxford, in 1250.

Balliol was summoned to Edward's court where he was told to supply money and men for the King's French war but the Scots would have none of it. Four Scottish bishops, four earls and four barons formed a council and in October 1295 concluded the first formal treaty with the French. The alliance was a constant feature of Scottish history over the next 500 years – so much so that it became known as the 'Auld Alliance'.

Edward was furious and in 1296 sent north an invading army who put the leaderless Scots to the sword, deposed Balliol and looted the Castle. The Stone of Destiny on which Scottish monarchs were traditionally crowned was removed to London from Scone. It forms part of the coronation chair in Westminster Abbey, on which monarchs are crowned today. For his ferocity, Edward earned the title 'the Hammer of the Scots'.

The fighting of these continuing wars of independence with the English came to a pause in 1314 when Robert the Bruce succeeded in defeating the English at Bannockburn. But the English returned to Scotland in 1322, under Edward II, and sacked Holyrood Abbey. Bruce prevailed and in 1329 gave his principal city its first recorded charter.

The charter gave the burgh and the Port of Leith (for 52 marks, about £34, a year) to the burgesses and recognition to the huddle of rough buildings sheltering by the castle.

After the death of Bruce, Edinburgh was once again in trouble. Edward III plundered the town and King Edward Balliol (who had no real claim to the throne) was forced to surrender his crown and in 1334 gave land in the southern counties to the English Crown.

The Scots were in despair and sent their boy king, David II, to France where he stayed until 1341. He was able to return only when Edward's attention was centred on the French throne and the Hundred Years' War between England and France.

Scotland, impoverished by war and disorder, needed peace and good government. David II gave neither. In fact he brought more war with the English and ended up lodged in the Tower of London. He was liberated by the promise to pay a 100,000 marks ransom to the English.

He returned to Scotland in 1357 and found the country wasted by constant war and the Black Death. There followed an uneasy truce with England and experiments in taxation which gave the burghs of Scotland more power. Edinburgh's port at Leith developed and the burgesses shook off the direct control of the financial officers of the Crown. The town, at last, began to prosper.

Records show that in 1376 the population of Edinburgh was about 2000 with 400 houses. The inhabitants must have been a hardy bunch, well used to adversity Richard II wrought more havoc in the city in 1385, and Henry IV laid siege in 1400.

In 1424, James I landed at Leith with his Queen and succeeded to the Scottish throne after 19 years as captive of the English.

The couple received a welcome and as they rode through the town James must have noted the tremendous changes. The houses of the Royal Mile were rising higher. Timber was giving way to stone and thatch was being replaced by sturdier roofing. But thatch had had its advantages. During the endless firings of the town by the English, the Edinburgh townsfolk would load all their goods and chattels on wagons and 'take to the heather' – and they took their highly inflammable roofing with them.

James I made Scotland a place fit to live in again. His legislation was aimed at keeping 'firm and sure peace' throughout the country and building a firm foundation for the economy. He also instituted a system for 'a poor man's advocate whose services went to 'any poor creature who could not pay for his own defence'.

But James was not without enemies and in 1437 two of his lords, eager to put the Earl of Atholl on the throne, had him stabbed to death at Perth, where he was spending Christmas.

James II became King of the Scots at the age of six. He had been smuggled from the Castle in 1438 in his mother's trunk and it was he who, some years later, gave a charter for a city wall starting below the northeastern rock of the Castle. The King also ordered that his pleasure garden should be swept away to create the Nor' Loch directly below the Castle as a defence.

But he too was killed – by one of his own cannon bursting at a siege of Roxburgh Castle near Kelso in 1460. He was followed by James III who fell foul of his power-grasping lords and was murdered in 1488.

James III had, though, in 1482, rewarded the loyalty of the Edinburgh burgesses by granting the provost and bailies (magistrates) important privileges including the almost complete control over the dispensing of justice – an independence they maintained until the Union of Parliaments in 1707.

At the beginning of the fifteenth century the King, his court, and courts of justice were itinerant. But by 1483 Edinburgh was the undisputed capital of Scotland: it was the permanent seat of government, and had the principal Royal residence – Holyrood – the central administration and the law courts.

Peace, prosperity and a new enlightenment reigned with James IV. 'There is as great a difference between the Scotland of the old time and the Scotland of today as there is between good and bad,' wrote a Spanish diplomat in 1498.

The King had an intelligent and questing mind. He was a patron of the arts and a great promoter of learning: he granted in 1506 a royal charter to the college of surgeons in Edinburgh and founded, among other institutions, the nation's third university at Aberdeen. He also granted a charter to two burgesses of Edinburgh, Andrew Myllar and Walter Chapman, to set up the first Scottish printing press for the purpose of producing books of laws, Acts of Parliament, chronicles, and Mass books 'after our Scottish use'.

This era of renaissance and chivalry – when jousting tourneys were held at the King's Stables area, west of the Grassmarket – came to an end with the tragedy of Flodden.

James had left his Queen and baby to lead his army against the English at Flodden Field in September 1513. The Scottish army was annihilated on the nation's blackest day and many Edinburgh men, including all the bailies, died with their King. When news reached the town lamentation was mingled with fear of immediate invasion by the English.

A town guard was formed and a new wall speedily thrown up, within which plague soon spread through the streets. Not for the next 250 years did the citizens dare build outside this Flodden Wall in case of invasion. Instead they built upwards, as the population increased, storey upon storey to a height of eight or ten floors – unmatched elsewhere in Europe.

James's body was found on the field at Flodden and taken to London where Henry VIII designed a splendid funeral. It did not take place. The royal corpse lay in its lead at Sheen until the house was ruined after the Reformation. Eventually the embalmed head was hacked off by Queen Elizabeth I's master-glazier who used it as a sort of pot until he tired of it!

James's infant son of 13 months became King James V and yet another bloody power struggle between the leading nobles ensued for control of the kingdom. The fight between English and French interests ended with a coup d'état, led by the Earl of Angus, which put James in nominal control at the age of 14.

The King grew to be greedy and brutal and succeeded in making himself the most disliked of the Stuart kings of Scotland.

It was during his reign that the first voices spoke out against Roman Catholicism.

The Roman Church had reigned supreme from the time of Malcolm II until 1559 when, a little behind the rest of Europe, Scotland was overturned by the Reformation. And as in the Reformations elsewhere it was more than a change in the Church system – it was also a political and economic revolt.

The Church in Scotland during the fifteenth and early sixteenth centuries had enormous political influence. It was far richer than the state – the revenue was 15 times that of the Crown – and the taxes it demanded of each commoner nurtured bitterness among the people.

Bishoprics were allocated by favouritism; bastardy, in a church that supposedly practised celibacy, was common among all ranks of the

Language

The speech of Edinburgh reflects the city's history as vividly as does its architecture. The stylized Morningside accent can be traced back precisely to 1761, when a group of citizens eager to ditch their Scottish accents engaged as their elocution teacher Thomas Sheridan, father of the playwright-actor and Irishman.

This would not have happened in Glasgow which never shared Edinburgh's Anglophilia or literary aspirations. The everyday speech of the rival cities, only a 45-minute train ride apart, differs widely. A naked child in Edinburgh is 'a bairn in his bare buff' and in Glasgow 'a wean in his bare scuddie'. Truant children in Edinburgh 'plunk or kip school' and in Glasgow they 'dog the school'.

The Scottish language, still in use, is mainly based on an Anglo-Saxon dialect and supplanted the historic language of Gaelic, still spoken in the highlands and islands. Scots was the national language until the Union of the Parliaments in 1707 and has been revived in literature over the past 60 years.

Naturally many common words were carried over from Gaelic, including *loch, glen, bog, cairn and caber,* as in 'tossing the caber'. But other words as distinctively Scottish as these are corruptions of continental languages introduced by settlers or traders. The famous Edinburgh cry to warn passers-by that rubbish and slops are about to fall on them from tenement windows above is 'gardyloo' from the eighteenth-century French, 'gare de l'eau', look out for water. The Auld Alliance between Scotland and France, lasting from 1295 until the Reformation, and the presence of numerous Norman settlers accounts for many Scots words of French origin – tartan from *tiretaine,* petticoat tails from *petit gateau* and Hogmanay from *aguillaneuf.*

Viking settlers bequeathed Norse words: *flit,* (move), as in 'moonlicht flit'; *lug,* (ear), as in 'lug-hole'; and the various 'k'-ending words, *kirk* for church, and *dike* for ditch.

In its turn the Scots language has given many words to the English-speaking world, including blackmail, canny, uncanny, cosy, eerie, flunkey, fogie, heckle, pony, and spate.

Scottish languages and dialects have survived four centuries of erosion by the English - erosion which can be traced back to the introduction of the English bible in the 1500s. In Edinburgh literary figures faced a particular dilemma: how to preserve their heritage and excel as Britons. The philosopher David Hume and novelist Robert Louis Stevenson solved it by speaking Scots but writing English and Walter Scott combined dialect and Standard English.

Today, when English with very rolled r's and a generous sprinkling of Scotticisms is the norm, visitors to Edinburgh often still find that written communication with the Scots is easier than the verbal variety.

priesthood; and priests failed in their pastoral duties.

The records of the Edinburgh Town Council in 1501 show that the civil bailies had to take legal action against the prebendaries of St. Giles to force them to say masses.

Pockets of reform, however, were emerging and found support among the less corrupt clergy and the nobility and merchant classes who controlled the council. The time was ripe for revolution.

Had the next monarch, Mary, been more far-sighted perhaps some of the ferocity of the coming years would have been avoided.

Mary, Queen of Scots, was proclaimed Queen as a seven-day-old child on the death of her father James V in 1542. Two years later Edinburgh was laid waste by Henry VIII's army, the houses put to fire and the countryside for seven miles around was ravaged – Holyrood Palace, the castles of Craigmillar and Rosslyn, the town of Leith and its pier, all were destroyed – simply because the Scots revoked an earlier agreement that Henry's son should be married to the young Queen. It was the beginning of Henry's 'rough wooing'.

The Queen's mother, Mary of Guise-Lorraine, appealed to her native France for help which came. But in return the Scots had to send their little Queen to Paris where she was bethrothed, and later married, to the Dauphin. The English, knowing they were outmanoeuvred, left Scotland.

With the English gone, the French stayed on to protect Catholic interests, but all that they achieved was the antagonism of the many Scots who already supported the new doctrines of Calvin and the reformed Church.

The new religious movement was also allowed its leader back – a tactical mistake on the part of Mary of Guise who had been made Regent in 1554. He was John Knox who had fled Scotland in 1547. The teachings of George Wishart had formed the basis for Knox's views on religion and politics. Wishart had set out the first principles of the reformed faith in his writings, stating that the only sources of truth were the Holy Scriptures; that the Pope's role was invalid; and that there were only two sacraments – Baptism and Holy Communion. He was burnt at the stake for heresy.

Knox spent most of his exile in Geneva at the church of John Calvin which Knox described as 'the most perfect school of Christ that ever was on earth since the days of the Apostles'.

The news of his return to Edinburgh on May 2, 1559, spread like wild fire through the streets: 'John Knox is come, John Knox is come' was the message and soon, by way of merchants, travellers, fishermen and shepherds, much of the country knew it too.

John Knox

Knox's powers of oratory stirred first of all the crowds in Perth to violent action – they sacked the town's monasteries, pillaged, burned and looted every friary in the city. Mary of Guise sent her troops into action but underestimated the support the new Church had. She was forced to retire.

Knox and his followers moved on to St. Andrews where Knox preached – lambasting the Church of Rome as the 'synagogue of Satan'; the Pope as that 'man of sin of whom the Apostle speaks'; the Virgin Mary as 'that Roman harlot'; and said the Roman Church was 'polluted with all kinds of spiritual fornication'. Once more the incited crowds ransacked all the religious establishments, burning 'idols' and sharing out the spoils of the friaries.

At the end of June they marched to Edinburgh and the Queen Regent retired to Dunbar. On July 1, 1559, Knox preached his first sermon from the pulpit of St. Giles. It seemed as if, in the space of two months, the Reformation had been achieved, but it was in fact only the start of a battle that continued for 130 years from the establishment of the reformed Church. Knox never witnessed a secure Kirk.

In 1559 a Protestant league known as the Lords of the Congregation turned to the new Queen in England, Elizabeth I, for help in their armed struggle against Mary of Guise. The French, who had heavily fortified Leith, were besieged. Mary, who had left Holyrood and had a sumptuous mansion at Leith, tried to arrange a truce but died of dropsy in June 1560 before it was achieved. The following month, in the Treaty of Edinburgh, it was agreed that all French troops should leave Scotland.

Shortly afterwards the city's council ordered that the Leith fortifications which faced Edinburgh should be demolished 'in caiss strangearis sall at ony time hereafter intruse thameselfs thairin'.

At a meeting in August, Parliament rejected the supremacy of the Pope. / Continued on page 18

Folklore

Headless phantoms, body snatchers, witches...and a faithful terrier

Edinburgh is a city of ghosts and goblins, horrors and hauntings, with a blood-steeped folklore handed down through the centuries and undoubtedly often embellished in the taverns of the town. There are tales of phantom squadrons of soldiers, a sword-wielding White Lady, a death coach drawn by headless horses, an evil major who rises from the grave, and a 'Street of Sorrow' where the spirits of plague victims roam in anguish.

In a chronicle laden with terror, witchcraft and bloodlust, one of the few folk characters remembered with fondness is Greyfriars Bobby, a Skye terrier who kept a 14-year vigil by his master's grave. He belonged to a shepherd named Jock Gray who died in 1858, and from then until his own death in 1872 Bobby maintained virtual freedom of the city in 1867. As recently as 1981 a new memorial was erected to Greyfriars Bobby and a pop song was written about him.

But villainy and nightmarish events predominate in Edinburgh folklore, none less than the story of Major Thomas Weir, Captain of the Town Guard and among the most respected of preachers. In a city-shaking scandal, the major suddenly confessed publicly in 1670 that he had dedicated much of his life to fornication, bestiality and incest with his sister. Outrage succeeded disbelief among his followers, and Weir and his sister were burned at the stake for making a compact with the devil. Long after his death the major was said to ride furiously

Right Body-snatchers Hare and Burke.
Below right William Burke's execution.
Below Deacon Brodie – the original Jekyll and Hyde.

through Leith – the district of his death – on a black horse and then vanish in a burst of flames while lights blazed miraculously in his empty house. Another character with two lives was Deacon Brodie, a city councillor and thriving businessman thought to be the inspiration of Robert Louis Stevenson's famous novel *Dr. Jekyll and Mr. Hyde*. His fortune dissipated by gambling, the Deacon went in for a night-time career of burglary and mayhem which led him to the hangman at the Tolbooth on October 1, 1788, watched by 40,000 people. His moaning apparition is said to linger at the site of the gallows, which he mounted three times before the gibbet worked.

The visitor who might happen to hear midnight drums and the tramping of feet on the Castle Esplanade can take some comfort from the fact that a ghostly squadron of troops has been on the move there since the days of Oliver Cromwell.

The mystery column was first seen in 1650, according to legend, by sentries guarding the Castle against a threatened attack by Cromwell's army. Ancient documents also record that in the same area a 'death coach' pulled by fire-flashing steeds races headlong from Holyrood to the Castle to warn of impending disaster.

The White Lady of Corstophine was Christian Nimmo, the wife of a prosperous merchant, who used to meet her lover under a sycamore tree and finally killed him with a sword for being drunk. She was beheaded in 1679, but the story goes that she still appears near the sycamore, wearing a stark white robe and carrying a bloody sword. The Street of Sorrow is Mary King's Close, whose residents were totally wiped out in the bubonic plague of 1645. The street, reputed to be the haunt of headless phantoms, still survives below ground. It can be seen from

Cockburn Street, its entrance barred by a gate.

Stories of witchcraft abound in the lore of Edinburgh, where hundreds of women were burned at Castle Hill during a Scottish national frenzy that took 17,000 lives between the years 1479 and 1722. Most were tortured and put to death for allegedly possessing magical powers, including in one instance the supposed ability to sink a royal ship.

But inevitably to the forefront of Edinburgh truth-legend is the case of the body-snatchers William Burke and William Hare, Irish labourers who strangled at least 16 paupers in 1827 and sold the bodies to surgeons for medical research. Hare testified against his companion during a sensational trial and escaped the gallows, but Burke was hanged on January 28, 1829. The story still grips the imagination of Edinburgh people more than the city's most supernatural tales.

Below The grave of Bobby's master 'Auld Jock' is in Greyfriars Churchyard **Left**. **Above** Nearby is the pub named after Bobby.

The Church

Centuries of bitter struggle established Scotland's spiritual capital

The hundreds of church buildings in Edinburgh give the visitor an immediate impression of a city in which religion has played a vital role – a role which at various times has brought both turbulence and reassurance.

From the year AD 563, when St. Columba established his monastery on the small island of Iona, Scotland was known as Christian, although it took three centuries to convert the native tribes. By the middle of the ninth century Scotland was ruled by a Roman Catholic monarchy, and it remained a

violence. The medieval cathedrals, abbeys and parish churches were taken over for Protestant worship or allowed to fall into ruin.

Knox's dream was not only to create a reformed Church in Scotland, and banish 'popery' from her shores, but also to strengthen democracy and to set up a system of comprehensive education. But it was to take almost 130 years of bitter struggle to achieve the religious transition.

Between 1559 and 1689 various monarchs attempted to reestablish the Catholic Church,

but the seeds of reform had been deeply sown, and the Covenanters, as they came to be called, fought steadfastly and determinedly for Knox's principles.

James I and VI and his son Charles I sought to make Scotland's ministers bring their Church more in line with the English Church. In 1637 Charles I attempted to introduce Archbishop Laud's new Service Book, based on the English Book of Common Prayer. As soon as the Dean of Edinburgh began to read from it he was bombarded with folding

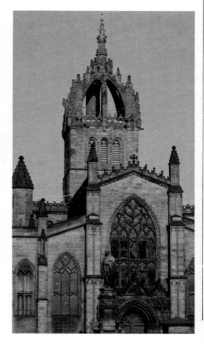

Catholic nation until the Reformation in 1559.

In sixteenth-century Scotland as in other countries, Church reform was urgently needed. Scotland forsook its traditional friendship with Catholic France, allied itself with England instead and accepted a Protestant Reformation. It was a radical reform but carried through without much

Right Central to the city's religious turmoil, St. Giles' Cathedral is over a thousand years old.

Above 1787, a meeting of the General Assembly.

stools, Bibles and anything else the congregation could lay hands on. Jenny Geddes, who made her living selling cabbages outside St. Giles, ensured herself a place in history by throwing the first stool and screaming 'Daur ye say mass in my lug!'

The heirs of Knox's reforms were determined that their religious freedom should not be jeopardized by a London monarch. In 1638 they gathered in the small churchyard of Greyfriars that was to become so closely associated with their fight and signed the National Covenant, swearing loyalty to the King but rejecting his rulings on the Church. And in 1643 the Solemn League and Covenant was signed, pledging its subscribers not only to preserve the reformed religion, but also to advance it in England and Ireland.

Meanwhile in England Cromwell deposed and executed Charles I and defeated the exhausted Scottish army. The Restoration of Charles II in 1660 again meant the reformed Church was threatened. It was not until the Dutch Calvinist William of Orange took the English throne in 1688 that Protestantism was assured of its survival. When in 1707 the two crowns were joined by the Act of Union, Scotland was granted its independent legal system, judicature and Church – the Church of Scotland.

But the Church was to suffer yet another blow to its confidence. At the 1843 meeting of the General Assembly nearly 500 ministers walked out to form the Free Church of Scotland, an action which became known as the Disruption.

In 1900 most of the Free Church and other Presbyterian groups joined to become the United Free Church and in 1929 the United Free Church reunited with the Church of Scotland, which had agreed to

Left Near the church where he so often preached is John Knox's House, reputed to be the oldest dwelling place in Edinburgh.

Above In the room where he died on November 24, 1572 is a stained-glass window of the fiery reformer.

abolish patronage by influential landowners. However, there was still a small minority who remained outside the union, commonly known as the 'Wee Frees'.

Catholicism had survived, however, chiefly in the northeast and the Highlands. The Relief Act of 1793 gave freedom to worship and own property, and Emancipation in 1829 res-

tored other rights. During the nineteenth century, great numbers of Irish settled in Scotland, so that now the Roman Catholic Church is strongest in the central belt, especially Clydeside.

But for the Reformed Churches, to which 80 percent of the people belong, Edinburgh has always remained the spiritual capital of the country.

The beautiful 18-year-old Catholic widow of the King of France, Mary, returned to Scotland in August 1561 to this civil and religious upheaval. She was given a tremendous welcome by the people while John Knox protested.

The sad catalogue of trouble with her nobles and her people; her confrontation with Knox and his followers on religion; her marriage to Darnley – by whom she bore James VI and I – and her husband's subsequent murder in an explosion at Kirk o' Field in 1567; her unpopular marriage to Bothwell (who was suspected of Darnley's murder) – were some of the ingredients in the period of turmoil that finally saw Mary imprisoned in Loch Leven Castle. She escaped to England, only to be imprisoned by her cousin Elizabeth, on whose orders she was beheaded.

After Mary's flight a group of nobles formed a coalition known as the Queen's Lords who resented the power of Regent Morton who ruled on behalf of the infant James. Civil war ensued: the governor of Edinburgh Castle, Sir William Kirkcaldy, allied himself with the Queen's men against the Regent. As a result the city suffered badly – the castle was under siege for five years.

It was finally defeated by the guns of the Earl of Morton. Five batteries of English guns opened simultaneously and the David Tower crashed down with men and guns to the rocks beneath, the debris choking the draw-wells of the Castle. Even so 13 hours of hand-to-hand fighting followed before Kirkcaldy surrendered the Castle and was hanged.

So, with the support of Elizabeth I of England, Morton had taken Edinburgh. But the Castle was destroyed and the city was thus undefended. Never knowing who might attack he had the Half Moon Battery built on the foundations of the ruined tower.

Morton was coerced into resignation in 1578 by a group of hostile nobles and James VI took the throne at the age of 17. But his mother, Mary, was still alive, although imprisoned.

The situation in Scotland was attracting international interest. Both Spain and France were uncertain whether to deal with Mary or James. Mary did not want to give up her part as champion of the Catholics but equally her staunchly Protestant son was the one with the power.

Fearing that France was deserting her she promised in 1580 to put herself and her son and the realm under the protection of the Spanish King Philip II – none of which endeared Mary to her English cousin who feared Mary's claim to the English throne. The result was that no one viewed Mary's death in 1587 with any great sorrow – apart from her diminishing band of Scots supporters.

James, well-educated and intelligent, very aware of his position, tried to bring peace to his nation by encouraging his feuding nobles to join forces. But he was also determined to cast himself in the Elizabethan mould and have power over Kirk as well as government.

He was soon in deep trouble with Knox's successor Andrew Melville who declared that there were two kingdoms in Scotland and that James was a subject of the realm of Christ.

The royal argument with the Kirk about power, political and religious, lasted until 1603 by which time James had determined to make the Scots Kirk conform more closely with the English pattern, with the monarch as head of the Church.

Despite his erudition and intelligence, James had a firm belief in sorcery and it is claimed that more witches were burned and strangled on Castle Hill than in any other area of Scotland.

The story of Elsie Peat, in 1589, was not an unusual one. She was an elderly woman who was often muttering to herself and so it was suspected that she was in league with the Devil and conversed with him. A 'dookin' was demanded.

It involved the suspected witch being thrown into Nor' Loch with her thumbs and toes tied. Her innocence would be assured if she sank and drowned but if she floated it would be proof that she was bedevilled. Poor Elsie's voluminous skirts filled with air and she floated – which gave the crowd the excuse they wanted to drag her to Castle Hill to her death.

*D*ucking in Nor' Loch was the punishment for fornication in these times. The tongues of perjurers were bored; drowning followed conviction for theft and when the Loch was drained in 1820 workmen found a large coffin containing the skeletons of a man and a woman, thought to be a brother and sister who were drowned in 1623 for incest.

Although punishments were hard on transgressors, measures were taken to help the poor. The problem of what to do with them came about with the dissolution of the monasteries which had provided alms and hospitals. The town council, carefully distinguishing between the 'deserving and the undeserving', issued badges to the former, authorizing them to beg, and banished the latter from the burgh.

James's capital also had the unsavoury distinction of being the filthiest city in Europe. The houses were crowded closely together round the Castle for protection and because of the terrain which restricted building on the eastern slope.

Streets were narrow, dunghills piled up and, as swine were kept by many householders in pens under the outside stairs, it was little wonder that the plague was rife.

George Heriot's School

And yet this century saw a new building for the twelfth-century high school and the foundation of the university in 1583; the Scottish Mint was moved from Holyrood and erected in the Cowgate; in lighter vein, James licensed comedians.

It also saw the rise of an Edinburgh goldsmith and friend to the King, George Heriot. He was symbolic of an age of building and of business. The war-torn capital was settling down and fear of invasion was a thing of the past. Foreign trade was increased enormously and goods coming into Edinburgh included fine woollens from England; luxury dress materials from France, Flanders and Italy; wine from Bordeaux and La Rochelle; fruit vegetables, spices and salt.

Heriot, meanwhile, was making his fortune too. He lent money to the impoverished King and his Danish Queen. 'Jingling Geordie', as he was called, was appointed goldsmith to the Queen in 1597.

When the childless Heriot died in 1612 he left his fortune to the municipality and clergy of Edinburgh to found and endow a hospital for the maintenance and education of fatherless boys and sons of freemen and burgesses in the town.

The school was started in 1628, completed in 1659, and is still one of the most striking buildings in the city, now the co-educational George Heriot's School. His example in founding the hospital for scholars was to be followed by many other prosperous citizens – notably George Watson, James Gillespie, William Fettes, Daniel Stewart, John Watson and Mary Erskine.

In 1603, a dramatic event changed the course of Scottish history. Elizabeth I of England died and James succeeded as her nearest heir. He took the road south and Scotland's capital lost its permanent royal presence and its court. He had promised to return every three years but involvements in England meant that he came back only once, in 1617. His departure meant loss of prosperity to many in the city.

There followed, however, a period of comparative peace until the ascension of Charles I in 1625. Charles celebrated his Scottish coronation in Holyrood in 1633, welcomed lavishly by the town council.

But the few following quiet years ended at a service in St. Giles after Charles, who had learned little about the Scots during his visit, had insisted on the use of the English Episcopal service book in the fiercely Presbyterian country.

On July 23, 1637, a crowded congregation in the cathedral – a title Charles had imposed which was to hold officially for only 50 years despite which it is still popularly called that – heard the new Dean of Edinburgh start to use the revised prayer book of the Anglican Church.

Uproar followed. And in the following year the National Covenant, calling on its supporters to renounce popery and resist all religious innovation, was drawn up and signed in Greyfriars Churchyard.

The city and the nation faced more civil war. In England Oliver Cromwell was stirring his forces to war. In 1642 the Scots joined the English parliamentarians in a league and covenant against the King.

The opposition of the Covenanters to the King had been a reaction to his hated religious policies but they were horrified at his execution. Six days after Charles was beheaded his son was proclaimed King in Scotland.

Before his barbarous execution in 1650, organized by the Earl of Argyll, the Marquis of Montrose had kept the royal banner flying in Scotland. He was hanged for three hours at the Mercat Cross in the capital, then his head was cut off and displayed on the Tolbooth; his legs and arms were removed to go on display in other towns, and the remnants of his body were finally buried.

In 1650 Cromwell invaded Edinburgh. The town's defensive wall was no match for Cromwell's military genius and the town council surrendered without a fight after the battle of Dunbar. Cromwell's troops, some of whom were billeted in the half-finished Heriot's Hospital, treated the city and its citizens with severity. But finally a working relationship between the city fathers and the Cromwellian regime emerged.

Despite cooperation with Cromwell there was a general rejoicing when Charles II was restored to the throne in 1660. However, when the celebrations were over the Scots found themselves facing a government committed to Episcopalianism with its structure of government-appointed bishops. The Scots Kirk wanted to elect its own leaders.

In 1662 an edict was issued ordering the use of Episcopal services and ministers were deposed for not doing so.

The Covenanters rose again only to be crushed by General Tam Dalyell and then by James Graham of Claverhouse. Martyrs faced death defiantly at the Grassmarket where their memorial stands, and the Covenanters were finally defeated at Bothwell Bridge in 1679.

About 1000 Covenanters were held in atrocious conditions for five months in what is now Greyfriars Churchyard. The man who led much of the prosecution against them was Lord Advocate Sir George Mackenzie, whose zeal won him the title of 'Bluidy Machenzie', the man who wrote a standard work on Scottish criminal law and founded the Faculty of Advocates' Library.

Life in the city was not entirely bound up with religious disruption: the *Edinburgh Gazette*, the city's first newspaper, started publication in 1679; two years later the Merchant Company was founded; in 1681 the Royal College of Physicians was chartered.

---

*I*n August 1686 James granted freedom of worship to Catholics in private houses and the following year Catholics and Quakers were allowed to worship more openly. In an attempt to counteract the unpopularity of these measures he granted the same rights to Presbyterians in June 1687.

But the proclamation failed to reduce anti-Catholic feeling; rather it increased mistrust and suspicion. It also made the Episocopalians feel that their royal support had weakened.

In the meantime, James's elder daughter Mary had married William of Orange who was himself a grandson of Charles I and, more to the point, a Protestant. Here was an alternative heir to those who hated Catholicism.

James's fate was sealed when his wife, Mary of Modena, produced a son – a Catholic heir – in June 1688. The 'Glorious Revolution' began. William's English anti-Catholic supporters encouraged him to come to Britain. James fled to France a month later.

In Edinburgh the mob showed its anti-Catholic feeling by sacking the Catholic Chapel Royal and driving the Jesuits from their school at Holyrood;

they also desecrated the tombs of the Stuart monarchs buried there.

Popular feeling and the arrival of Protestant William brought about the reinstatement of the Presbyterian Church government in Scotland.

The Stuarts and their Catholic cause seemed at an end. The rightful heir, James Francis Edward, was denied the Crown – the usurpers William and Mary sat firmly on the throne. This led, in 1715 and 1745, to two uprisings by supporters in Scotland but neither achieved the return of the Stuarts.

By then the nations of Scotland and England had been joined under one parliament.

The union was partly due to a huge financial disaster in Scotland that brought the people to a psychological and monetary misery.

A company was formed in 1695 for trading with Africa and the Indies – an attempt to break the monopoly of the English East India Company. It was a cause that excited the Edinburgh imagination and in which William Patterson, who conceived the idea of the Bank of England, was a driving force. Eager subscribers put up 400,000 Scottish pounds.

A group of Scots colonists were landed on the coast of Darien, possibly the unhealthiest part of the Isthmus of Panama, and after a few years of unprofitable struggle were finally driven out by the Spanish in 1700.

The venture was the worst commercial undertaking in Scotland's history. There was no glory and the loss of pride and money were enormous. Scotland's exchequer and storehouses were empty and the challenge to English mercantilism was a mockery. Nine ships that the company had bought or chartered were lost; the huge capital had disappeared without profit and 2000 men, women and children had died in Darien, been abandoned in Spanish prison, or become indentured servants to English colonies.

When news of the Darien Scheme reached Edinburgh the mobs took to the streets to vent their fury at their lost hopes and fortunes and their wrath against the English who had failed to help the colonists in favour of keeping on good terms with the Spanish who had claimed Darien. The disastrous scheme so impoverished Scotland that many concluded the nation would only be successful financially if it had equal trading rights with England. In 1707 the Scottish Parliament cut its own throat by passing the Act of Union.

It was finally ratified in the Edinburgh Parliament by 110 votes to 67 and when the treaty passed through Westminster without opposition the Parliaments of Scotland and England ceased to exist. In their places was one Parliament of Great Britain with 513 English representatives and 45 Scottish in the House of Commons. In the Lords 16 elected Scottish peers would sit.

$\mathcal{S}$ome independence remained: it kept the Kirk, the system of education, the courts and legal code, and the royal burghs with their special privileges. However, the administration did move south and with it Scotland's political, cultural and economic force.

'Bought and sold for English gold' sang the Jacobite ballad of the day and, indeed, Queen Anne paid £20,000 to reduce the arrears of the Scottish government; bribes and inducements had no doubt passed hands during the long arguments. But without the union and the financial benefits it brought it is possible that Scotland would not have survived.

The General Assembly and the Court of Session stayed in Edinburgh, but the men of influence and talent moved to England. Streets like the Canongate, where the nobility had lived, declined.

But the city did not die: horse racing was still popular, cock fighting at Leith Links and other venues was a public obsession and concerts were held at Bailie Fyfe's Close every Saturday during the winter. Gentlemen exercised themselves playing golf, tennis and shooting bows and arrows.

The Jacobites revived Catholic hopes in 1715 and 1745 but their efforts never achieved return of the Stuarts and a Catholic monarchy. In 1715 they tried to put James, the 'Old Pretender', on the throne. A raid on the Castle was beaten off and the uprising, with little support in southern Scotland, died in spite of French backing.

It had never been easy to maintain order in Edinburgh and over the years various attempts were made to control crime and riot. At the end of the seventeenth century the city had appointed a city corps of guards, nicknamed by the people as the 'Toun Rats'.

Their reputation was never good but it sank to an all-time low, along with the name of the town's magistrates', when the Edinburgh mob took to the streets once more in April 1736.

It was then that the Grassmarket became the scene of a virtual lynching which has gone down in the history books as the Porteous Riot. Captain John Porteous was a Captain of the town guard who had the unsavoury reputation of relishing public executions. On April 14, a demonstration broke out when he presided over the hanging of a popular smuggler named Andrew Wilson. Wilson was highly regarded for having accepted full personal responsibility for robbing an excise officer, and thus allowing an equally guilty colleague to go free. Members of the town guard opened fire on the crowd, killing nine people and wounding many others. In the outcry that followed, Porteous was put on trial for murder and was condemned to death by the High Court. But on September 7 word spread through the city that he was about to be reprieved by royal decree. An angry mob broke into the Tolbooth jail, dragged Porteous out in his nightgown and hanged him from a pole which marked a dyer's premises, close to the scene of the shooting. The pole, symbolizing perhaps the most dramatic example of Grassmarket law and legend, stood in front of Hunter's Close on the south side of the rectangle. Porteous's body was laid to rest in nearby Greyfriars Churchyard. Except for a post inscribed P. 1736, his grave remained unmarked for 237 years. Then, in 1973, a headstone replaced the post, providing the extra information: 'John Porteous, a Captain of Edinburgh City Guard, murdered 7 September 1736. All passion spent.'

$\mathcal{R}$ebellion and violence came again to Scotland with the second Jacobite uprising of 1745 which sought to place Bonnie Prince Charlie, the 'Young Pretender', on the throne.

When news of his arrival from France reached the city a band of 1000 men was raised to defend the town. The 'Young Pretender's' army of Highlanders camped in Holyrood Park and a large crowd went out to meet the Catholic Prince, whose official recognition lay with the Pope.

The Highlanders easily entered the city and subsequently the Lord Provost Archibald Stewart had to face trial for failing to offer stiff enough resistance to the Jacobites. Their cause, though, died on the moors of Culloden the following year and the Prince fled into humiliating exile.

His supporters paid heavily for their loyalty. Apart from the blockades of the navy and revenge of the English army which hounded Culloden's survivors, about 120 of the prisoners were executed – peers by the axe and the others by the rope. A further 1150 were banished or transported and the fate of another 700 is still unknown.

Politically Scotland was also repressed. The office of Secretary of State was abolished and the post of Lord Advocate came to represent royal power in Scotland under the direction of the Secretary of the Northern Department.

Rigorous laws were passed against Episcopalians; the wearing of kilts and playing of bagpipes were banned. Some lands were annexed to the Crown.

Trustees were appointed to run the forfeited estates of Jacobite supporters and order was restored; schools were established; land tenure for crofters was improved; cottage industries were introduced and the Scottish economy began to flourish.

Continued on page 26

The Law

A unique tradition marries the two great schools of European law

*N*ot Proven – it's a court verdict you will not hear in any other part of the world. But it symbolizes a tradition of fiercely independent Scottish law born out of repeated wars with England and the Auld Alliance with France. Often quirky, sometimes at variance with the legal system in other areas of the United Kingdom, the law of Scotland stands proudly alone.

In no other part of Britain can a jury declare that the case against a defendant has not been proved. Such a verdict means simply that there was insufficient evidence to estab-lish that the accused person was guilty or not. He or she leaves court without penalty but not without suspicion. It is a unique finding, in that few people who stand in the dock elsewhere ever walk away without being declared guilty or innocent.

'Not Proven' undoubtedly carries a kind of stigma – the notion that someone has been clever enough to get away with something – but the Scots regard it as merely a sign of commonsense. Perhaps there were genuine doubts back in June 1852, when a truly sensational trial took place in Edinburgh.

High-born Madeline Smith, her story re-enacted a hundred times in books and films, stood accused of murdering her French lover with liberal doses of arsenic. The verdict was 'Not Proven' – and Madeline went on to live to a ripe old age in the United States.

Between its close ties to France and proximity to England, Scotland has created its own coherent legal system – incorporating Roman law, feudal law, canon law, special customs and local practices. A wealth of experience went into the Scottish law first defined in the seventeenth century by Sir

James Dalrymple, later Viscount Stair. His formula persisted through the 1707 Act of Union with England to remain the basis of the law of the land. But that was also when Parliament in London began infusing its own flavour.

Critics still feel that acts of Parliament do not always take account of Scottish precedent, one of the mainstays of the system practised north of the border. The courts will always pay high regard to judicial opinions passed down in similar cases decided many years earlier.

Until 1820 the bulk of Scottish law owed its origin to those Roman regulations, feudal laws and ancient customs – in common with France and Germany and most of the then developed world, but distinct from the great common law systems of England, the United States and the majority of Commonwealth countries. Since then, Scottish law has moved away from its Roman base and taken a middle ground between the continental system and the common law of England.

In modern times Scotland has administered its own criminal law since 1926, although civil law ultimately comes under the jurisdiction of the House of Lords at Westminster. The London government appoints a Lord Advocate, usually a lawyer–politician, who represents the state in all criminal proceedings. These range from Scotland's supreme criminal tribunal, the High Court of Justiciary, to local hearings in Sheriff's and District courts. Most High Court cases are heard by a judge sitting not with 12 but 15 jurors – another unique aspect of Scottish law.

The Edinburgh Sheriff's Court stands north of the High Street, opposite St. Giles' Cathedral. But don't expect large-scale drama there – a two-year jail sentence is the limit they can impose.

Far left The Great Hall of Parliament Hall, home of the Scottish Parliament until 1707 and now a meeting place for lawyers from the adjacent courts. The great stained glass window dates from 1532 and shows James V, one of the great protectors of Scottish law, together with Abbot Mylne, first Lord President of the Court of Session.
Above The Advocates' Library, founded in 1682. It now houses the legal collection of the National Library. **Right** Examples from the library's valuable collection of books and documents.

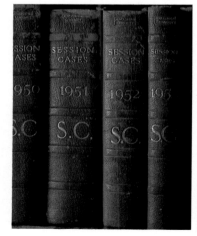

Literature

Great men of letters rose from the tradition of ancient Celtic bards.

Edinburgh remembers its writers and poets. And is remembered by them. Its first poet, the sixteenth-century William Dunbar, described the city as 'nobill toun'; Burns as 'Edina! Scotia's darling seat'; Scott as 'mine own romantic town' and for Stevenson, far away in Samoa, it was 'a precipitous city' whose gusty winds could make it 'scowling'.

Its characters, too, are recalled. The merchants of Dunbar's days were castigated by him for their wares which cluttered the streets and fouled the air with the 'stink of haddockis and of scattis' (skate). Allan Ramsay portrayed Lucky Spence, the madame who kept a brothel in the Canongate of the eighteenth century; Stevenson found inspiration for Dr. Jekyll and Mr. Hyde in Deacon Brodie, a respectable city councillor by day and burglar by night; Conan Doyle modelled Sherlock Holmes on the Edinburgh surgeon Dr. Joseph Bell.

The Celts have a long and revered literary heritage in their myths, legends and bardic poetry but an international seal of approval was set on the capital in the late eighteenth and early nineteenth centuries.

It was, as Smollett said, 'a hotbed of genius', when the brilliant circle of literati lived and met under the acknowledged leadership of David Hume (1711-1776), historian, philosopher, religious sceptic and humanitarian. With him were the likes of Adam Smith (1723-1790), economist and author of *The Wealth of Nations;* Adam Ferguson (1723-1816), philosopher and historian; William Robertson (1721-1793), historian and principal of Edinburgh University and Dugald Stewart (1753-1828), philosopher.

They started the popularity of literary clubs such as the Easy Club, The Cape Club and the Speculative Society, which met at the taverns tucked away in the wynds and lanes of the Old Town. They frequented the booksellers like William Creech, Burns' Edinburgh publisher, and Blackwood's 'great lounging book-shop'.

39

Sir Walter Scott's signature and the small statue of the author reading which marks the house in Castle Street where he moved in 1801. The printing press below is the one James Ballantyne used to print the first editions of Scott's Waverley Novels.

A segment of Burns' script of his poem 'Scots Wha Ha'e', dated 1795; the 'heaven-taught ploughman's' signature; and the statue of him that stands in Lady Stair's House, a museum dedicated to three great Scottish men of letters.

There was Robert Fergusson, born in 1750, who died of drink and madness in an asylum at 24, hailed by Burns as 'my elder brother in the Muse' and by others for his part in the revival of Scottish poetry.

Burns spent time in the city,' lionized by the literati as 'the heaven-taught ploughman', amused by his landlady's complaints about the prostitutes in the flat above.

Edinburgh also attracted, over the centuries, many other writers: Daniel Defoe was here in 1710 as a government spy sent to report on Scottish attitudes to the recent Act of Union and later wrote about the 'stench and nastiness' of the Old Town; Oliver Goldsmith studied medicine here but was more interested in the social life and beauty of Scots women; Dr. Johnson visited on his way to the Hebrides with his biographer James Boswell and gave the Scots an opportunity to get their own back on him after all his insults about them.

Wordsworth, an admirer of Walter Scott, stayed as Scott's guest after a tour of the Highlands; Thomas Carlyle attended the university and trained for the ministry; Thomas de Quincey contributed to *Blackwood's Magazine* and Blackwood published his *Confessions of an English Opium Eater* in 1822; J. M. Barrie was at the university; and John Buchan became Lord Chancellor of the university.

Of all native Scots writers Sir Walter Scott and Robert Louis Stevenson are probably best known. Scott was born in 1771 and as a sickly child read poetry and romances when confined to bed. He was a prolific writer and while he wrote his old tomcat and his favourite dog, Maida, kept him company. He wrote long into the night, by hand, page after page and, in one period of three weeks, completed the last two volumes of Waverley.

Stevenson was another invalid child and his physical weakness drove him from Edinburgh to the sunnier shores of the South Pacific. But childhood memories remained with him and led to his collection of poems, *A Child's Garden of Verses*, with the much-loved Leerie the Lamplighter. He also went to university in Edinburgh and was something of a rebel, giving up his middle-class family life to spend his time with the dubious characters in the pubs and brothels of Lothian Road and Leith Walk where he was often seen with notebook and pen in hand.

The city still inspires its authors: Muriel Spark, born in 1918, was educated in Edinburgh and her novel *The Prime of Miss Jean Brodie* might well have been based on her own school – James Gillespie's School for Girls. The Scottish Renaissance Movement of the 1920s and 1930s injected new life into poetry with the appearance of writers like Hugh MacDiarmid. The Abbotsford Bar in Rose Street, the Cafe Royal near Register House and Milnes Bar in Hanover Street became meeting places for the new literati – men like Sydney Goodsir Smith (1915-1975), Robert Garioch (1909-1981) and Norman MacCaig (born in 1910), who have all written about their lives in the capital.

This statue of Robert Louis Stevenson stands in his boyhood home at 17 Heriot Row, and the handsome brass plaque that marks the spot is inscribed with a verse from his children's poem 'The Lamplighter.' The author died at the age of 44 in Samoa where he lived for three years presiding like a native chief in his adopted land.

Edinburgh was now beginning to burst at the seams. Around the time of 'the forty-five', conditions for the 51,000 citizens were very mixed. One estimate shows that ten percent lived in houses in the streets, 60 percent in the tight closes, 20 percent in dugouts or sheds and the remaining ten percent straggled homeless through the streets, seeking shelter wherever they could.

The city buildings of Edinburgh were still concentrated around the spine of the High Street and down the slopes of the Grassmarket and Cowgate. By the middle of the seventeenth century high tenements were standard, pushing upward, restricted from spreading outwards by the ancient city walls.

Flats of six or seven rooms were common – with a great mixture of tenants in any one building. Merchants and bankers lived in this sort of building on higher floors and the poorer people took the dark ground floors.

As a result of this gross overcrowding – one story tells of 11 adults crammed into one room – small developments were starting to open outside the walls – like Nicholson and George Squares to the south.

St. Giles and the Old Town

*T*he push came from an extraordinary visionary, George Drummond, six times Lord Provost of Edinburgh.

In 1752 he was largely responsible for drawing up 'Proposals for carrying out certain public works in the City of Edinburgh' which in 7500 words outlined the overcrowded conditions of the city and suggested an extension of the town.

He then, in September 1753, as Grand Master of the Scottish Freemasons, laid the foundation stone of the Royal Exchange in the High Street (the building later became the City Chambers). He had also been instrumental in launching in 1729 an appeal fund for an infirmary which grew into one of the world's greatest teaching hospitals, the Royal Infirmary, now standing in Lauriston Place.

Ten years after the 'Proposals' were published, Drummond managed to persuade the town council to hold a competition for a plan of a new town on the far side of Nor' Loch.

It brought in six plans and the winner, announced in 1766, was 23-year-old James Craig, son of an Edinburgh merchant, who won a gold medal and the freedom of the city – as well as overnight fame.

His plan was symmetrical; a gridiron of three main streets balanced at either end by a square. Today its shape is basically unaltered from Princes Street to George Street and Queen Street, although the houses which once lined Princes Street have all but vanished

On the original plan Princes Street was named St. Giles Street but the name was altered. In the end the whole plan was dedicated to the House of Hanover and claimed to represent the new union between England and Scotland.

The first houses of the New Town were built in Thistle Court – where they still stand – and by 1774 the foundation stone of the magnificent Register House was laid. The designs for the building were drawn by the distinguished and fashionable Adam brothers.

Robert Adam was commissioned to provide a plan and complete elevations for Charlotte Square and, in doing so, one of the world's gems of Georgian architecture was started in 1792.

The New Town was largely built of grey Craigleith stone in a neo-classical style, influenced by the Greek revival then holding the interest of the nation's intellectuals.

It gave enormous opportunities to the architects of the time – like the Adam brothers, William Playfair, William Sibbald and Robert Reid and James Gillespie Graham – whose fame spread throughout Britain.

Reid, Sibbald and Playfair made their mark on the second phase of the New Town where the grand terraces of Royal and Regent Terraces were built and the monuments on Calton Hill sprang up.

'Forty years saw the Old Town changed as respects population,' wrote Robert Chambers the publisher. 'One after another its nobles and gentry, its men of the robe, its writers, and even its substantial burghers, had during that time deserted their mansions in the High Street and Canongate, till few were left.'

The Lord Justice Clerk's house was occupied by a woman who sold furniture, the Lord President's by a French teacher, a duke's house taken over by a wheelwright – changed days indeed.

It was the town where James Boswell practised as an advocate; where Robert Fergusson died in Edinburgh's Bedlam at the age of 25 leaving some remarkable poetry and leaving another poet, Robert Burns, to appreciate its excellence and arrange for a headstone on Fergusson's grave in Canongate Kirkyard.

It was said you could stand at the Mercat Cross and take 'fifty men of genius and learning by the hand'. And yet it was a town where the household slops (and worse) were hurled from upper windows into the open gutters below.

Figures of genius were many and varied in this, Scotland's golden age, when Edinburgh earned a reputation as a brilliant intellectual and artistic centre, prompting even the cynical Voltaire to write: 'It is from Scotland we receive rules of taste in all the arts from the epic poem to gardening'.

There was the judge Lord Kames, a philosopher and jurist; William Creech, bookseller and publisher and one-time Lord Provost; David Hume, the philosopher, who went to university at the age of 12; Adam Smith, author of *The Wealth of Nations*; Henry Raeburn, the painter; Francis Jeffrey, founder of *The Edinburgh Review*, Walter Scott and Burns among the writers.

It was the time when Scotland, with a population a quarter of England's, had four universities to England's two; schools, hospitals and technical colleges were founded and produced brilliance in every direction: James Watt with his steam engine; Simpson and his discovery of chloroform – inventions and discoveries seemingly endless.

In 1790 the First Statistical Account of Scotland was under way and the publisher Creech was given his say in a comparison of Edinburgh in 1763 and in 1783.

Although he might be accused of a little exaggeration, he reported that in 1763 'five or six brothels and a very few of the lowest and most ignorant order of females skulked about the streets at night' but 20 years later 'brothels increased twenty-fold and women of the Town more than a hundred-fold'.

'Housebreaking was extremely rare' in 1763 but 1783 saw that 'housebreaking theft and robbery were frequent. Many of the crimes were committed by boys whose ages prevented them from being objects of capital punishment.'

Although bookselling was his trade, Creech was interested in all sorts of shops. 'Perfumers have splendid shops in every street. Some of them advertise they keep bears, to kill occasionally for greasing ladies' and gentlemen's hair, as superior to any other animal fat.'

Yet amid all the brilliance of the golden age which also brought a revival of pride in things Scottish and in the Gaelic language, there was still a shortage of grain in the city markets in 1800 and talk of famine among the poorer citizens as the population steadily increased. By 1811 it was 103,143 and, although the city increased in size

George Street

from its original site of 138 acres (55 ha) to several thousand acres, the Old Town was still grossly crowded and those who could not afford to move to the New Town suffered gruesome conditions.

The new century was not a peaceful one in the early years. New Year riots broke out at the end of 1811 and a policeman and clerk were killed: three youths hanged in consequence.

In 1824 one of the most disastrous fires ever to hit the city broke out. On November 15 smoke and flames burst from a house in Assembly Close off the High Street and spread rapidly to engulf the whole tenement. And before the fire was out, the entire area from the High Street below St. Giles to near the Tron Kirk and down the hill to the Cowgate was devastated. Shortly afterwards, the first municipal fire brigade in the world was founded under the direction of James Braidwood.

The city was rocked by public scandal in the late 1820s, with the Burke and Hare murders. William Burke faced trial for murdering to provide bodies for the anatomy classes run by Dr. Robert Knox. Burke and partner first filched bodies from new graves to give to the doctor but soon turned to murder to provide the anatomy subjects.

Hare turned King's Evidence and, after Burke's execution in 1829, a crowd of 24,000 went to see his body on the dissecting table at Surgeon's Hall. His skeleton is still preserved in Edinburgh University's Medical School.

The mob reacted with their customary speed and violence to the scandal and gathered to throw stones and sticks at Dr. Knox's house. They also coined a ditty:

Down the close and up the stair
But an' ben wi' Burke and Hare
Burke's the butcher, Hare's the thief,
Knox the man that buys the beef.

Through pioneers like Dr. Knox, however, Edinburgh had a huge reputation for medicine and hospitals. But balanced against this is a sorry tale of disease and neglect.

The scourge through the years was smallpox. Inoculation was practised as far back as 1745 in the city but between 1740 and 1742 a smallpox outbreak claimed 17 percent of all deaths in Edinburgh. Typhus fever also struck, and cholera outbreaks in 1831-1832 and 1838-1840 increased public concern about the squalor in the dark, insanitary houses in the Old Town.

There was pressure for the appointment of a public health officer but it was only after the collapse of a tenement in the High Street in 1861, which killed 35 inhabitants, that the town council were forced to act.

Dr. Henry Littlejohn took the post, which he

Bakehouse Close

held for the next 46 years, in 1862. Three years later he produced his first report in which he proved that Edinburgh's high death rate, for adults and babies, and all the disease was due to the insanitary and appallingly cramped conditions.

His recommendations for action were to pave and drain the closes; improve accommodation by introducing water and gas, cleaning common stairs and repairing houses; limit the number of people in each apartment; remove tenements that were in danger of collapse; and open up the worst of the narrow closes.

His ideas were backed by the Lord Provost William Chambers who did much to implement them and, by degrees, conditions improved.

The greatest impact the Industrial Revolution had on Edinburgh was probably in transport. The efforts of Thomas Telford, the engineer, and John Macadam, who invented his road surfacing, improved travel on the roads and the building of canals made transport speedier.

But it was the railways that were the most effective innovation. Edinburgh's first line was planned by Robert Stevenson to connect the coalfields of Midlothian with Edinburgh and the sea. It opened in 1831 and by 1834 passenger services were running.

Traffic on the Glasgow-Edinburgh line started moving in 1842 when the Edinburgh-Newhaven route also opened. Edinburgh and Berwick were connected to London in 1846. 'Railway mania' had begun. The Granton to Burntisland line saw the world's first train ferry – over the Forth.

Horse tramcars arrived in the city in 1871 and the system spread until, by 1891, there were 300 cars and more than 1000 horses in operation.

Cable cars were introduced in 1888 and ran down Hanover Street and Dundas to Canonmills and Goldenacre. Another opened two years later along the Stockbridge route. They were pulled by cables driven by a power station in Henderson Row.

Eventually the system, the fourth largest of its kind in the world, extended throughout the city with four power stations driving 52 miles (84 km) of cables through a 26-mile (42 km) network of routes.

Edinburgh had prospered with the Victorian industrial expansion: there was brewing, distilling, printing, baking and confectionary, the manufacture of glass and chemicals.

The city also took to the morality and formality of the Victorians which appealed to the ethics of Knox's followers. But there was still dissension in the Kirk. In 1843 four hundred ministers took about a third of the Kirk's members to establish the Free Church because they felt that the Church of Scotland had become too liberal. And again in 1892 a group split away – this time from the Free Church to set up the Free Presbyterian Church on the grounds that the Free Church had become insufferably liberal!

Morality was also the basis for the enormous support that William Ewart Gladstone found in his father's native Scotland. He conducted his Midlothian campaign in the city in 1879, and paid for the return of the Old Mercat Cross to its present site.

Gladstone also toyed with the idea of all-round devolution for Britain and, although his energies were devoted to Irish Home Rule, the Scots responded with enthusiasm. Nationalism had already been inflamed by the vast numbers of English troops which virtually occupied Scotland after the uprisings of 1715 and 1745 and it was helped along by the intellectual interest in Scottish language and history of writers like Burns and Scott.

In the 1880s a demand was made – and met – for a Scottish Secretary to deal exclusively with Scottish affairs, and a Scottish Home Rule Association sprang up.

From 1906 onwards there was an almost annual

Pier at Newhaven

Government of Scotland Bill but it was never successful because the parties in power failed to push it through Parliament. Had World War I not intervened it is possible that the government would have been forced to honour its pledge.

The Scots started a New Home Rule Association in 1917 and by 1928 the National Party of Scotland was formed. But it did not meet with quite the popular enthusiasm its leaders had hoped for, perhaps because it was too left wing and wanted total separation from England.

The agitation over the years did lead to the move of the Scottish administration to Edinburgh from Whitehall in 1939 and gradually, after World War II, the administrative powers were widened.

The Scottish Nationalist Party won its first by-election in 1945, only to lose the seat in the subsequent general election a few weeks later. It had to wait another 20 years or so before another Nationalist sat in Westminster. In 1974 there were seven SNP members in London and it seemed that the time was ripe for a referendum on devolution. It was taken in 1979 and the feeling was such that Edinburgh spent £3 million on converting the old Royal High School, built in 1825 on Calton Hill, for the Scottish Assembly. But the vote was indecisive and the school remains empty.

While Scottish nationalism flowered, literature and the arts blossomed too. Between the two World Wars, Edinburgh was still a great city for bookshop browsing and artists and writers were busy in the city – busy enough to start a 'Scottish Renaissance' in the 1930s with poets like Hugh

Universities

*E*stablished under royal charter by James VI in 1583, Edinburgh University is the sixth oldest in Britain. Beginning with ninety freshmen, it now has over 11,000 full-time students, and over 50,000 members of its General Council (living former students). Its size is obvious: it is spread throughout the city making it the largest private owner of buildings in Scotland.

The university's founding principles were based on the firm doctrines of Calvinism and students were encouraged to attend the university to gain 'the manners of morality and virtue'. This was to be achieved by study within the college but residence 'in the presence of their friends'. Thus it was not until 1887 that Edinburgh's – and Scotland's – first hall of residence was established. This hall, Patrick Geddes (at number 2 Mound Place) was recently renovated and is occupied by students today.

The university has always been non-collegiate (there is no system of colleges) and offers no multitude of lawns, chapels and stairways. Rather, it is the buildings in which the students were taught, the austere Georgian proportions of the Old College (on the corner of Chambers Street and South Bridge) and the Medical School (in Teviot Place), that provided the architectural and educational heart of the university.

In 1582, the Town Council purchased the Kirk o' Fields on which the Old College now stands. From the outset the Council financed building and teaching alike, beginning a long involvement with the university. In 1789, the university was granted an independent coat of arms but it was not until 1858 that autonomy from the Council was achieved.

From the beginning, university students took a four year MA degree in the General Arts. Only then could they enter the Divinity School – the only other faculty. It was only later that Medicine (1705) and Law (1722) were established.

Originally, Edinburgh adopted the regent system of teaching, taken from the great university of Leyden. Each student was assigned a regent (or tutor) who taught him throughout his degree. This system was replaced in 1708 by the professorial system of today.

The demands upon the students were exacting. There were no set examinations; the regent or professor who did not examine his students daily was failing in his duty. 'Dictates' (given at dictation speed) began at five am (six am in midwinter) and continued until evening. The only break was two hours of compulsory exercise – the regent's parade – in midafternoon. The students were forbidden to attend the public hangings in the Grassmarket. Even funerals – except those of eminent councillors – were deemed too frivolous for attendance. Only the month of August was permitted for vacation. Calvinism reigned supreme.

This rigorous system of education did not, however, subdue all students. In 1680, Robert Brown, an Englishman, publicly burnt an effigy of the Pope in the Kirk o' Fields. This protest was directed at the Catholic heir-presumptive Duke of York who was in residence at the Palace of Holyroodhouse. The Old College and Town Guards could not prevent a student revolt from supporting Brown. The Privy Council charged the college with treason and closed it down. Brown was expelled. From this incident arose a pledge, which all students must sign today upon matriculation, agreeing to accept expulsion if

McDiarmid and Albert Mackie bringing pride back to things Scottish. And while writers wrote through the 1930s and 1940s a new idea in cultural expression came to the capital in the form of the International Festival of the arts.

It was launched in 1947 under the leadership of the Lord Provost Sir John Falconer and was an act of inspiration and faith after the gloomy days of World War II. It brought, as intended, international stars and companies to the city. Now the Festival attracts about 100,000 visitors each year and, in turn, the visitors stimulate the town's tourism, restaurants, shops and hotels.

Dr. Johnson once wrote that the best sight for a Scotsman was the road to England. It is now a road that takes the financial and trading talents of the Scots all over the world.

Edinburgh has become a major centre for banking and insurance – Charlotte Square is said to be among the richest squares in the world so many are the headquarters there. Traders like Jardine Mathieson, of Hong Kong fame, had their beginnings in Edinburgh, and the 'black gold' from the North Sea has brought more financial work for the capital.

The capital is flourishing and still has great beauty. And it retains an impression of mystery and magic of which Robert Louis Stevenson wrote: 'There is no Edinburgh emigrant, far or near, from China to Peru, but he or she carries some lively pictures of the mind, some sunset beneath the Castle cliffs, some snow scene, some maze of city lamps, indelible in the memory and delightful to study in the intervals of toil.'

---

they break the university laws or bring it into disrepute.

Throughout the nineteenth century the university continued to expand. The Divinity School, now the largest in Britain, was rehoused in the New College, where the assembly of the University meets annually each May.

The nineteenth-century Prime Ministers Lord Palmerston and Lord John Russell (son of the Duke of Bedford) studied here. Other students included Mungo Park, James Boswell, Thomas Carlyle, Oliver Goldsmith, Charles Darwin, Sir Arthur Conan Doyle, Sir Walter Scott and Robert Louis Stevenson. David Hume was refused a professorship for publicly professing disbelief in God. From 1920-1929, successive Rectors of the University were David Lloyd George, Stanley Baldwin, Sir John Gilmour and Winston Churchill. Churchill had failed in his first Rectorial election in 1905. Their predecessors included the Liberal Prime Ministers Gladstone and Lord Rosebery. University Chancellors have included the literary figures Sir James Barrie, Bt., and Lord Tweedsmuir (John Buchan). HRH the Duke of Edinburgh is the present Chancellor.

Among the eminent teachers today is John Erickson, Professor of Politics and adviser to President Ronald Reagan on vital issues of strategic arms and defence. Professor Geoffrey Beale of the genetics department is also a widely respected expert in his field.

Today, Edinburgh University's reputation in the fields of medicine and science remain pre-eminent. The modern science complex at Kings Buildings undertakes far-reaching and invaluable research, whilst many an advocate has studied within the traditional grandeur of the Old College. If the university offers no immediately recognizable identity perhaps the answer lies in its size. For character, humour, endeavour and achievement abound here

– even if the university chooses to keep quiet about it.

The main part of Edinburgh's second university, the Heriot-Watt, stands in the woodlands of Riccarton estate on the western side of the city. Founded in 1821 as a school providing evening classes in basic science for young artisans, it later took the name of the Watt Institution and School of Arts in memory of James Watt, developer of the steam engine. From a rented hall in long-demolished Adam Square, it moved to premises in Chambers Street where, in 1885, it became the Heriot-Watt College as a result of an amalgamation with George Heriot's hospital. The college achieved university status in 1966.

Thomas Shepherd's nineteenth-century view of Edinburgh University.

Medicine

From the horrors of plague rose a city renowned for medical research

For centuries Edinburgh has had the reputation of being a great centre of medical progress – but it was once one of the unhealthiest, dirtiest cities in Europe. From the earliest times disease was rife and the streets were clogged with refuse and sewage tossed at night from high tenement windows to the cry of 'gardyloo'.

In 1504, despite attempts at quarantine, bubonic plague hit the city badly. Victims were removed forcibly from the city, mass graves were excavated in areas like Bruntsfield Links. For the first time efforts were made to clean the city and King James IV, who was a keen amateur dentist founded the Incorporation of Barber-Surgeons later to become the world famous Royal College of Surgeons of Edinburgh.

But another major plague devastated the city in 1645. Ten years later Oliver Cromwell was so concerned at the filth that he appointed a Town Scavenger to clear the main streets.

By this time, though, ideas from Europe were filtering through to Edinburgh. Robert Sibbald set up a practice with Andrew Balfour and in 1670 established a Physic Garden which had more than 1800 plants in it to supply the town's 20 or so physicians with their prescription ingredients. The garden formed the basis of the Royal Botanic Garden, the second oldest of its kind in the British Isles.

In 1681 Sibbald founded the Royal College of Physicians under a patent from Charles II. Sixteen years later Edinburgh surgeons opened their first fully equipped anatomy theatre giving the public a chance to view dissection. Only hanged criminals could be used for such purposes but body-snatching soon provided plenty of corpses and became so widespread that in 1725 the enraged townsfolk rioted. The snatching went on, however, and 100 years later Robert Knox, whose dissections were well-attended social occasions, found his career in ruins when the news spread of his use of bodies brought in by the murderers Burke and Hare.

Progress in medicine speeded up in the eighteenth century: the first dispensary for the poor was opened at its start; in 1729 Lord Provost George Drummond helped physicians open a hospital which later grew into the largest voluntary hospital in the British Isles – the Royal Infirmary; and in 1737 Andrew Duncan founded a medical students' club which

Joseph Lister, who pioneered antiseptics, used this carbolic spray and these surgical tools. Above is the first edition of the *Edinburgh Medical Journal.*

The death mask of William Burke who, with his partner William Hare, committed between 16 and 30 murders to provide bodies for dissection. The pocket book was made from Burke's own skin.

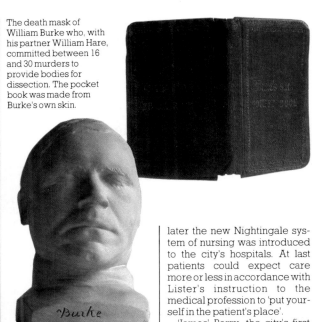

woman doctor, was awarded a medical degree in 1812. Throughout her life she had assumed the male identity necessary to achieve her goal. It was only at the autopsy that her sex was revealed.

In the early twentieth century medicine became more specialized, with the opening of the first post-graduate courses for specialists at the Royal Colleges and the University.

Today the city's reputation for medical research is still high.

The fine buildings of the Royal College of Surgeons and Physicians with their libraries and museums are evidence of their distinguished history, and the research units in the University Clinical Departments and in Edinburgh's hospitals ensure that these high traditions are carried on into the future.

later the new Nightingale system of nursing was introduced to the city's hospitals. At last patients could expect care more or less in accordance with Lister's instruction to the medical profession to 'put yourself in the patient's place'.

'James' Barry, the city's first

later became the Royal Society of Medicine.

The teaching of medicine also forged ahead as William Cullen taught the classification of diseases by symptoms for the first time and started lecturing in English rather than Latin.

In 1805 the *Edinburgh Medical and Surgical Journal* – the first of its kind – was published with articles by the two great surgeons Robert Liston and James Syme. Syme's assistant was Joseph Lister who pioneered the use of carbolic acid in surgery to prevent wounds going septic and later was the first medical peer.

James Young Simpson discovered the anaesthetic properties of chloroform. Legend has it that his first 'guinea pigs' were guests at a dinner party at his home. His wife came in to find the assembled group literally 'under the table'.

In 1807 Andrew Duncan set up a hospital for the treatment of the insane and 50 years or so

Anaesthetics pioneer James Young Simpson owned this medicine chest, pill box and primitive stethoscope.

Cooking

From Bawd Bree to Bubblyjock – a distinctive culinary repertoire

The visitor to Edinburgh who associates Scottish cooking with such deadly sounding dishes as haggis and black bun is in for a pleasant surprise. Blessed with a wealth of natural produce from its rich land and teeming waters, Scotland has developed a culinary repertoire of exceptional quality and variety. Partridge, grouse and pheasant from the rolling moorlands, venison from the red deer running wild in the mountains, salmon and trout from Highland rivers, succulent beef from the Aberdeen Angus herds, shellfish of all kinds – with ingredients like these, only a truly lamentable cook could fail to come up with a feast.

Edinburgh folk tend to look back to bygone days when the streets of the capital rang to the cries of 'oyster wives' and vendors of everything from hot peas to Het Pints – a brew of ale, eggs and whisky flavoured with nutmeg and sold from a steaming copper kettle. Those were the times when a fish dinner, including ale and perhaps a dozen oysters, cost little more than one cigarette does now. As far back as the thirteenth century, salmon was so plentiful that it was pickled for export to London to be fed to the poor, and only a hundred years ago servants in big houses had contracts stipulating that it was to be served to them no more than three times a week.

But those are bygone days indeed. The allure of traditional Scottish fare, however, has carried through to modern times in all but price. Breakfast and tea have a special place in Scottish cooking, and the visitor who might think of these meals as something light has another think coming. It was Dr. Samuel Johnson who wrote: 'If an epicure could remove by a wish in quest of sensual gratification, he would breakfast in Scotland.' Oatmeal is still a staple of the national diet, and certainly most of the older people start the day with a bowl of porridge – flavoured with salt, not sugar, please. Then come the soft warm rolls known as baps, kippered herring from Loch Fyne or smoked haddock ('smokies') from Aberdeen and Arbroath, scones and oatcakes with heather honey, jams, jellies and marmalade, claimed by Scots as their own invention. Tea is the occasion for another mam-

moth spread of cold meats and eggs, potato scones, crunchy shortbread and such delicacies as Dundee cake, a fruity concoction strewn with almonds.

An elaborate dinner or late supper will bring out the matchless smoked salmon, rich dark venison or feathered game, roast beef or tender mutton, perhaps lobster from the Firth of Forth. Auld Alliance, a savoury of creamed cheese laced with whisky and served with hot buttered toast, can be a superb climax to the meal.

The visitor who comes across haggis or black bun should not be put off by the unappetizing names. Haggis consists of the heart, liver and lights of a sheep, cooked with oatmeal and onions inside its stomach bag. Hard to believe, but it's delicious. Black bun, also known as Scotch bun, is a tasty cake made with raisins, cur-

rants, almonds, ginger, cinnamon and brandy.

The names of many Scottish delicacies are nothing if not colourful. A few examples: Bawd Bree (hare soup), Bubblyjock (roast turkey), Cock-a-Leekie (chicken and leek soup), Inky-Pinky (beef and carrot stew), Stovies (sliced potatoes cooked with onions and lamb) and Melting Moments (biscuits in rolled oats).

Scottish food at its best – the supreme high tea with the delights of bannocks and baps; Finnian haddie topped with poached egg for breakfast; and a fine brew from an ancient house to ease the evening.

Edinburgh Castle

The impenetrable fortress of Edinburgh Castle has been besieged and attacked numerous times in its 1300 year history but it has rarely been overwhelmed. It stands today as a memorial to the turbulent history of a nation.

This drawing of Edinburgh Castle, perched high above the Grassmarket, is by the artist Thomas H. Shepard and was published in 1829.

Edinburgh Castle dominates the city below. This is no accident but a deliberate strategy of its many military designers and part of the secret of its success as a fortress. For nearly 500 years the stone edifices topping Castle Rock were regularly under siege and, though famine and maybe even betrayal led their garrisons to surrender, the Castle was never once successfully stormed.

Twentieth-century visitors can pass freely through these once impregnable defences but can only penetrate the castle's mysteries by understanding its history. It has served as a fort, palace, prison, garrison, arsenal, armoury and as a repository for the State regalia.

Castle Rock is the basalt core of one of the five extinct volcanos in the Edinburgh area. It rises 435 feet (133 m) above sea level and Ice Age glaciers made the north and south sides almost vertical. The summit can only be easily approached from the ridge on the east, and the west side, steep enough to be defended, providing grazing for animals. These factors, plus the presence of springs of good water, made it a natural stronghold.

However, though there is a wealth of evidence of prehistoric man in Holyrood Park there is none on the rock. The Romans do not appear to have made much of its potential either, although it was marked on Ptolemy's second-century map of the Roman Empire as Castrum Alatum, because of its supposed similarity to an outspread eagle. Accounts of its occupation by Picts and Saxons are mainly guesswork though this occupation lasted almost a millenium. It is widely thought the Picts held the rock until 452 when the Saxons of Northumbria took over and it changed hands frequently thereafter. A Welsh poem, the *Gododdin*, records a sixth-century king of the region feasting in his fortification of Dun Edin before setting out to attack the Anglo-Saxons; this probably refers to Castle Rock. Over this period the Saxons are believed to have had more influence than the Picts in this southern area of Scotland and, though the connections are hardly direct, Edinburgh is still the most Anglicized of Scottish cities.

It was the Saxon queen, Margaret, wife of Malcolm III, who can be held partly responsible for Edinburgh's development in the eleventh century. In the Middle Ages the capital moved around the kingdom with the court. Malcolm Canmore, son of Shakespeare's Duncan and successor to Macbeth, had his capital in Dunfermline but his wife thought civilization lay further south. The crude fortress on the hill was converted to a royal residence and the name Castle Rock originates from this period. Margaret's own chamber there was said to have been furnished more luxuriantly than any in Scotland at that time. She was living there when the news of her husband's and eldest son's deaths in England reached her in 1093 and she died on the rock the same year.

Her death was followed by events to be repeated frequently in the nation's history – a disputed succession and siege of the Castle. Both attempts failed and her youngest son was crowned Scotland's next king in 1124. David I is thought to have built the summit's only surviving twelfth-century structure, a chapel dedicated to his mother's memory. But he also shaped the first real settlement around the Castle which stretched as far as the present intersection of High Street and South Bridge. David I was the first to use the Castle for the assembly of earls, barons and churchmen which later became the Parliament of Scotland.

The pattern of alternating occupation of the fortress by Scots and English started in the late twelfth century. It was held by an English garrison between 1174 and 1186 but was safely back in Scots hands when their first official parliament was convened there by Alexander II in 1215. His son, Alexander III, made it a repository for the kingdom's records and regalia. On his death the succession to the throne was disputed and the English king, Edward I, called in as umpire, settled this by burning the town and seizing the castle in 1296 after a three-day siege. The Scots virtually razed the Castle to the ground in 1313 to prevent further domination by their foes from this stronghold. Only St.

Margaret's Chapel was left standing.

The Castle began to take on more of its present form in the late fourteenth century. King David II returned from captivity in England in 1356 and built a 60-foot-high tower on the site of the present Half Moon Battery to protect the Castle's east side. This defence, known as David's Tower, was so strong it withstood a major attack by Henry IV and succumbed only to the massive bombardment of English cannon in 1573.

The next monarchs strengthened David's fortifications along the east, extending them to end in the Constable's Tower. In the 1430s James I moved the royal accommodation out of David's tower stronghold to the site of the present palace block. This move did not prove as fatal for James I as his choice of Perth as a centre for his court and parliament. His assassination there in 1437 increased the importance of Edinburgh as its Castle was considered the safest in the land.

Perhaps it was safe for the nation's rulers but not for others with any claim to the throne. In 1440 when the boy King James II lived there, his regents Crichton and Livingstone lured two rivals, the young Douglas brothers, to a feast in the Castle's hall. When the food was brought to the table, the main course was a black bull's head, a symbol of death. The boys were taken from this meal, since known as the Black Dinner, to a mock trial, after which they were beheaded.

James III was so suspicious of his own brothers claiming his crown that he kept them imprisoned, holding the Duke of Albany in David's Tower in 1479 while he lived in the adjacent royal apartments. But Albany escaped after luring his guards into his chamber to drink wine before a blazing fire, killing them when they became drow-

sy and roasting them in full armour on the fire. Ironically, before long James III was imprisoned for two months in David's Tower, to be released by the intervention of his former captive brother, Albany. Under James III, Edinburgh was finally declared the chief town in the kingdom and the permanent seat for the Scottish Parliament.

After the crowing of James IV in 1489, life took on a brighter look at the Castle and its tournaments brought it fame throughout Europe. His building programme included the splendid Great Hall which still stands, mounted on a vaulted structure over the southern rockface. Though the Palace was also improved, the Castle was no longer used as the Royal household's main residence. This era of success ended on Flodden Field in 1513 when James IV and his army of more than 100,000 suffered, at the hands of the English, the worst military disaster in Scottish history.

James V is thought to have taken little interest in the Castle. However, during his reign the Castle's captain built a bake house and a brewery near the well house. The Flodden Wall was begun as a defence against the expected invasion of the English. But when the army arrived a full 31 years later it was still unfinished and drawings made by an English agent in 1544 show the eastern defences still dominated by David's Tower. The castle was not seriously harmed in this attack but an Italian engineer was nevertheless engaged to build an artillery bastion before the crosswall, using the latest Italian techniques.

By the time Mary, Queen of Scots began her reign, Edinburgh Castle was the nation's main armoury, making and storing gunpowder and artillery. In 1566 the armaments included at least 25 cast bronze guns, many of which were used in sieges

The huge vaults, built to create a level surface for the Great Hall above them, are best known for holding foreign prisoners-of-war. The Hall was built in James IV's time for communal living. It became a barracks in 1650 and later a hospital. The restoration, rather too romantic, was done between 1887 and 1891.

1 Esplanade
2 Statue of Robert the Bruce
3 Statue of William Wallace
4 Gatehouse
5 Gateway to the Castle
6 Portcullis Gateway
7 Disused stables
8 Forewall Battery
9 Lang Stairs
10 Saint Margaret's Chapel
11 Water reservoirs
12 Foog's Gate
13 Scottish United Services Museum
14 Dury's Battery
15 Vaults/French Prisons
16 Great Vault/Mons Meg
17 Great Hall
18 Palace
19 Half Moon Battery
20 Twentieth-century Naafi building
21 Seventeenth-century ditch
22 Crown Square
23 Scottish National War Memorial
24 The Well

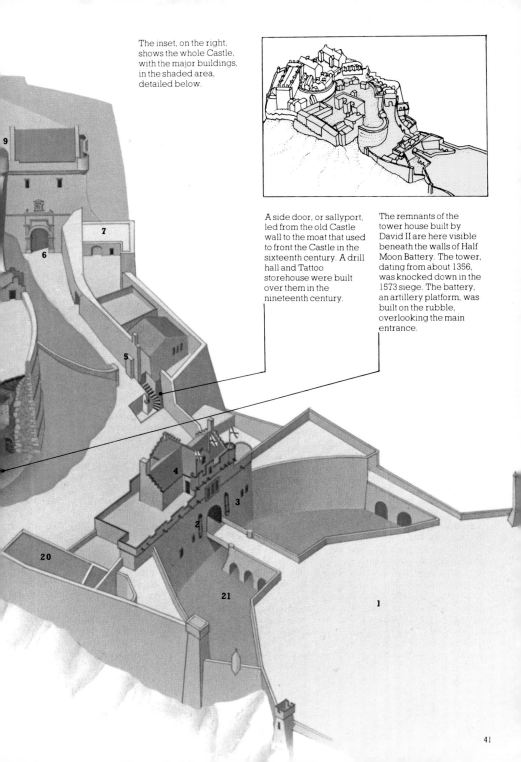

The inset, on the right, shows the whole Castle, with the major buildings, in the shaded area, detailed below.

A side door, or sallyport, led from the old Castle wall to the moat that used to front the Castle in the sixteenth century. A drill hall and Tattoo storehouse were built over them in the nineteenth century.

The remnants of the tower house built by David II are here visible beneath the walls of Half Moon Battery. The tower, dating from about 1356, was knocked down in the 1573 siege. The battery, an artillery platform, was built on the rubble, overlooking the main entrance.

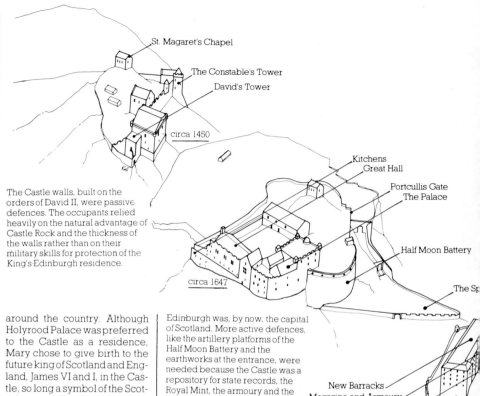

St. Magaret's Chapel

The Constable's Tower

David's Tower

circa 1450

The Castle walls, built on the orders of David II, were passive defences. The occupants relied heavily on the natural advantage of Castle Rock and the thickness of the walls rather than on their military skills for protection of the King's Edinburgh residence.

Kitchens
Great Hall

Portcullis Gate
The Palace

Half Moon Battery

circa 1647

The Sp

New Barracks
Magazine and Armoury
Governor's House

Queen Anne Barracks
St. Margaret's Chapel extended

circa 17

around the country. Although Holyrood Palace was preferred to the Castle as a residence, Mary chose to give birth to the future king of Scotland and England, James VI and I, in the Castle, so long a symbol of the Scottish crown. The Castle was the last place to uphold Mary's cause in the most destructive siege in its history.

Sir William Kircaldy of Grange held the Castle against incredible odds for three years for the exiled Queen. There is a suspicion that he finally turned traitor as the attackers sent suddenly for help from Queen Elizabeth I. These reinforcements included 30 cannon sent by sea and by May 1573 five batteries were set up surrounding the Castle. David's Tower eventually collapsed, blocking the Castle's main well and within weeks there was no food, water or provisions. The Castle surrendered but contrary to the agreement made, Kirkcaldy and other leaders were hanged, beheaded and their heads displayed.

The Castle was put in the

Edinburgh was, by now, the capital of Scotland. More active defences, like the artillery platforms of the Half Moon Battery and the earthworks at the entrance, were needed because the Castle was a repository for state records, the Royal Mint, the armoury and the Royal Household.

hands of Regent Morton and he rebuilt the eastern defences much in their present form. Records show the massive Half Moon Battery cost £743 6s 6d and the expense led Morton to devalue the Scots currency. The Castle became a fortress seldom visited by kings, although huge sums were spent to extend and redecorate the Palace for the homecoming of James VI.

The Castle came under serious siege three times within 50 years during the seventeenth century, though no assault breeched the walls. Most impact on the defences was made by the Covenanters Army, Presbyterian loyalists,

besieging a company of English soldiers. They held out for three months and were allowed to leave with honour.

In 1649 and 1650 the Castle was made even more impregnable when the citizens of Edinburgh were used as forced labour to demolish the spur in front of it. Though the Castle, ammunition and provisions all seemed to be holding up against Cromwell's attack in 1650, General Dundas surrendered to him. The Castle's reputation was redeemed by the Duke of Gordon, holding the Castle for the exiled Old Pretender in 1689 against the forces of William and Mary. In three months the brave and steadfast Duke cost his attackers 500 lives before famine and disease forced him to give in.

The guns of the Castle fired in March 1707 then the Act of

The Unions of Crowns in 1603 and of Parliaments in 1707 had taken the Royal Court and administration south so the Castle was no longer needed for defence. The Scottish Army used the Great Hall as a barracks and Napoleonic War prisoners were kept in the vaults.

Union was read to the last Scottish Parliament; the Scottish Honours, including the Crown Jewels, were taken to the Palace building and immured. Sir Walter Scott, who played a major part in their rediscovery, said this was because 'these emblems, connected with so many galling and hostile recollections of past events, could be no safe spectacle for the public eye, while Men's minds were agitated by the supposed degradation of Scotland beneath her ancient enemy .'

The Castle came under attack only twice more, both attempts made by Jacobite forces and neither coming near to success. The first was in 1715 when a bold plan was formulated to scale the Castle's wall by night and prepare it for the Highland armies en route to England. But a combination of betrayal and bad planning turned this assault into a fiasco. Bonnie Prince Charlie fared no better in 1745. He was wel-

comed by the citizens of Edinburgh but the Castle troops fired first on Holyroodhouse, then on the houses nearby, giving one the name Cannonball House from the shot embedded in its gable. The Stuart colours finally reached the Castle, displayed as spoils of war after the Young Pretender's defeat at Culloden.

A regular army, an innovation introduced in the mid-seventeenth century, kept a permanent garrison at the Castle from that time. Now the fortress's main military function was as a barracks and prison, especially during the Seven Years' and Napoleonic Wars with France. At the beginning of the nineteenth century as many as 1000 prisoners of war were kept in the Castle. Most were lodged in the vaults under the Great Hall, since known as the French Prisons. Their skill in carving can be seen in graffiti on the vault walls and handiwork made for sale, now on

The War Memorial was built and restoration work, begun by an Army officer, Gore Booth, in the late nineteenth century, was continued. Statues of the national heroes, Wallace and Bruce, were also erected and the Castle's popularity as a tourist attraction grew.

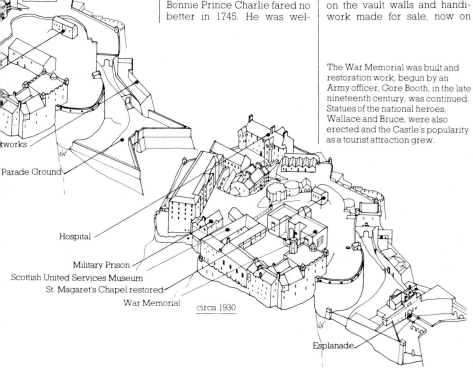

tworks

Parade Ground

Hospital

Military Prison

Scottish United Services Museum

St. Magaret's Chapel restored

War Memorial   circa 1930

Esplanade

view in the Castle's military museum. But they also carved mutton bones to make watermarks on forged banknotes. So skilful were these forgeries that advertisements appeared in the press offering rewards for information on the prisoners' lucrative sideline.

The prisoners were said to be kept in humane conditions but soldiers stationed at the Castle did not enjoy a much higher standard of accommodation. Up to 1000 could be lodged in barracks there at once and a 1791 census includes 159 women and 131 children. A mid-nineteenth century report described the married quarters as the worst in the United Kingdom, with no privacy and so insanitary that epidemics were rife. Even the New Barracks completed in 1799 are very austere. Troops were stationed at the Castle before serving overseas in India, North America or the Continent. The Castle was a major barracks until 1923 when the Redford Barracks south of the city were opened.

The process of restoration of Edinburgh Castle, begun in the nineteenth century, owes much to Sir Walter Scott's interest in it. He was named on a royal war-

rant, along with the Scottish Officers of State, allowing them to break open the oak chest in the Crown Room which was thought to contain the Scottish Honours. The Crown, Sceptre and Sword of Scotland were found inside, intact but dusty, and have only been hidden from public view twice since – during the two World Wars.

St. Margaret's Chapel was discovered by accident, as was the true nature of the Great Hall. Restoration work on the latter deviated rather a long way from its original state, but with far less damage to the Castle than would have occured if other grandiose Victorian schemes for 'improvements' had been allowed.

The age-old connection between Edinburgh Castle and military life still continues. It is the site of the National War Memorial and houses the Scottish United Services Museum. It is the headquarters for the Lowlands and the Scottish Division and the Regimental Headquarters of the Royal Scots and Royal Scots Dragoon Guards. It also has the only Army School of Piping in the country and is the real home of a few fortunate families of warders. Since 1947 the Castle has achieved international

fame through its annual Military Tattoo, held on the Esplanade. But today the only invaders besieging Edinburgh Castle are tourists.

Castle Rock

Visitors to Castle Rock today need an active imagination to see why the site was an obvious choice for a defensible stronghold. The buildings of the Old Town nestle snugly up towards the defences and the North Loch has been filled in and turned into Princes Street Gardens and the railway station. But throughout most of its history Castle Rock had a far more cragged appearance and the broad terraces and sweeping approach roads are products of extensive levelling in the eighteenth and nineteenth centuries, when the fortress' working life was almost over.

The Esplanade

The Esplanade did not exist when the Castle was under siege. It was built as a parade ground in 1753 using earth from the foundations of the Royal Exchange building to level and widen the ridge formed by glacial action. The ornamental walls were added in 1812 and 1820. The Esplanade, with its

Surmounted by the Royal Arms of Scotland and flanked by statues of Robert the Bruce and William Wallace, this gatehouse was built as an entrance worthy of the Castle rather than as a true fortification.

Above The cannon standing on the Half Moon Battery are 18-pounders made at the Carron Iron works near Falkirk.

Right This staircase links the remnants of the vaults in David's Tower with the battery platform above.

magnificient views of the city and its surroundings, has a blaze of glory each year when it is used for the Military Tattoo, but otherwise serves as the Castle car park.

The Gatehouse

The Gatehouse is not part of the real defences of the Castle but a symbolic entrance way built in 1887; its statues of Robert the Bruce and William Wallace were added in 1929. However, the ditch in front of it was started by Cromwell in the mid-seventeenth century, and only completed a century later. Its unusual shape allowed coverage from the walls and this three-sided form is echoed in the design of the later gatehouse. The retractable drawbridge was the last ever built in Scotland.

Eastern Defences

The rounded Half Moon Battery facing East is built over two storeys of the fourteenth century David's Tower, all but demolished in the great siege of 1573. Its artillery platform is at the same level as the principal buildings of the summit and the vaults were long used as a cistern to hold the Castle's water supply. The Forewall Battery extends northwards, incorporating a wall built in the 1540s. It ends in the Portcullis Gate, built over the gate-tower erected by Robert II. This had a residence for his constable on top and so was called the Constable's Tower.

The Portcullis Gate is also known as Argyle's Tower because the 9th Earl was imprisoned there before being beheaded. The upper part is an architectural oddity as it was added in Victorian times; it has openings for archers but artillery was the weaponry in use when the lower part was erected. Renaissance decoration on the original part of the gateway includes the arms of Regent Morton who rebuilt the Eastern defences in their present form, mainly in the late 1570s. Their commanding position can best be appreci-

ated by surveying from above the field of fire their guns command and then examining their invulnerability from the area below. Nevertheless, they did not survive the Civil War intact and needed to be repaired after Cromwell laid siege to the Castle in 1650.

Northern Defences

The Argyle or Six Gun Battery was constructed in the 1730s for Major General Wade. He had been called to the Scottish highlands to control the Jacobite insurgence and suggested also strengthening the north-western and northeastern approaches to Edinburgh Castle. Wade is well known in Scotland as many of the military roads and bridges he instigated were named after him. Mill's Mount Battery also looks north, giving fine views of Princes Street Gardens and the New Town, although when it was built these did not exist. The one o'clock gun is fired from its artillery platform every day. Below these batteries is

Left The Governor's House was erected in 1742. Today the main body of the house is used as the Officers' Mess of the Garrison although the right wing is still the Governor's residence. **Right** These vaults beneath the Great Hall are known as the French Prisons. **Inset** the imposing rough-hewn walls of the French Prisons.

the Low Defence, artillery outworks first built in the mid-sixteenth century but rebuilt in the seventeenth and eighteenth. This terrace was once used as the Governor's garden.

Cart-shed

The mid-eighteenth century cart-shed with its double pitched roofs has been frequently modified to serve different purposes. Formerly a barrack and an ammunition store it now serves as the Castle's tea room.

Governor's House

Several of the buildings inside the walls of the Castle are in styles pre-dating the era in which they were erected. In the case of the Governor's House with its crow-stepped gables the result is a happy one. Built in 1742 with wings to house the Master Gunner and Storekeeper, it is still in active use as an Officer's Mess while the right wing is the Governor's official residence.

Hospital

A side road leads to the Hospital, a series of buildings started in the eighteenth century but extensively remodelled as a hospital in the 'improvements' era of the late nineteenth century. The north block was then reconstructed in an early seventeenth-century style but the south block retains many of its earlier features.

Western Defences

Surrounding this range of buildings are the Western Defences built on two separate levels. The lower walls follow the natural line of the rock and mostly originate in the 1730s, although a walkway existed along this level in the mid-seventeenth century. This terrace has two sentry boxes and the northern one is named the Queen's Post. The upper terrace on the north and west sides of the Hospital replaces a simpler earlier wall. The two levels are joined by a stair inside a turret at the southern junction of these defences.

Southern Defences

The Southern Defences were built to prepare the Castle for a Jacobite attack in the early eighteenth century. They were the work of Scotland's military engineer, Theodore Dury and the highest battery bears his name. The other, Butts Battery, is so-called because the bow butts used for archery practice were nearby. These two batteries were five-gun emplacements connected to the Old Back Parade by steps. The defences were completed by 1713 and withstood the Jacobite assault two years later.

The Military Prison

The Military Prison was built about 1842 for offenders from all over Scotland. The exterior is carefully designed to fit into its historic setting and the interior

to allow all prisoners to be kept in solitary confinement. The cells are grouped around a central stairway and all can be centrally heated.

The French Prisons

When James IV wanted to build his Great Hall he obtained sufficient level ground for it by constructing a vaulted substructure on the rock face. These vaults extend under the hall and further west and have had many uses, including an arsenal, barracks, bakehouse and stores. But they are now known as the French Prisons, commemorating their use for prisoners of war in the eighteenth and nineteenth centuries. At the main entrance opening on Dury's Battery is graffiti carved in the stonework. They also put their carving skills to more practical use and an impressive ship model is currently displayed in the Scottish United Services Museum.

The vaults now contain 'Mons Meg', a huge siege gun which is one of the pair given to James II by his uncle in marriage, Phillip, Duke of Burgundy, in 1457. It consists of wrought-iron bars welded into a cylinder over a wooden core and bound with iron hoops. It was probably used as a muzzle loader and could fire a 500-pound stone nearly two miles. It was moved to sieges around the country, its wheels greased with Orkney butter and tended by more than

Left Eighteenth-century graffiti. The name of *Proyol Prisonnier nee Natiffe de Bourbourg* is engraved for ever in the stonework of the French Prisons' west entrance.

Right Mons Meg, an iron siege-gun, was forged in Flanders in 1449. It took 100 men, five carpenters and a large number of oxen to move the five-ton Meg.

Below Foog's Gate is the only archway leading to the upper enclosure. After many names, including 'foggy' and 'fogo', the mysterious 'foog' has stuck.

100 men. 'Mons Meg' burst while firing a birthday salute in 1681 but was later restored.

Hawk Hill

Hawk Hill is the second highest point in the Castle enclosure and came into especially heavy use in the eighteenth century. The New Barracks, which Sir Walter Scott likened to a vulgar cotton mill, was built in 1798. Earlier structures on the site included a guardhouse and artillery battery.

Foog's Gate

The road leading from Hawk Hill to the upper enclosure of the Castle passes through the protective wall by a small opening, Foog's Gate, placed so that it could be easily covered by fire from the nearby wall. This is of unknown origin but predates Charles II.

Crown Square

Crown Square is the centre of the medieval citadel but only two of its flanking buildings date from this period.

The Great Hall

The Great Hall was built by James IV and completed in the early years of the sixteenth century, but its interior has been over-imaginatively restored to the Victorian image of a medieval hall. Nonetheless it is remarkable so much survived as the building was crudely subdivided and used as a barracks and hospital for two centuries before its historic importance was realized. This hall was the meeting place of Scottish Parliaments until 1640. Earlier halls serving as communal living for the Castle household are mentioned in records but no traces survive. James IV used his hall for state ceremonial occasions and banquets. The King and his courtiers sat at the east end while the door at the west end was screened by draught-excluding timber screens. One of the hall's finest features is the hammer-beam roof, lost to view for two centuries. The restoration work done in 1887 to 1891 was financed by the publisher William Nelson.

There are many ancient and decorative features in the Great Hall.
Above The elaborate open-timbered roof.
Left A stone carving of a combined rose and thistle motif.
Below The hall has a fine display of arms and armour.

Right The Scottish Crown was remodelled in 1540 by order of James V. Together with the Sword of State and the Sceptre it is part of the Scottish Regalia.
Below In Queen Mary's Room the Old Pretender, father of Bonnie Prince Charlie, looks down from the oak panelling.
Below right The Royal Palace dates from the fourteenth century. The stair turret was turned into the Castle's main flag-staff in the early nineteenth century.

The Palace

The exterior of the Palace Block fronting Crown Square shows a compilation of styles due to the huge number of modifications made by monarchs through the ages.

Royal residences have been built on this site since James I but the basis of the present building was shaped by James IV. Two storeys and the classical windows were added between 1615 and 1617 for James VI's homecoming. The rather overbearing extension of the central turret for a flag staff was built in the early nineteenth century.

One of the most fascinating rooms inside the royal residence is the tiny bed chamber where Mary Queen of Scots gave birth to James VI of Scotland, later crowned James I of England. The entwined initials of Mary and Henry Darnley, MAH, are engraved outside the

door with the birthdate – 1566. For the birth it was hung with blue velvet and taffeta but the present decorations mostly stem from the preparations for James VI's homecoming. Also of great interest is the Crown Room where the Scottish Regalia, including the Sceptre and Sword and the Crown made for James V are on display. These were walled up inside the room for over a century after the Unions of Parliaments.

The Scottish National War Memorial

The Scottish National War Memorial was created after the First World War in honour of the 150,000 Scots who died. The basic structure is an eighteenth century barracks standing on the site of the medieval church of St. Mary's which had been put to use as a munitions store. Sir Robert Lorrimer transformed the interior of the barracks into a vaulted hall with the casket holding the names of the dead at the hall's focal point. The elaborate interior includes fine stained-glass windows by Douglas Strachan. The exterior was kept simple, with most decorative detail by the entrance. The memorial was opened by the Prince of Wales in 1927 and aroused such public interest that for some months queues of visitors stretched down to the Esplanade.

The Scottish United Services Museum

The Scottish United Services Museum was founded in 1931 to house weapons, uniforms, medals and insignia of the Armed Forces, some for display and others to be kept for military historians' research. It occupies some rooms in the Palace block and also in a separate museum. This building, originally officers' quarters, was erected in 1708 over a vaulted substructure.

Saint Margaret's Chapel

St. Margaret's Chapel is the oldest building in the Castle and in Edinburgh. Its Romanesque architecture dates it as early twelfth century and it was probably built by David I in memory of his mother, Queen Margaret, who was canonized in the thirteenth century. It was a royal chapel until after Mary Queen of Scots' reign but then was linked up with other buildings and put to secular use, ending up as a powder magazine. In 1845, the garrison chaplain noticed a font-like piece of stonework which turned out to be the socket of a pillar for a chancel arch. Queen Victoria urged its restoration but the chapel became, before long, little more

The oldest structure on Castle Rock, Saint Margaret's Chapel was the only building to survive when the Castle was captured by the Earl of Moray who razed it to the ground in 1313. **Above** The simple interior of the Chapel. After three centuries as a gunners' storehouse the Chapel was rediscovered in 1845 and rededicated in 1934.

than a souvenir kiosk. It was completely refurbished and finally rededicated in 1934. Though unremarkable on the outside, the interior features an arch with exquisite zig-zag ornamentation.

The Lang Stairs

The main medieval approach to the Castle's upper enclosure

was a steep winding staircase which has been continued to form the Lang Stairs.

Finally, no visitor to the Castle should fail to spend time admiring the magnificent view of Princes Street Gardens, the New Town and the Firth of Forth. On a clear day Fife can be seen in the distance.

The Royal Mile

The Royal Mile, a sequence of four connecting streets running roughly west to east from Edinburgh Castle to Holyrood Abbey, is the area of the city that is most steeped in history. Crossing the Esplanade below the Castle, you enter into Castle Hill, the oldest street in Edinburgh. Here you can see the development of a city from its medieval beginnings. Clustered at the start of Castle Hill and continuing along the ridge that comprises the Royal Mile are some of the most enticing sights and monuments of the city, detailing its gradual rise to one of the premier urban centres of the realm.

Castle Hill

The first building on the south side of Castle Hill is Cannonball House, built c. 1630. It derives its name from the cannonball lodged in the west wall, which tradition claims was fired from the Castle during the siege of 1745. Another explanation is that the ball marked the level to which water could rise by gravitation from the city's first piped-water system. The water was piped from Comiston Springs into the Castle Hill Reservoir, completed in 1851. It stands on the site of the first city water supply (1681) and is still in use.

To the north is Ramsey Garden, built on the site of the poet Allan Ramsay's house, which was referred to by local wits as 'Goose-pie'. Ramsay Garden is a shrine for town planners worldwide. Built in 1893 by Sir Patrick Geddes, it is the earliest example of organized town planning as we know it.

Back on Castle Hill is the Outlook Tower or Camera Obscura. Built in the seventeenth century, it was extensively altered in the 1850s by an optician who installed a camera obscura – a lens system which on a clear day projects an image of Edinburgh onto a concave white table. The lens and mirror were replaced in 1945 with a much improved system. Sir Patrick Geddes owned the

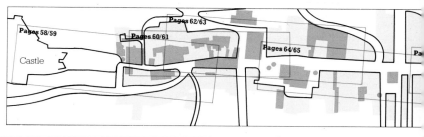

house from 1892 and created one of the first museums designed to teach people about other parts of the world. Much like an old-fashioned encyclopedia, there were rooms on geography, history and natural science among others.

Opposite is Boswell's Court, a seventeenth-century tenement which is named after the uncle of James Boswell, Dr. Johnson's biographer. Just to the east of Boswell's Court is The Highland Church of Tolbooth St. John's, completed in 1844. Designed by James Gillespie Graham and Augustus W.N. Pugin, this Gothic Revival pile is topped by the highest spire in the city (240 feet/73 metres). On Sunday afternoons, services are held in Gaelic.

Crossing the street once again, you come to Semple's Close. The mansion at the foot of the close, dated 1638, was the home of Grissel, Lady Semple, widow of the 8th Lord Semple. Once a garden enclosure, these 'closes' were gradually filled in as land be-

came scarce in the walled city. The narrow lane leading from the street took on the name close.

To the east is the site of the 'Palace' of Mary of Guise, demolished in 1861 to make way for the Church of Scotland General Assembly Hall, whilst across the road at the junction of Castle Hill, Lawnmarket and Johnston Terrace is the site of the Weigh House (demolished in 1822) and commemorated by a circle of 'setts' or rectangular stone blocks. This was the place for the weighing of butter and cheese for the use of the city.

Opposite is Milne's Court, an early attempt to create some open space in the Old Town. It was created by James Mylne, master mason to Charles II in 1690. Further down and set back from the street is James' Court. Built in 1725-1727, it was once a fashionable area, with a roster of distinguished tenants. Probably the best known was the philosopher David Hume.

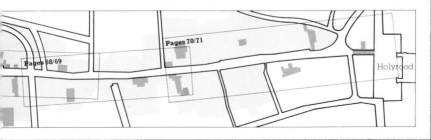

Continuing down the same side is Gladstone's Land. The original building dated from 1550, but in 1617, Thomas Gledstanes acquired the property and rebuilt it into a six-storey tenement. The only block of flats in Edinburgh with the original arcaded front, original painted interior decorations of the early seventeenth century still survive. Part of the National Trust of Scotland since 1935, it has recently been furnished much as it might have appeared in the last quarter of the seventeenth century.

Lawnmarket
You are now actually in The Lawnmarket (land market), originally the *agora* or marketplace of the Old Town. Here produce, butter, cheese, milk, meat and other edibles were displayed in stalls, with the exception of Wednesdays, when a special sale of linen and woollen cloth was conducted.

The close at the side of Gladstone's Land leads to Lady Stair's House, constructed in 1622 by Sir William Gray of Pittendrum. Owned in the early eighteenth century by Elizabeth, Countess Dowager of Stair, widow of the 1st Earl of Stair, it now houses memorabilia and manuscripts of three great Scottish men of letters: Robert Burns, Sir Walter Scott and Robert Louis Stevenson.

Across the Lawnmarket will be found Riddle's Close and Court, rebuilt by Captain George Riddle after 1726. David Hume lived here before moving to James' Court. In the inner court is the late sixteenth-century mansion of Bailie John McMorran, shot to death by one of the students of the high school. The Bailie's house was nevertheless of high repute, and was borrowed in 1598 (three years after his death) by the Town Council for a banquet in honour of James VI and his Queen.

Next to Riddle's Close is Brodie's Close. One of the more colourful characters in the history of Edinburgh, Deacon William Brodie (son of Francis, after whom the Close is named) was a respected cabinetmaker and member of the town council by day and a burglar by night. His success was not without hazard however. On October 1, 1788, along with an accomplice, he was hanged at the Tolbooth on a scaffold of his own design. Robert Louis Stevenson used Deacon Brodie as the model for *Dr. Jekyll and Mr. Hyde.*

Just past the George IV Bridge, you will find one of the last remaining wells in the Old City. At one time ten public wells existed in different locations.

In front of St. Giles' Cathedral is the site of the Edinburgh Tolbooth, marked by a brass plaque in the roadway and a heart-shaped design of setts. The Tolbooth may well have dated from the last years of the fourteenth century. Since then it has accommodated the Scottish Parliament, Edinburgh Town Council and the Courts of Law, as well as being used for executions and as a prison. As a jail, it was immortalized by Sir Walter Scott in *The Heart of Midlothian.*

Though a church has existed on the site of St. Giles' Cathedral since AD 854, the present structure dates, in this form, from 1829, when the exterior was clad in ashlar. However, the four central pillars date from about 1120 and the crown spire was completed in 1495. Actually, it is more appropriate to refer to the Church as the High Kirk of Edinburgh since it was a cathedral proper only for the five years following the introduction of bishops to the Presbyterian Church of Scotland by Charles I. After the Revolution of 1688, the title remained. The rather gaudy Chapel of the Order of the Thistle was added in 1911. The name St. Giles derives from a Greek hermit who settled in Provence in the sixth century.

Commemorated in the interior, amongst others, are the Regent Moray, who was assassinated, and two implacable enemies, the 1st Marquis of Argyll and the 1st Marquis of Montrose, both of whom were executed.

Behind the cathedral are located Signet Library and Parliament Hall. The Library is reached by passing through the narrow passage to the top half of Parliament Square. The Upper Hall is perhaps one of the finest bits of Georgian interior design in all of Edinburgh. The buildings themselves were finished in 1815 and are still in use by the Writers to HM Signet, now the principal body of solicitors in Scotland.

Parliament Hall was built at the behest of Charles I. It was the home of the Scots Parliament from 1639 to 1707 and the Treaty of Union. Since that time it has been the seat of Scotland's supreme courts.

The Hall contains a magnificent seventeenth-century hammer-beam roof and stained-glass windows depicting the inauguration of the Court of Session by James V in 1532. Below the Hall is the Laigh (low) Hall which Cromwell once used as a stable.

Two statues beside Parliament Hall are worth your attentions. To the west is a figure of John Knox by Pittendrigh McGillivray, erected in 1906 not far from Knox's grave; whilst to the east is the oldest lead equestrian statue in Britain, erected in 1688, of Charles II. Due east of the façade of Parliament Hall is the Mercat Cross. This marks the spot where merchants gathered to conduct business. Also the scene of assorted executions and other public celebrations, the Cross was the place from which Royal Proclamations were read. The Cross itself is nineteenth century with only a small section of the shaft left from the original sixteenth century erection.

High Street

The stretch of the Royal Mile from the Cathedral to opposite John Knox's House is known as the High Street.

The most imposing building on the High Street is the City Chambers, erected in 1761 as the Royal Exchange. It is now the meeting place of the Edinburgh City District Council. Within the arches facing the street are war memorials for 1914-1918 and 1939-1945.

New Assembly Close, opposite, leads to a courtyard containing the Edinburgh Wax Museum. From 1736 to 1784, members of 'society' staged charity balls here. Later used by the Commercial Bank of Scotland,

the building was opened as the Wax Museum in 1976. The famous and infamous figures of Scotland's past are members of the cast, alone and in historical tableaux: Mary, Queen of Scots, John Knox, Robert Burns and Burke and Hare.

Tron Church (Kirk) founded in 1637 and opened for worship in 1641, was meant for the part of the congregation for whom there was not room in St. Giles. Named after the 'trone' or salt-weighing machine standing to the north, the great fire of 1824 destroyed the spire and did other extensive damage. The present steeple was erected in 1828. Closed as a church in 1952, and with the exterior restored, Tron Kirk is still the congregation point on Hogmanay; Old Year's Night.

Further down the hill at the bottom of the High Street, next to John Knox's House, is to be found Moubray House, with traces of the structure going back to 1477. The painter George Jamieson lived here in the 1630s, and Daniel Defoe edited the *Edinburgh Courant* from here in 1710.

John Knox's House is the last house on the street to retain its top storey wooden gallery, saved by the supposed connection with the great religious reformer when plans for widening the street were proposed in 1849. Inside are displays on his life, and the architecture is a classic example of domestic structures of the time of Mary, Queen of Scots.

On the other side of the street is the Museum of Childhood, the first museum in the world devoted solely to childhood history, which contains one of the world's finest collections of toys, model dolls, hobby items and memorabilia of children.

The Canongate

The Canongate derives its name from the time when King David I gave the Augustinian canons of Holyrood permission to build on either side of their path or 'gait' between the abbey and the Royal Burgh of Edinburgh. In fact, it was a separate town, so to speak, until 1636 and did not come under the aegis of the Edinburgh Town Council until 1856. Unlike Edinburgh proper, the Canongate was never a walled town and suffered accordingly. However, after James IV began building the Palace of Holyroodhouse, the area became increasingly fashionable as a residential sector for members of the court. After 1800, with the move to the more chic New Town, Canongate degenerated into a slum. After World War II, Robert Hurd led a crusade to save the Canongate houses, and the area has been restored and given a new life. Once again it has become a fashionable residential district,

'Chessel's Court, built in 1748 by Archibald Chessel, was advertised as 'neatly finished and fit to accommodate a genteel family'. In turn the building housed the Scottish Excise Office. A burglary here in 1788 led to the arrest of Deacon Brodie. Almost opposite is the Effigy of Moor, a remembrance of the tenement once here known as Morocco Land. The legend has it that in the early seventeenth century, Andrew Gray, the younger son of a noble family, was sentenced to death for leading a riot. Escaping to sea, he made a fortune in Morocco, returned to Edinburgh in the disguise of a Moor and threatened to sack the city. Instead, he cured the Lord Provost's daughter (his cousin) of the plague, married her and set up house on the spot where the cure had been effected.

Old Playhouse Close is named after the theatre opened here in 1747. The scene of several riots from passionate audiences, the theatre was closed in 1767. At its peak, the box office draw was reputedly as much as £70 per night. Box seats cost half a crown and the pit cost one and sixpence. The theatre succeeded in spite of clerical opposition and Sarah Siddons played here.

Smack in the middle of the Canongate outside Old Playhouse Close is the site of St. John's Cross, indicated by a circle of setts in the roadway. Charles I, making his ceremonial entrance into Edinburgh in 1633, was greeted by the provost, whom he knighted

in the time-honoured fashion on the spot.

Moray House, constructed about the time of Charles I accession to the throne, remained in the possession of the Moray family until the middle of the nineteenth century. Cromwell stayed here twice. The seventeenth-century plaster ceilings are in a remarkable state of preservation. In that same century the gardens were particularly famed. Now part of a teacher-training college, Moray House stands as one of the monuments to a more gracious age.

Across the street is Bible Land. Built in 1677 by the Incorporation of Cordiners (shoemakers) of the Canongate, the tenement is named after the sculpture above the stair entrance, quoting the first verse of Psalm 133. Also upon the shield are to be found the crown and rounding knife of St. Crispin, the patron saint of the shoemakers, who practised their craft within these walls. Note particularly the gables and termination of the stair tower.

Canongate Tolbooth, built in 1591 in the Franco-Scottish style, was the centre for the collection of public dues, the courthouse, the prison and the municipal affair centre for the independent borough of the Canongate. The motto of the armorial bearing of the Canongate is *Sic itur ad astra* (This is the path to the stars). Now used as a museum, it contains the J. Telfer Dunbar Tartan Collection, temporary exhibitions and a brass-rubbing centre. Here, visitors can make rubbings of moulded replicas of medieval brasses and Pictish inscriptions.

Canongate Church was built in 1688 with funds willed by Thomas Moodie of Edinburgh for the purpose of providing an alternative place of worship for parishioners displaced from the old parish church in the Abbey of Holyrood. The churchyard contains the remains of many famous Scots including the economist Adam Smith, the poet Robert Ferguson (the stone paid for by Robert Burns), and Mrs. Agnes McLehose, Burns' Clarinda. The Fergusson marker contains a verse by Burns:

No sculptured Marble here nor pom-
pous lay
No Storied Urn nor animated bust
This simple Stone directs Pale Scotia's way
To pour her Sorrows o'er her Poet's Dust.

The original Canongate Mercat Cross is
now located in the churchyard.

Across Canongate are located the Huntly
and Acheson Houses. Built in 1570 for John
Acheson, Huntly House was originally three
separate houses as can be seen from the
gables above. Restored in 1932, it is now the
museum of the local history of the city. Located within are a splendid collection of
silver and glass and the National Covenant
of 1638, signed by citizens as a protest
against Charles I's attempt to establish Epis-
copacy in Scotland and introduce a new
service into the Church. Huntly House is also
known as the 'speaking house', because of
the inscriptions displayed on sixteenth-
century plaques on the front of the building,
supposed to have been placed there to
answer criticisms as to the magnificence of
the structure.

Acheson House, to the east, dates from
1633 and was built for Sir Archibald Acheson, a councillor to Charles I. Since 1952 it
has been the headquarters of the Scottish
Craft Centre. In a rear courtyard is a doorway topped with Sir Archibald's crest – a
cock surmounting a trumpet – and the motto
'Vigilantibus' with the date, 1633.

On the north side of the Canongate, extending east from Canongate Church, are a
number of interesting sites. The seventeenth-century garden, reached through
Dunbar's Close, is a reconstruction of the
formal gardens of the time. Panmure House,
reached by way of Little Lochen Close, and
once the town house of the Earls of Panmure,
was the home of Adam Smith, author of *The
Wealth of Nations,*

Reid's Court, named after an eighteenth-
century coachmaker, was built c.1690 and
was the Manse of the Canongate until 1832
and again from 1958. The Site of Golfers'
Land was supposedly erected by a
shoemaker, John Paterson, with his share of
the winnings from a golf match. The game
took place on the Leith Links and his partner
was the Duke of York, later James VII and II.
Whitefoord House, now home for veterans,
was built in 1766, but stands on the site of
'Seton Palace' where Lord Darnley stayed
on his first visit to Edinburgh.

Across from Whitefoord House stands
Queensberry House, erected in 1681 by
Lord Hatton. Now a hospital for the elderly,
Queensberry House was bought a few years
later by William, 1st Duke of Queensberry.
His son, James, was the principal promoter
of the Treaty of Union of 1707, a part played
to the displeasure of nearly everyone in
Scotland. Supposedly, when he was out
gathering signatures for the treaty his eldest
son, Lord Drumlanrig, who was thoroughly
mad, roasted a Canongate kitchen boy and
was found devouring his flesh

Just before the Canongate runs off into
Abbeyhill stands the Site of Girth Cross,
marked by a circle of setts in the roadway.
Known to exist until 1750, the Cross was the
scene of many executions and marked the
sanctuary area (western boundary) that surrounded the Abbey and Palace

White Horse Close was named after the
White Horse Inn, which occupied the building (1623) at the rear of the close. Now
restored, this was the main coaching house
for travellers to and from London.

Finally, before entering the precincts of
the abbey and Palace you come to the
Abbey Strand and Sanctuary, once the residence of aristocratic debtors. The 'Abbey
Lairds', as they were known, were safe from
arrest withing these precincts, including
Holyrood Park and Arthur's Seat. Only on
Sundays could they venture safely forth. The
sanctuary was in effect from around 1128
until 1880 when imprisonment for debt was
abolished.

And so, after a leisurely journey through
the history of a city, you now stand at the
gates of Holyroodhouse.

▲1 Ramsay Lodge
This row of remodelled
Georgian houses in a
highly romantic late
Victorian style was built
on the site of the gardens
of Ramsay Lodge.

▶2 Ramsay Gardens

THE
ROYAL
MILE

Castlehill

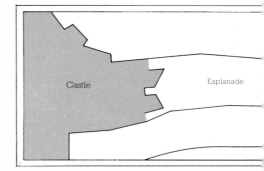

◀6 Castle Gatehouse
The gatehouse was built
in 1887 to create a fitting
entrance to the Castle,
without much heed to any
military logic. The
drawbridge was the last
built in Scotland.

▶▲7 Canonball House
Legend says the ball,
lodged in the bricks, was
fired from the Castle in
the 1745 rebellion but
another theory claims it
marks the gravitation
height of the first water
supply.

▲ 3 Witches Well
The iron fountain marks the spot where hundreds of witches, 'some evil, some misunderstood', were burned to death between 1479-1722.

◀ 4 Outlook Tower
An optician, Maria Theresa Short, installed a camera obscura here in the 1850s. A new lens and mirror were added in 1945 and the camera still gives a fine panoramic view of the city.

▼ 5 Tolbooth Kirk
The kirk was built in 1842-1844 for the General Assembly of the Church of Scotland and the Tolbooth congregation. It has the tallest spire in the city – 240 feet (73m).

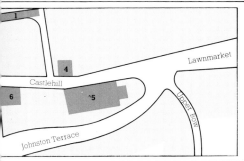

▼ **2 Riddle's Close**
2 Riddle's Close
King James VI and his
Queen attended a
banquet here in 1593, not
long after it was built by
burgess George Riddell.

◄▲ 1 Wardrop's Court
In 1790 a burgess and
wright of the city, John
Wardrop, built a
tenement here. Four
dragon figures guard the
entrance and Lady Stair's
house rises from within.

THE
ROYAL
MILE

Lawnmarket

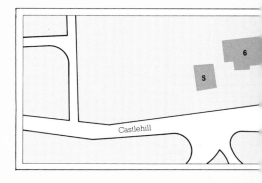

Castlehill

6

5

◄ 4 Gladstone's Land
This six-storey tenement,
completed in 1620,
housed burgess Thomas
Gledstanes. The main
rooms now show a typical
seventeenth-century
home and the original
shopbooths display
period goods.

▶ 5 Milne's Court
This reconstruction of the
city's first open square
was named after the
Master Mason to King
Charles II, James Mylne,
who designed the
extensions to
Holyroodhouse and the
Castle.

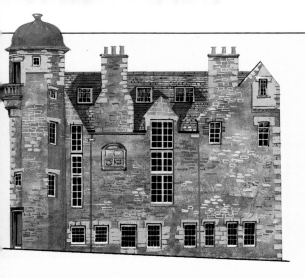

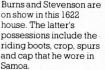

◀▼ 3 Lady Stair's House
Relics of the writers Scott, Burns and Stevenson are on show in this 1622 house. The latter's possessions include the riding boots, crop, spurs and cap that he wore in Samoa.

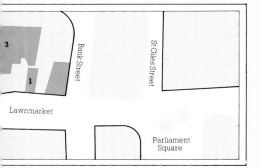

◀ 6 James' Court
David Hume and James Boswell both lived here; Adam Smith and Dr. Johnson were visitors. The court, which has three entrances, was built between 1725 and 1727 by a wright, James Brownhill. The original, destroyed in 1857, was rebuilt.

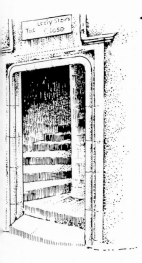

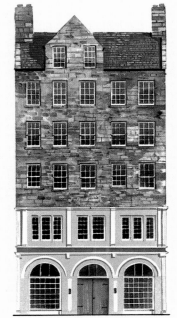

▲ 7 Deacon Brodie's Tavern
This tavern was named after the infamous William Brodie, respectable citizen by day, burglar by night.

Across the street is Brodie's Close, named after William's father, a glass-grinder and burgess of the city. William lived there before his hanging in 1788.

► 1 Parliament House
▼ and Statue of Charles II

This is the only surviving equestrian statue in Britain of this king. The building was completed in 1639 for the Scottish Parliament and used by it until the Union in 1707. It is now part of the Law Courts.

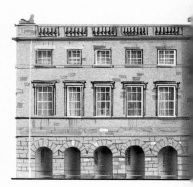

THE
ROYAL
MILE

High Street

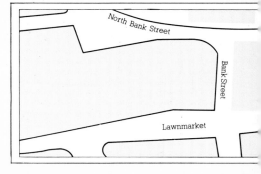

North Bank Street

Bank Street

Lawnmarket

▲ 3 The Heart of Midlothian (The Old Tolbooth)

The granite blocks embedded in the road mark the entrance to the old Tolbooth prison, demolished in 1817. The old custom of spitting on the heart survives today.

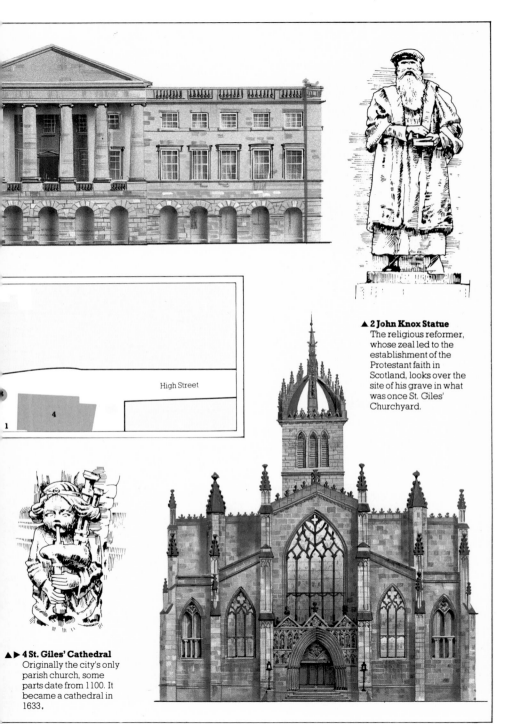

High Street

4

1

▲ **2 John Knox Statue**
The religious reformer,
whose zeal led to the
establishment of the
Protestant faith in
Scotland, looks over the
site of his grave in what
was once St. Giles'
Churchyard.

▲▶ **4 St. Giles' Cathedral**
Originally the city's only
parish church, some
parts date from 1100. It
became a cathedral in
1633.

◀ 1 City Chambers

The City Chambers were built as the Royal Exchange with coffee houses, flats and a printing press between 1754 and 1757. The Town Council took it over in 1811.

▶ 2 Edwardian placard

One of a series of enamelled Edwardian advertisements on the front of the Waverley Cameron Pen Company Building in Blair Street.

THE
ROYAL
MILE
High Street

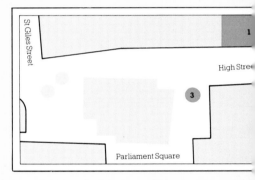

St Giles Street

High Street

1

3

Parliament Square

EDINBURGH WAX M

▲ ▶ **3 Mercat Cross**
The first cross, a focus for
the market where royal
proclamations were
read, dates from 1365.
The present one, paid for
by Gladstone, used the
shaft of a cross
demolished in 1756.

◀ 5 Tron Kirk
Founded in 1637 by
Charles I for those
displaced when St. Giles
became a cathedral, this
church is named after a
tron, or weighing
machine, that stood on
the site.

North Bridge

High Street

5

Hunter Square

4

2

**◀▼ 4 Edinburgh Wax
Museum**
The 1766 New
Assemblies Hall now
houses the city's Wax
Museum based on the
work of the Gems family.
Mary, Queen of Scots,
and a scene from *Alice in
Wonderland* are included.

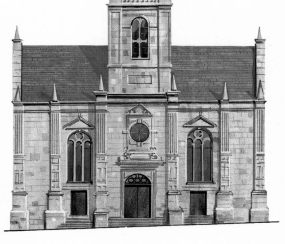

◀ 1 Museum of Childhood
This sign gives a taste of
the charms of a large and
varied collection of
historic dolls, games and
hobbies inside.

▲ 2 Paisley Close
These words, above the
entrance to the close,
were the cry of a boy
trapped under rubble
when tenements nearby
collapsed in 1861.

THE
ROYAL
MILE

High Street

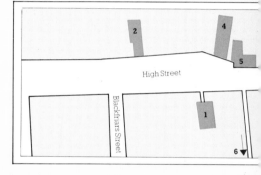

High Street

Blackfriars Street

◀ 5 John Knox's House
The house, possibly the
oldest dwelling in the
city, dates from 1490. It
belonged to Mariota
Arres and her husband
James Mosman and their
initials decorate the

outside. Knox may have
lived here from 1561 to
1572. It was bought by the
Church of Scotland,
became a museum in
1853 and was again
restored in 1958.

3 Netherbow Port

The brass plate marks the position of the last Netherbow Port, one of six city gates, built in 1513 and demolished in 1764. The heads of criminals and preachers were displayed there.

▶ 4 Moubray House

Built around 1462, this was a tavern in the eighteenth century, Daniel Defoe's office, and later Constable's bookshop. In 1890 the upper floors were a temperance hotel.

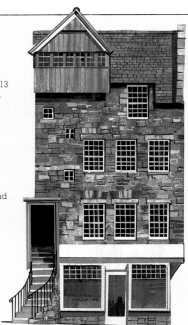

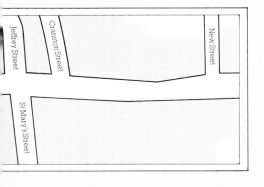

◀ 6 St Patrick's Church

Like many of the later public buildings of the Old Town, St Patrick's Church is tucked away in a close. Originally a Church of England chapel, it was consecrated as Episcopal Church, Cowgate in 1771; it changed its name to its present one in 1856, when it became a Roman Catholic church.

1 The Tolbooth

Built in 1591 as a council chamber, court house and jail, the tower of the Tolbooth is set with fearsome, but useless, gun ports. The clock was added in 1884.

Canongate

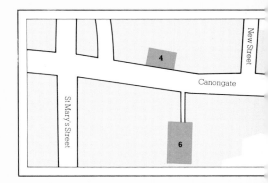

◀ 3 Bakehouse Close

A property in the close was once owned by the Incorporation of Bakers of the Canongate. The archway was formed in 1570. Records from 1851 show that 230 people lived here.

▶ 4 Morocco's Land

This tenement is named after the stone, life-sized figure of a Moor, which was probably a late seventeenth-century merchant's sign, but the motto has long since been erased.

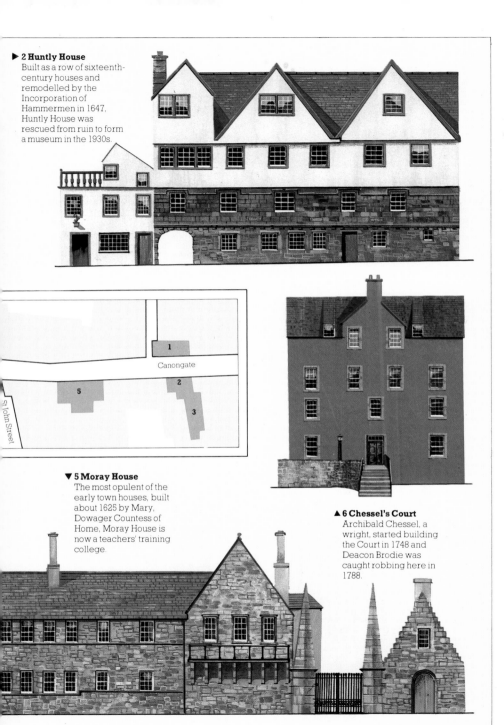

▶ **2 Huntly House**
Built as a row of sixteenth-century houses and remodelled by the Incorporation of Hammermen in 1647, Huntly House was rescued from ruin to form a museum in the 1930s.

Canongate

St John Street

1

2

3

5

▼ **5 Moray House**
The most opulent of the early town houses, built about 1625 by Mary, Dowager Countess of Home, Moray House is now a teachers' training college.

▲ **6 Chessel's Court**
Archibald Chessel, a wright, started building the Court in 1748 and Deacon Brodie was caught robbing here in 1788.

◀▲ 1 Canongate Church
This church was built in
1688 for those displaced
when James VII and II
converted the abbey at
Holyrood for the use of
the Knights of the Thistle.

THE
ROYAL
MILE

Abbey Strand

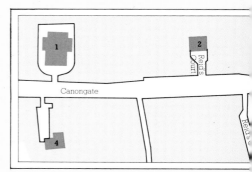

Canongate

◀ **3 White Horse Close**
This close was used as
the Royal Mews in the
sixteenth century and in
1623 a merchant built an
inn and coaching stable
here, naming it after
Queen Anne's white
palfry. Jacobite officers
used the inn as
headquarters in the 1745
rebellion. the close was
restored In 1965.

Canongate Manse
uilt in 1690 as a coaching
n, this building became
manse in 1789 and
mained one until 1832.
fter having fallen into
isrepair it was restored
1958, and once again
ecame the home of the
inister of the Canongate
hurch.

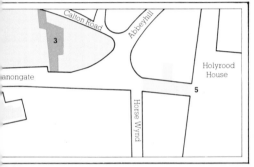

▲ **4 Acheson House**
Sir Archibald Acheson,
one-time Secretary of
State for Scotland under
Charles I, built this house
in 1633. It was restored in
1937.

◀ **5 Holyroodhouse Gates**
Set at the entrance to the
magnificent palace, the
wrought-iron gates were
part of the 1922 national
memorial to King
Edward VII.

At the foot of the Royal Mile stands one of the most imposing royal residences in the world. For over nine centuries Holyrood has been the scene of pomp and glory – and of bloodshed and turbulence. It is still the official Scottish home of Britain's Royal Family.

The Palace of Holyroodhouse

The splendid royal palace that conceals a gruesome and grisly past

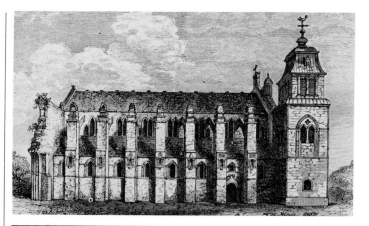

Left Today the ruined nave and the northwest tower are all that remain of the mediaeval splendour of the Abbey of Holyrood. The vaulted ceiling collapsed under its stone roof in 1768.
Below This isometric engraving of the Royal Palace appeared in Maitland's *History of Edinburgh* in 1753, an

*G*littering pageantry vies with a notorious murder and a splendid but grisly funeral in the crowded history of the Palace of Holyroodhouse, official Scottish residence of Britain's Royal Family. Down the centuries, the palace has seen dark events as well as grand designs, riot combined with revelry, fire and bloodshed along with the splendours of court life.

Bonnie Prince Charlie, Mary, Queen of Scots, Oliver Cromwell and the King he beheaded, Charles I – a note of grimness and tragedy runs through many of the names so inextricably linked with the fortunes of the Palace. It came into existence as a guest house associated with the medieval abbey which was founded in 1128 by King David I after a hunting accident that he barely survived. According to legend, the King was knocked from his horse and wounded in the thigh by a stag which then tried to finish him off. But a cross miraculously appeared between its antlers, the King clutched it, and the animal slunk away, suitably crushed. In thankfulness for his deliverance, David bequeathed the land to Augustinian canons then living in Edinburgh Castle and he

ordered them to build the Abbey of Holyrood, known as the 'Church of the Holy Cross'.

The guest house for royal visitors was built to the west of the now-ruined abbey. Scottish kings lodged there in its earliest use as a royal residence, and James II was born, crowned, married and buried within its walls. In 1501 James IV decided to transform the guest house into a palace fit for a king and spent large sums on new buildings. An imposing four-storey corner tower was built with a gabled roof and balustrade – it is the northwest tower

of the present building and still the most eye-catching feature. After James IV's death at the battle of Flodden Field, his son carried on the work of creating royal apartments and had reception rooms and bedchambers built above the ground floor vaults.

It was on the second floor that Mary, Queen of Scots had her rooms, and some of the original decoration survives in the painted ceilings and freize of her bedchamber. Mary, regarded by Catholics as the rightful Queen of England, was dining in her small supper room

authoritative work 13.9 inches thick.

Right An aerial view of the Palace of Holyrood House, with the ruined abbey in the foreground. Originally built in the forests east of the town, the Palace was much more secluded than it is today. Salisbury Crags can be seen in the background.

in the west turret on March 9, 1566, along with guests who included her Italian secretary – and hated favourite – David Rizzio. Protestant plotters accompanied by Mary's second husband, Henry, Lord Darnley, burst in over the Queen's protests and dragged Rizzio to an antechamber where they stabbed him to death. His body was left with 56 dagger wounds. A brass tablet marks the spot.

The early Palace was only about 30 years old when, in 1544, an invading English army burned down most of it – and the adjoining abbey for good mea-sure – while laying waste to the countryside around Edinburgh. The great tower survived the flames, however, and after it had been repaired and extended the Palace buildings surrounded three courtyards occupying roughly the same site as the present ones. The palace stayed largely unchanged until 1650, when an accidental fire reduced it to ruin except for the tower, whose massive walls saved it for the second time. Oliver Cromwell, who had quartered some of his troops there earlier that year while subduing the rebellious Scots, ordered major rebuilding but in a style regarded as highly inferior to the original, and it stayed that way until the monarchy was restored with Charles II.

In 1661 Holyrood saw one of the most spectacular funerals in Edinburgh's history. The royalist Marquis of Montrose, who had been executed by Cromwell for high treason and his limbs cut off for display around the country, was rehabilitated for a grand ceremony of farewell. One of his legs was brought from Aberdeen in an elaborate casket, his head from a spike in the capital, his other leg and his arms from Glasgow, Stirling and Perth, and the rest of his remains from the local gallows. After four months' lying in state in the chapel of Holyrood, the pieces of the Marquis were paraded through the crowded streets in a coffin carried by 14 earls and buried in the Kirk of St. Giles.

Although he never actually entered Holyrood, Charles II – the Merry Monarch – began building the existing Palace in 1671. It was a massive reconstruction which involved tearing down Cromwell's handiwork and erecting a new façade flanked at one end by the old tower put up by James

The Palace of Holyroodhouse.

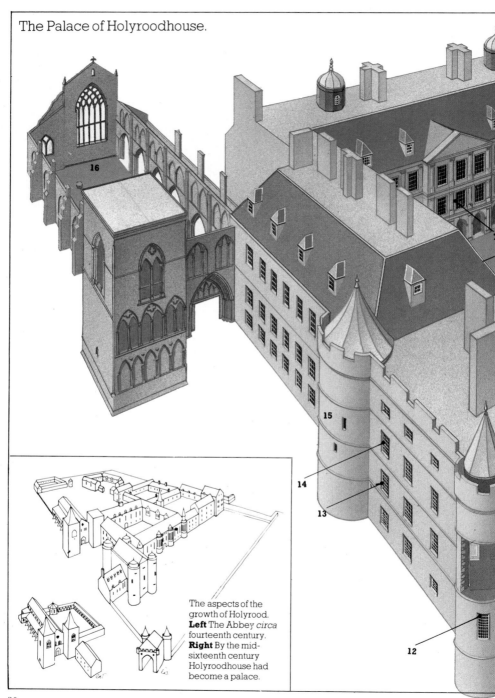

The aspects of the growth of Holyrood. **Left** The Abbey *circa* fourteenth century. **Right** By the mid-sixteenth century Holyroodhouse had become a palace.

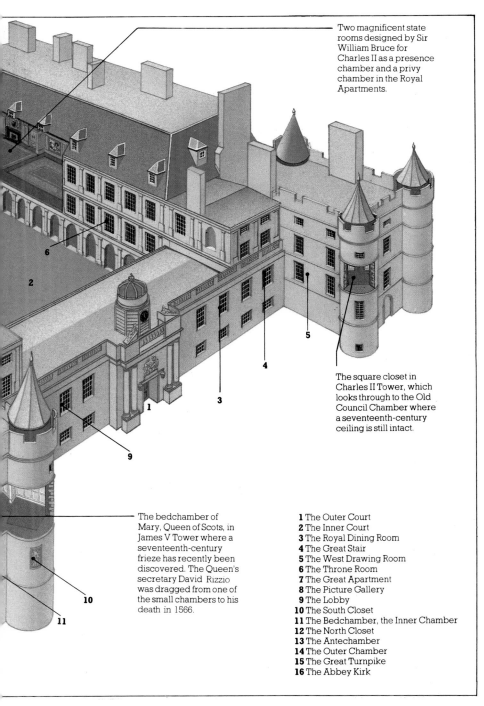

Two magnificent state rooms designed by Sir William Bruce for Charles II as a presence chamber and a privy chamber in the Royal Apartments.

The square closet in Charles II Tower, which looks through to the Old Council Chamber where a seventeenth-century ceiling is still intact.

The bedchamber of Mary, Queen of Scots, in James V Tower where a seventeenth-century frieze has recently been discovered. The Queen's secretary David Rizzio was dragged from one of the small chambers to his death in 1566.

1 The Outer Court
2 The Inner Court
3 The Royal Dining Room
4 The Great Stair
5 The West Drawing Room
6 The Throne Room
7 The Great Apartment
8 The Picture Gallery
9 The Lobby
10 The South Closet
11 The Bedchamber, the Inner Chamber
12 The North Closet
13 The Antechamber
14 The Outer Chamber
15 The Great Turnpike
16 The Abbey Kirk

IV more than 150 years earlier. The plans were drawn up by Sir William Bruce, a proven loyalist and fine architect, and the King's Master Mason, Robert Mylne, was called in to translate the design into stone. The total cost, sky-high for that time, was £57,000.

The Palace is built round an elegant, Italian-style courtyard quadrangle with an arcaded loggia and superimposed Doric, Ionic and Corinthian orders. On one projection there is a pediment bearing the Royal Arms, with its Scottish elements to the fore. The west front combines the medieval tower, which Charles II was anxious to retain, with the Renaissance-classicism of the grass-covered courtyard. To achieve the effect he wanted, Bruce designed a matching tower on the southwest and linked the two with a screen dominated by a grand entrance of four Doric columns surmounted by the Royal Arms of Scotland. The motto 'In Defence' is emblazoned above the crest, while at its base are the Latin words *'Nemo Me Impune Lacessit'* (No one provokes me with impunity), motto of the Most Noble Order of the Thistle. The general style of Palace architecture is French, of the time of Louis XIV. The north side of the quadrangle contains the renowned Picture Gallery, with the State Apartments on the southern side.

Work on the new Palace was well under way by 1676 and three years later it was largely completed, with the truncated abbey becoming the Chapel Royal. The clock on the cupola over the gate bears the date 1680. A variety of non-Scots took part in the interior finishing. Two Englishmen did the ornamental plasterwork, a Dutchman was responsible for the carving, and the decorative painting was by another Dutch-

Left This splendid fireplace of black veined marble is in the Morning Drawing Room. *Cupid and Psyche* are enclosed within the ornately carved wooden chimneypiece

Below The largest of the historical rooms, the Picture Gallery is still used for many state functions. Set into the panelling are the portraits of 111 Scottish monarchs.

man, Jacob de Wit.

De Wit's major legacy is to be found in the Picture Gallery – framed portraits of 111 Scottish kings and queens. A deed drawn up between Hugh Wallace, His Majesty's Cashkeeper, and de Wit 'binds and obleidges him to compleatly draw, finish and perfyte The Pictures of the Haill Kings who have Reigned over this Kingdome of Scotland... and to make them like unto the Originalls which are to be given to him'. De Wit set to with a will, but doubts have been cast on the accuracy of the likenesses he produced between 1684 and 1686 with the aid of old portraits supplied by the government. He was paid £120 a year for the work, which begins with King Fergus in the fourth century and ends with James VII – James II of England. A good deal of imagination seems to have gone into his masterpiece; more than 30 of de Wit's kings apparently never existed. Sir Walter Scott described the gallery as 'long, low and ill-proportioned, hung

Right The atmosphere of the seventeenth century is recaptured in Charles II's State Bedroom. The grand canopied bed dates from 1672.
Above The elaborate plasterwork on the ceiling is the work of Dunsterfield and Hulbert. It surrounds de Wit's *Apotheosis of Hercules*.

with pictures affirmed to be the portraits of kings who, if they ever flourished at all, lived several hundred years before the invention of painting in oil colours'. Undaunted, today's Royal Family holds state ceremonies in the gallery, which is the largest of the palace's 'historical apartments'. Representative peers of Scotland were elected in the gallery, which measures 150 feet (45 m)

long, 24 feet (7·2 m) wide and 20 feet (6 m) high. It was here that Bonnie Prince Charlie – otherwise Charles Edward, the Young Pretender – held sparkling levees during a stay in Edinburgh in 1745.

From the Picture Gallery, the State Apartments of the James IV tower are entered through a chamber known as the Duchess of Hamilton's Drawing Room, which has ornamental ceilings and oval panels containing the cypher of Charles II. The Throne Room and drawing rooms all feature fine paintings, tapestries, furniture, panelling and ceilings. In the older part of the Palace are Lord Darnley's Rooms, consisting of an audience chamber, bedroom and dressing room with fireplaces of marble and Dutch tiles, portraits and ancient tapestry.

Queen Mary's corresponding apartments on the second floor are reached by a turnpike stair from Darnley's audience chamber. The public, by the way, has no access to a small private staircase by which the murderers of Rizzio entered the Queen's rooms on that fateful night in 1566. The supper room, where the attack on the Italian was mounted, is perhaps the most interesting of these apartments, at least for students of history Coffered ceilings of oak are among the few fixed features left from Mary's time at Holyrood, but two panels embroidered in cross-stitch on linen canvas were genuinely

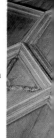

The richly carved ceiling of the Inner Chamber, or Queen's Bedroom, in James IV Tower is emblazoned with the initials of James V and his wife, Mary of Guise, mother of Mary, Queen of Scots. The panels were painted later, in the seventeenth century, and bear monarchs' emblems.

David Rizzio

Lord Darnley

Mary, Queen of Scots

The murder of Rizzio

Mary, Queen of Scots chose for her second husband in 1565 her cousin Henry Stuart, Lord Darnley. He was handsome and amusing and his claims to the English throne could bolster her own, but he was also violent, arrogant and had talents for making enemies. The royal pair soon quarrelled and when Mary was six months' pregnant with Darnley's child, he accused her of an affair with her Italian secretary. Jealous of the Queen's affection for the accomplished David Rizzio, Darnley found support for his hatred in those who thought the foreigner an undeserving, ambitious upstart. One cold night in March 1566 Darnley and his cohorts climbed the dark, hidden steps to Mary's chambers and dragged the screaming Rizzio from the Queen's supper table. In the corridor outside they stabbed him again and again. Rizzio died at Mary's feet with more than 50 wounds in his body. Darnley's dagger stood deep in his heart, left there for all to see by Darnley's accomplice, Lord Ruthven. Mary was distraught at the Italian's death but suspected that Darnley had wanted her dead too. He was killed by his enemies in an explosion at Kirk o'Field in 1567.

worked by the Queen during her imprisonment in England, where she was eventually put to death at the order of Elizabeth I. Her work is signed with her monogram, MR.

The outer room, known as Queen Mary's Audience Chamber, 24 feet (72 m) long and 22 feet (66 m) wide, has a splendid display of heraldic symbols representing the arms of James V, King of Scots; his Queen, Mary of Guise; Mary, Queen of Scots; her first husband, the Dauphin of France; and his father, King Henry II of France. At the east end there is an oratory, and part of the freize which adorned the walls in Mary's time has been uncovered. Other panels contain the crowned initials of James V and his Queen. The initials recur in the inner chamber, called Queen Mary's Bedroom, which has panelled compartments with the emblems of Scottish sovereigns in the ceiling. The walls are hung with tapestry. More tapestry, much decayed, hangs in a small dressing room

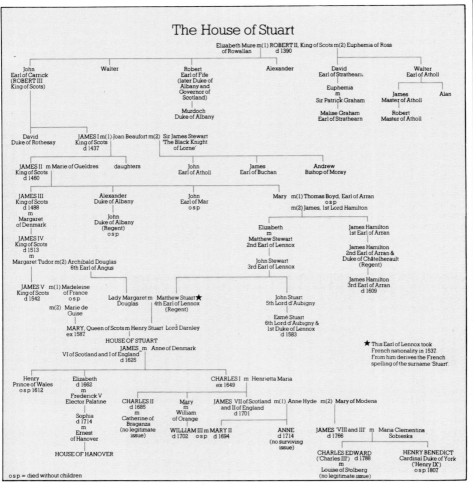

The House of Stuart

Elizabeth Mure m(1) ROBERT II, King of Scots m(2) Euphemia of Ross
of Rowallan — d 1390

- John, Earl of Carrick (ROBERT III King of Scots)
- Walter
- Robert, Earl of Fife (later Duke of Albany and Governor of Scotland)
  - Murdoch, Duke of Albany
- Alexander
- David, Earl of Strathearn
  - Euphemia m Sir Patrick Graham
    - Malise Graham, Earl of Strathearn
- Walter, Earl of Atholl
  - James, Master of Atholl
  - Robert, Master of Atholl
  - Alan

David, Duke of Rothesay

JAMES I m(1) Joan Beaufort m(2) Sir James Stewart 'The Black Knight of Lorne'
King of Scots
d 1437

JAMES II m Marie of Gueldres — daughters — John, Earl of Atholl — James, Earl of Buchan — Andrew, Bishop of Moray
King of Scots
d 1460

JAMES III — Alexander, Duke of Albany — John, Earl of Mar (osp) — Mary m(1) Thomas Boyd, Earl of Arran (osp) m(2) James, 1st Lord Hamilton
King of Scots
d 1488
m
Margaret of Denmark

John, Duke of Albany (Regent) (osp)

JAMES IV
King of Scots
d 1513
m
Margaret Tudor m(2) Archibald Douglas, 6th Earl of Angus

Elizabeth m Matthew Stewart, 2nd Earl of Lennox
John Stewart, 3rd Earl of Lennox

James Hamilton, 1st Earl of Arran
James Hamilton, 2nd Earl of Arran & Duke of Châtelherault (Regent)
James Hamilton, 3rd Earl of Arran d 1609

JAMES V m(1) Madeleine of France (osp)
King of Scots
d 1542
m(2) Marie de Guise

Lady Margaret m Matthew Stuart ★ 4th Earl of Lennox (Regent)
Douglas

John Stuart, 5th Lord d'Aubigny
Esmé Stuart, 6th Lord d'Aubigny & 1st Duke of Lennox d 1583

MARY, Queen of Scots m Henry Stuart Lord Darnley
ex 1587

HOUSE OF STUART
JAMES m Anne of Denmark
VI of Scotland and I of England
d 1625

★ This Earl of Lennox took French nationality in 1537. From him derives the French spelling of the surname 'Stuart'.

Henry, Prince of Wales (osp 1612)

Elizabeth d 1662 m Frederick V Elector Palatine
Sophia d 1714 m Ernest of Hanover
HOUSE OF HANOVER

CHARLES I m Henrietta Maria
ex 1649

CHARLES II d 1685 m Catherine of Braganza (no legitimate issue)

Mary m William of Orange
WILLIAM III m MARY II d 1702 osp d 1694

JAMES VII of Scotland m(1) Anne Hyde m(2) Mary of Modena
and II of England d 1701

ANNE d 1714 (no surviving issue)

JAMES 'VIII and III' m Maria Clementina d 1766 Sobieska

CHARLES EDWARD ('Charles III') d 1788 m Louise of Stolberg (no legitimate issue)

HENRY BENEDICT Cardinal Duke of York ('Henry IX') osp 1807

osp = died without children

which adjoins the bedroom and occupies the eastern turret of the tower. Tapestries in the State Apartments came from the looms of Flanders, Brussels and Paris in the sixteenth and seventeenth centuries, but much of the furniture dates from a later period.

Sir William Bruce's scheme for the State Apartments involved more rooms than Charles II finally decided to have. Bruce wanted to keep to the tradition of a separate suite of rooms and private stairs for the King and Queen. In each suite there was to be a guard hall, a 'presence chamber', a bedroom, dressing room and closets, planned so as to bring the bedrooms near to each other. But the King chose the eastern section for his apartments because he wanted to look out towards a garden he had made on the site of the demolished abbey's cloister. Except for her bedroom, the Queen's rooms were constructed in the southern range of the Palace. Charles also ruled out having the private chapel on the ground floor of the tower, insisting that the chapel should be at the eastern end of the long gallery where private family prayers could be said near his presence chamber.

With the building near completion, work was held up by political uncertainties and a lack of funds. The south and west quarters of the Palace were left unfinished, and a good deal of the oak panelling and plasterwork to be seen now is modern. But it fits in well with the original work – sympathetic treatment which has been credited to the Royal Family's interest since the Palace became their home in Scotland's capital.

A sun dial made in 1633 by a royal master mason graces the garden to the northwest of the James IV tower. It has carvings of various royal heraldic badges and the crowned initials of Charles I. The fountain in the palace forecourt was put up by Queen Victoria, and a small building called Queen Mary's Bath House stands in a corner of the one-time garden. She was reputed to have bathed there in wine.

During Bonnie Prince Charlie's stay in 1745, the Palace became the focus of a glittering court life, most notably the grand levee he staged in the long gallery. But then Holyroodhouse fell into disuse as a regular royal residence. The Duke of Cumberland lived there for a short time in 1746 after a punitive campaign in

Scotland, but 50 years then went by before royalty came back in the person of a refugee from the French Revolution, Count d'Artois. He lived there for four years and later returned as the exiled King Charles X, staying for three more years. James Boswell, the author and traveller, described Holyrood as 'a virtuous place where no monarch dwells'. The tide turned in 1822, however, when George IV – the first Hanoverian king to set foot on Scottish soil – held a levee in the Palace but failed to take up residence because he found it uninhabitable. Queen Victoria and Prince Albert stayed in the royal apartments in 1850 and enjoyed their visit so much that they made a habit of resting at Holyroodhouse on their travels to and from Balmoral Castle.

Repair works prevented King Edward VII and Queen Alexandra from moving into the Palace in 1903, a year after their coronation, but they delighted Edinburgh society by holding a levee there. Holyroodhouse came more frequently into royal use with the accession of King George V and Queen Mary, who paid seven state visits between 1911 and 1934. Much redecoration and renovation were authorized by the royal couple, who had several

The sumptuous bedchamber of Mary, Queen of Scots was linked to Lord Darnley's below by a private staircase in James IV Tower. The Queen's room has since been changed and the bed moved to the King's Suite in the newer part of Holyrood Palace commissioned by Charles II.

Mary worked two of these panels when she was in the custody of George Talbot, 6th Earl of Shrewsbury. The cat and mouse expressed her own situation. Bess of Hardwick, George's wife, embroidered the third.

uncompleted state rooms panelled in oak to harmonize with the original designs. The kitchens were entirely remodelled and Queen Mary personally directed the refurnishing of many rooms. More lavish and colourful ceremonial revived under King George VI and Queen Elizabeth, the present Queen Mother. They took up residence and held a whole series of state functions in the Palace shortly after their coronation in 1937. Their many further visits have been emulated by the present Queen and Prince Philip, Duke of Edinburgh, since she succeeded to the throne.

Since 1929, the palace has had the official designation of the Palace of Holyroodhouse, a title first used centuries ago. Since its triumphant return to royal favour, the days seem long past when Robert Louis Stevenson wrote in 1896: 'The Palace of Holyrood has been left aside in the growth of Edinburgh and stands grey and silent in a workmen's quarter between breweries and gas works.'

However, all that now remains of the glory of the medieval 'fair Abbey of Holyrood' is reflected in its ruined nave. Only a section of the north wall and the roofless nave are from the original twelfth-century chapel. The magnificent window of the east wall dates back to the seventeenth century, when the abbey was partially restored for the coronation of Charles I. The abbey's story is one of destruction and violence. The transepts and choir were brought down by church order in 1569 and the vaulted ceiling of the nave collapsed during a storm in 1768, felling the main arcading on the north side. The western front is generally in the English style, with intrusions of later Gothic. Gravestones pave the floor of the nave, and among the tombs is that of Sir James Douglas, who killed the Earl of Arran in 1596 and was himself stabbed to death by Arran's nephew in the High Street of Edinburgh 12 years later.

Rioters played their part in the abbey's long descent to ruin. The trouble erupted after James II fled from his throne and William and Mary arrived from Holland in the 'bloodless revolution' of 1688. Supporters of the Dutch Orangeman overwhelmed a company of musketeers defending the Palace and rampaged through the royal apartments, tearing out all the furniture and ornaments of the private chapel. Then, in a passion to purge the abbey of Roman Catholic ornaments, they burst into the kirk and smashed it up. The lids of lead coffins in the royal burial vault were stolen for their high market value, and the bones of kings and princes were said to have been left exposed for many years. The mob built a huge fire in the outer court, burning books, images and every last symbol of Catholicism – or so they thought. In fact, the altar vessels were saved and are now held by the Scottish hierarchy of the Catholic Church. The royal vault was restored by Queen Victoria in 1898. Occupying the east end of the south aisle, it contains the remains of such Kings of Scots as David II, James II, James V and of Lord Darnley, consort of Mary, Queen of Scots.

For almost four centuries the abbey was a haven for debtors – not only paupers but professional men like doctors and lawyers who had fallen on hard times. Even the exiled King Charles X of France stayed there at one time. Debtors began seeking refuge in the abbey in the 1530s, and a small township grew up nearby with shops, taverns and markets. Inhabitants were under strict rules: they had to secure a place to sleep and report to the man in charge, the bailie, within 24 hours of arriving, but after that they were safe from the law.

The leave was allowed between midnight on Saturday and midnight on Sunday, and one debt-ridden minister used to walk 20 miles to preach in his parish and then trudge back again within the time limit. The last debtor recorded as having entered the abbey for sanctuary was an Edinburgh solicitor in 1880.

When it was founded in 1128, the abbey was in fact part of a sanctuary stretching from the base of the present-day Royal Mile to Duddingston Loch and covering what is now known as Holyrood Park. Today, despite its ravages, it remains an oasis of peace and serenity not far from the bustle of the city.

The Old Town

The tumult of ages has bequeathed old Edinburgh a brooding appeal.

Winding alleys, dark lanes and thoroughfares steeped in history make up the Old Town of Edinburgh. It stretches from the Castle to the Palace of Holyroodhouse down the Royal Mile, main street of the medieval burgh. Romantic and picturesque, the Old Town is the very core of Scotland's capital, rescued from one-time squalor and restored to city pride. Built on a ridge ending with the towering Castle Rock, where Picts first founded a settlement in pre-historic times, it has captured the imagination of travellers through centuries of high drama. Washington Irving, the nineteenth-century American author who spent seventeen years in sojourns throughout Europe, was especially captivated. He wrote of the Old Town that '... the shadows of a thousand sad memories mingle with the light of other days upon it, sombre, sublime, silent in its age'. The antiquity and charm of this area have never been overshadowed by the New Town, the spacious and graceful city extension conceived in 1752. The main reason has to be a brooding appeal which stems from its history of violent death, of folly and betrayal, of noble patriotism and religious dedication.

Perhaps most evocative of the good – or bad – old days are the Grassmarket and the Cowgate, lying south of the Castle and the High Street. Cowgate, an extension of Holyrood Road leading from the Palace, was originally a country lane along which cattle were driven to pasture. This narrow and somewhat sombre road has known its ups and downs in the life of the Old Town. In the fifteenth century it began to be a fashionable suburb with lavish mansions and private wells to provide acceptable drinking water for the gentry. Cowgate was described by the writer Alexander Alesse in the early sixteenth century as the place 'where the nobility and chief citizens dwell and the greatest in the land have their palaces, where nothing is cheap or mean but all things are magnificent'.

Some of the rich residents apparently disliked the road's somewhat earthy name, and the street degenerated over the years to the point where traveller Alexander Smith wrote in 1865: 'The inhabitants are morally and geographically the lower orders. They keep to their own quarters and seldom come up to the light of day. Many an Edinburgh man has never set his foot in the street. The condition of the inhabitants is as little known to respectable Edinburgh as are the habits of moles, earthworms and the mining population.' At the eastern entrance to the Cowgate stands the Magdalen Chapel, which was erected about the middle of the sixteenth century and contains what are regarded as the best examples of rare pre-Reformation stained-glass windows in Scotland. The windows represent the Royal Arms, encircled with a wreath of thistles. The chapel now serves as the University Chapel of Heriot-Watt University.

Farther to the east stands St. Cecilia's Hall, which has a world-famous collection of over 30 keyboard instruments including harpsichords, clavichords, fortepianos, spinets, virginals and chamber organs.

On the south side once stood the Blackfriars Monastery, a Dominican friary founded as far back as 1230.

Cowgate then passes under an arch of South Bridge and into a valley between the Heriot-Watt University on the south and the National Library of Scotland to the north. The library, opened by Queen Elizabeth II in 1956, contains more than three million books and manuscripts, the largest and most valuable collection of its kind in Scotland.

Take note of Guthrie Street, on the south side. Sir Walter Scott was born there in 1771, in a house long demolished and now marked by a stone tablet. After passing under George IV Bridge, Cowgate opens into the Grassmarket, a stately 230-yard (210 m) long rectangle standing in splendour under the lofty heights of the Castle. The tree-lined Grassmarket is a pleasant place now, but it has to be set against a bloody backcloth of murder and execution. At the east end, a small enclosed garden marks the place where the public gallows stood until 1784, when a halt was ordered to executions in the Grassmarket. 'Common criminals' died in

their hundreds on this spot, along with high-born leaders and rebel Covenanters – of whom at least 100 were hanged between the years 1661 and 1688. The site of the gallows is marked by a St. Andrew's Cross, in rose-coloured cobblestones, which bears the inscription: 'For the Protestant faith on this spot many Martyrs and Covenanters died.' The particular irony of the inscription is that, in the complex religious divisions of that era, it was other Protestants who ordered the executions. When one Covenanter stood on the gallows and refused to recant his faith in the face of death, the Duke of Rothes is said to have remarked: 'Then let him glorify God in the Grassmarket.'

The Grassmarket's most notorious inhabitants were infamous murderers. In Tanner's Close, long vanished, William Burke and William Hare carried out their trade of supplying corpses to surgeons for medical research. They lured paupers and prostitutes to their lodging house and strangled them. Hare finally turned against his companion in crime and got away with murder, but Burke was hanged in the Lawnmarket on 28th January 1829. The judge who sentenced him said in court: 'I trust that if it is ever customary to preserve skeletons, yours will be preserved in order that posterity may keep in remembrance your atrocious crimes.' The judge's remark was heeded, and Burke's body was delivered to the Department of Anatomy at Edinburgh University, where many of his victims had ended up. His skeleton may still be seen there today.

Murders, riots and executions apart, the Grassmarket had an important trading role in the life of the Old Town. In 1477 King James III granted a charter for a weekly market which was held regularly until 1911, when it

Spires emerge from the Old Town, viewed from above Calton churchyard.

was removed to Saughton in the west of the city. Circuses, cockfighting and other so-called entertainments were once a feature of the bustling market-

place nestled into a hollow at the base of Castle Rock. A plaque commemorating the 500th anniversary of the charter was unveiled in the west end of

area was so crowded that travel was almost impossible between the Grassmarket and the Cowgate leading to Holyroodhouse Palace. And yet this is still the largest open space in the Old Town. From the West Bow, so named because it was within arrow shot of the Castle, it extends just over 230 yards (210 m) to King's Stables Road.

In the heart of the Old Town you find tall, crammed buildings, dating from the fifteenth to the seventeenth century and almost Dutch in appearance. But only the occasional summer fair brings back the atmosphere of the ancient market. Perhaps the best example of the Grassmarket's age and architecture can be seen halfway down the north side, before you reach Castle Wynd. A stairway entrance, only three feet (0.9 m) across, carries the inscription: 'Blessed by God for all his giftis.' Shops selling clothes and antiques are the main attraction of the Grassmarket today. Fascinating little shops abound, some offering rare books, others selling kitchen utensils, some telling visitors that it's their last chance to pick up a really good brush or broomstick.

In a passage at the southwest corner of the Grassmarket is a section of the Flodden Wall, which was painstakingly built around Edinburgh after the Scots suffered a dreadful defeat by the English at the battle of Flodden Field in 1513. Some authorities say that the legendary caution of Edinburgh folk is exemplified by the fact the wall took the best part of 50 years to build. Nevertheless, it defined the limits of the burgh for 250 years; it now serves as the western boundary of the grounds of George Heriot's School, founded and endowed in 1628 by the goldsmith to King James VI.

There is another special sight to see on the north side of the Grassmarket. It is the White

the Grassmarket in 1977.

What a marvellous place the old marketplace must have been. Printers, tanners, brewers, tobacconists, corn merchants and 'such trades as prepare cat gut from the intestines of animals' all lived, worked and sold their goods there. On Fridays, the main market day, the

Hart Inn, an early eighteenth-century hostelry which has beautiful wallhead gables to the front and two semi-octagonal stair towers at the rear. Among noted guests at the inn were the poets Robert Burns and William Wordsworth.

Before leaving the Grassmarket, do have a look at the new Mountbatten building of the Heriot-Watt University, which was erected in 1968 on the site of the old Corn Exchange.

At its southeast corner the Grassmarket joins ancient Candlemaker Row and the southern part of the Old Town; it connects with the fragment of West Bow which now runs into Victoria Street West Bow, formerly led to the heights but was remodelled in the nineteenth century to join the George IV Bridge.

At the upper end of Victoria Street stand the India Buildings, erected in 1867 and now used mostly as a magistrate's court.

Candlemaker Row was named in recognition of one of Edinburgh's great crafts, which flourished from 1488 until gas lighting emerged early in the nineteenth century. The hall of the ancient Corporation of Candlemakers can be found at the head of the row. It was built in 1722 and restored in 1929. At the road junction in front of the hall is a memorial to 'Greyfriars Bobby', the Skye terrier who kept a 14-year vigil at the grave of his master in the adjoining churchyard. The main entrance of the churchyard, once the garden of a Franciscan monastery, can be reached through a lane at the top of Candlemaker Row.

More than any other place of worship in Edinburgh, Greyfriars Kirk reflects the turbulent history of the Church of Scotland from the Reformation in 1559 to the establishment of the Protestant faith in 1689. Its his-

The old craft of candlemaking revived with a modern touch.

tory is particularly closely associated with the Covenanters. The church was opened in 1620 – the first built in Scotland since the Reformation. It owned two 'repentance stools' on which worshippers with a record of unseemly behaviour were forced to sit during services. One of these stools has survived and is now to be seen at the National Museum of Antiquities in Queen Street. During the 1650s, when Oliver Cromwell's troops occupied Edinburgh, Greyfriars was used as a barracks. The congregation was unceremoniously kicked out. The church suffered badly at the hands of the soldiers, and a collection for repairs was taken at all the places of worship in Edinburgh when Greyfriars was handed back to the congregation in 1653. The church suffered yet again in 1718, when gunpowder stored in the tower by the city fathers exploded. The event was recorded by the Court Clerk in this way: 'On Wednesday the 7th of May instant 1718, about a quarter of an hour before Two of the Clock in the morning, the Grayfrier Church Steiple was blown up, which Surprized and allaramed the whole City, more particularly the Grayfrier Congregation. By which the Gray-

frier Church sustained so great damage as it was rendered unfit for the Congregation to assemble therein for publick worship...' After fresh repairs the kirk was reduced in size and a new church was built as an extension in 1721, with a dividing wall. It also suffered serious damage in a fire in 1845. Eventually the entire church was restored, the dividing wall was removed in 1938, and now the united congregations worship in the Kirk of the Greyfriars.

Today the church is architecturally quite unremarkable, a somewhat featureless oblong with an interior in a simple Gothic style. Its unbroken nave extends for 150 feet (45 m). But it stands in an historic enclosure – the churchyard occupying a spectacular site between the George IV Bridge and the Grassmarket. Its fame is chiefly associated with the signing of the National Covenant in 1638. Here, on February 28, in what is now the churchyard, the entire congregation gathered with Edinburgh's noblemen and merchants to put their names to the Covenant, which pledged all its signatories to fight anyone trying to establish the 'papist' religion in this country.

In effect, it professed loyalty to King Charles I but warned him not to interfere in the affairs of the Scottish Kirk. The Covenant, which also called for a free Scottish Parliament, was said to have been signed on a tombstone in the churchyard – sometimes in blood. Copies were later signed in churches all over Scotland.

On the side of the churchyard backing onto Candlemaker Row is the Martyrs Monument, erected in 1688 to the memory of Covenanters who had been executed in Edinburgh more than 20 years earlier. Its inscription reads, in part: 'Here lies interred the dust of those who stood 'gainst perjury, re-

Public executions were witnessed from these windows on the north side of the Grassmarket.

sisting unto blood, adhering to the Covenants and laws… Their lives were sacrificed unto the lust of prelatists and abjur'd.'

The majority of the martyrs were buried in the churchyard, ironically not far from the tomb of the man who ordered their torture and execution. He was Sir George Mackenzie, a Lord Advocate – or royal prosecutor – who came to be known as 'Bluidy Mackenzie'.

In the southwest corner of the churchyard is the Covenanters' Prison, now barred and locked. Some 1200 Covenanters, captured at the battle of Bothwell Bridge, were imprisoned here for five months here – under open skies and through the grim Edinburgh winter of 1679.

Rigorously guarded, the inmates were allowed a daily ration of one 'penny loaf', but in many ways they were better off than their leaders – who were condemned to enslavement in the American plantations.

Round the churchyard walls are a range of stately monuments and ornate tombstones commemorating famous citizens of old Edinburgh. Here are the last resting places of William Adam, the classical architect; Joseph Black, renowned physicist and chemist; George Buchanan, tutor to Mary, Queen of Scots; John and George Watson, who founded the hospitals that bear their names; Gaelic poet Duncan Ban McIntyre; James Craig, architect of the New Town; and Dr. Thomas McCrie, church historian and biographer of John Knox. But it must be said that most visitors head straight for the grave of Greyfriars Bobby, the faithful terrier. The spot is marked by a headstone provided by the 'American Lovers of Bobby'.

To the south, on the western side of the quaintly named Middle Meadow Walk, stands one of Britain's leading hospitals, the Royal Infirmary. It started in a humble way in 1729 as a 'hospital for the destitute sick', with only six beds. The site is marked by a plaque at the top of Infirmary Street. A second royal infirmary was completed in 1748, starting with about 70 beds but growing as funds increased. Between 1762 and 1765, according to medical records, 15,600 patients were admitted, of which about 75 percent were discharged as cured. The records show that about 750 patients died under treatment, and quite a few 'left of their own accord'. The foundation stone of the present building was laid in 1870 by the Prince of Wales, later Edward VII, and the new hospital was opened nine years afterwards. There was a major extension in 1939, when the Royal Simpson Maternity Pavilion was opened. Nowadays the Royal Infirmary is one of the most important centres in the country for training doctors. Thousands are treated each year at the hospital, which has a number of associated homes and clinics.

There is quite an inspiring story about the building of the first infirmary. Its true creator was George Drummond, who was elected six times as Lord Provost (Mayor) of Edinburgh and is regarded as the father of the city. Drummond struck a chord among the residents when he appealed for funds to meet this crying need in eighteenth-century Edinburgh. Money poured in from firms as well as individuals, from church-door collections and social groups who had the name of 'dancing assemblies'. Well-off citizens provided cash in response to Drummond's appeal. Landowners and quarrymasters gave stone, slates and timber. Farmers supplied carts for carrying materials to the site. Some English companies gave glass for the windows – and many Edinburgh workmen toiled there without wages for one day a month. The sacrifices were made out of a genuine desire for progress – and one wonders whether such dedication could emerge today in a different but no less traumatic climate.

The New Town

*T*he prime mover for the New Town, its inspiration and drive, was the city's Lord Provost, George Drummond.

Drummond, who had the idea from one mooted at the time of Charles II a century earlier, started planning the extension to the city when he was first elected Lord Provost in 1725. In his biography the Reverend Thomas Somerville quotes a fascinating conversation he had with Drummond:

'I happened one day . . . to be standing at a window (in the Old Town) looking out to the opposite side of the North Loch, then called Barefoot's Parks, in which there was not a single house to be seen. "Look at these fields," says Provost Drummond. "You Mr. Somerville are a young man and may probably live, though I will not, to see all these fields covered with houses, forming a splendid and magnificent city. To the accomplishment of this nothing more is necessary than draining the North Loch and providing a proper access from the Old Town. I have never lost sight of this object since the year 1725 when I was first elected Provost.'

But it was not until 1752 that his 'Proposals' were published and 14 years later a competition for the final plans opened. It was won by an unknown 23-year-old architect, James Craig, son

Detail of a Charlotte Square window (**above**) and the Moray Estate (**left**).

of an Edinburgh merchant. Only six had entered the contest and the prize was the freedom of the city and a gold medal. For James Craig there was also overnight fame.

The cause of all the planning was the great increase in population (the Scots economy was improving) to about 50,000 who were crammed within the ancient city walls on an area of 138 acres (55.2 ha). Conditions were gruesome, disease rife and crime high. It was clear something had to be done.

Drummond, six times Lord Provost between 1725 and 1764, was met by plenty of traditionalist opposition to his visionary ideas but he was shrewd enough to push them through in well-spaced stages.

First came the publication of the 'Proposals' in 1752, setting out the intention to build on the green fields overlooking the city to the north. Then in 1765 a contract was awarded for the building of North Bridge to take a new road across the valley of Nor' Loch to the port of Leith – and at the same time give access to the New Town land (much of which had been bought already by speculating city officials).

A year later, the year of Drummond's death, the competition was announced and in 1767, only two weeks after Parliament in Westminster had passed the Act to extend the city limits, Craig's win was announced.

The first stage

Craig's plan was classic and grand, with its grid-iron pattern of squares, gardens and parallel streets. But it was simple, too, and without any detailed drawings for the rows of houses that were to come. That was left to other architects.

The street names were an integral part of the design and symbolized the parliamentary union between England and

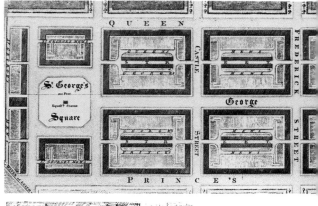

Above Craig's triumphant design in the 1776 competition for a New Town plan. **Left** The 23-year-old winner at work. **Far right** The architect Robert Adam in profile. **Below** One of the finest examples of his genius, Register House, designed in 1772. **Right** Interior of Register House.

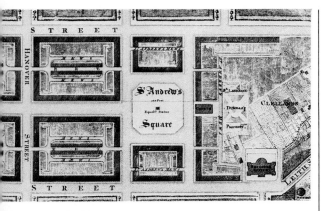

Scotland, glorifying George III and the House of Hanover. George Street, the main axis, linked two magnificent squares that were to be St. George's and St. Andrew's, the patron saints of England and Scotland, but Queen Charlotte thought differently and the former was soon renamed after her.

The outer streets were Princes and Queen Streets and were crossed by Frederick (George's son), Hanover and Castle. The ones in between, where the trades and craftsmen were to thrive, were Thistle and Rose Streets, named after the national emblems of Scotland and England.

There was, though, a reluctance on the part of the townspeople to build in the New Town area and the city's council soon came to the conclusion that incentives would have to be offered.

Mr. John Young, who built his house at Thistle Court, off St. Andrew's Square, was awarded £20 for being the first to make his home in the New Town. The silk merchant John Neale was exempted from city rates when he built the first house in Princes Street in 1769.

In 1777 advertisements invited plans 'by which buildings might be erected in the most regular, handsome and commodious manner'. Plain-fronted tenements, double flats and houses began to spring up but there was no uniformity of style and by 1782 the city decided to impose a few rules. Every house on the main streets, for example, was to be three-storeyed with a sunk basement and a frontage of not more than 48 feet (14.4 m). Failure to comply meant a £30 fine and immediate removal. But the more elaborate houses were designed by the notable architects of the day and the New Town became the fashionable place to live.

By now Robert Adam had

Above Charlotte Square in detail from the air; and the original elevation plan drawn by Robert Adam for the north and south sides (only the north was built). **From the left**: The view of West Register House from the square, the square's surroundings; intricate old street lamps; and an elegant doorway.

made his reputation as a stylish young architect in England and had made some very influential friends. But he returned to his native Scotland (which he had left calling it 'a narrow place') for the chance to design great public buildings.

Register House, where the historic and administrative records of state are kept, was started in 1774 from designs of Robert's and his brothers James and John. Robert did not actually move to Edinburgh but, as the building progressed, John kept an eye on it and Robert visited. It took more than 12 years to build and cost the government £31,000 but it is still one of the most remarkable architectural features of the city with its huge dome and splendid frontage. The former home of Sir Laurence Dundas flanks the east side of St. Andrew's Square. This square is one of the richest in the world due to the number of banks and insurance headquarters there. In the centre is a statue of Henry Dundas 1st Viscount Melville, a powerful Scottish figure in the 1780's.

At the other end of George Street, balancing St. Andrew's Square, is Charlotte Square, the most spectacular and beautiful of Adam's achievements. It was designed by Robert Adam who had been commissioned by the town council in 1791 to produce a unified scheme of frontages for the houses in the square – something quite new to a city where only a similarity in style had been attempted.

Robert died the following year and a letter written by his brother James afterwards asks for payment on account of a promise to Robert of 200 guineas for the elevations for Charlotte Square. But, accounting difficulties aside, the building went ahead and the rectangular square, with streets entering at each corner, one side of elegant frontages mirroring its opposite side and

The beauty of the Royal Bank of Scotland, formerly Sir Laurence Dundas's home, designed by Sir William Chambers in 1772. The star shapes cut in the ceiling allow light in. Light, this time at night, illuminates the Assembly Rooms (**right**).

the gardens in the middle, is a major achievement in European civic architecture.

Princes Street, once regarded as the most beautiful street in Europe, grew up rather haphazardly, starting at the beginning of the building of the New Town and not ending until 1805. It has a glorious open view on the south side across the gardens to the Castle. But this now much-admired view was once under threat. Town officials, greedy for the profits

of development, discussed a plan to enclose the south side of the street and, after a running battle, the gardens' owners were smart enough to take out a 99-year lease on the land in 1771, which prevented any building at all.

During the building of Princes Street's north side the excavated earth from it, and other streets, was used to fill in the already drained Nor' Loch to make private gardens for the residents. These were jealous-

lost his fortune after a divorce and a disastrous second marriage.

It was Miss Burns' custom to take an evening walk along Princes Street where she attracted much attention. But it was her behaviour at her home that caused enormous trouble – particularly to a Lord Swinton whose back windows overlooked hers. The matter ended in court where Bailie – later Lord Provost – Creech heard the case and expelled her from the city on pain of six months in a House of Correction, a 'drumming' through the streets and further expulsion. But she appealed to higher courts and won the right to stay.

Bailie Creech's dislike of the 20-year-old beauty was well known and the matter prompted comment from many. Even Robert Burns has his say on the lady:

> Cease, ye prudes, your
> envious railing:
> Lovely Burns has charms –
> confess:
> True it is she had one
> failing:
> Had a woman ever less!

The second stage
By the close of the eighteenth century the New Town had become the fashionable place to live and in the 1820s the Governors of Heriot's Hospital, who owned the land immediately to the north, embarked upon a speculative extension to the New Town. This second stage was largely residential and has remained so. The scale therefore is more homely and the downhill sloping site gave magnificent views across the Forth to Fife. The whole development was largely under the control of Robert Reid, the Master of the King's Works in Scotland, and William Sibbald, Superintendant of Works in the City, and thus has more architectural unity than the first stage.

ly guarded from the public – possibly because it was the owners who had to pay for planting and laying them out.

The garden owners were issued with keys, for £1 each, to get into the gardens but it was not long before a Rose Street locksmith was producing replicas and a builder of houses in Castle Terrace gave his buyers keys which just happened to fit the garden gates!

The Mound, which divides the gardens, was begun by a Lawnmarket clothier, George Boyd, in 1781 as a shortcut for his New Town customers. His mud brig was officially sanctioned by the Town Council and more than two million cartloads of soil from the foundation of New Town houses were dumped there in his time.

Rose Street was also the centre of a scandal which shocked the local residents. In about 1789 a young lady called Miss Burns moved to the street from Durham where her father had

It too is based on a grid system. The outward-looking Heriot and Fettes Rows flank Northumberland, Cumberland and Great King Streets, which lead onto the massive open spaces of Drummond Place and Royal Circus.

Royal Circus was the work of William Playfair, possibly the most prolific and influential of Edinburgh's architects. He was born in London in 1789, the son of a Scots architect, and when his father died in 1793, William was sent to Edinburgh to his uncle John, professor of mathematics and, later, of natural philosophy, at the city's prestigious university.

William first gained attention when he won a competition for a design which would complete the university, largely planned by Robert Adam. He went on to do a massive amount of work until his death in 1857. Donaldson's Hospital was his largest work but the others were scarcely inconsiderable: the National Gallery, the Calton Hill scheme, the National Monument and New Observatory, the Royal Institution (now the Royal Scottish Academy), the Royal College of Surgeons. The list is almost endless – even the Princes Street railway line was his design.

This phase, too, met with great opposition. Robert Chambers, writing his *Walks in Edinburgh* in 1825, says the building of Heriot Row was thought by many to be a mad speculation. And an English traveller, Sir John Carr, said the fine view from Queen Street was beginning 'to be interrupted by the recent elevation of new streets and particularly by the houses on a piece of ground called Heriot's Row'.

The lesser streets run parallel to the main ones, and Northumberland and Cumberland Streets, which have marvellous Georgian features, have been recently restored.

Another, Jamaica Street, was inferior and deteriorated so badly that it was eventually demolished. But it did have one claim to posterity. For a time, the young Thomas Carlyle tried to find the tranquillity he needed for his writing in a top flat there but his window overlooked Royal Circus and he wrote, in 1821, that 50 masons were 'chipping away'. He moved to more peaceful rural surroundings in Spey Street on the road to Leith.

The East End and Calton Hill
The area that earned Edinburgh the title of 'Athens of the North' is Calton Hill. There is an odd array of buildings and monuments, begun in 1776 and finished in 1830.

The Old Observatory came first, designed by Craig and made to look, it is said on the suggestion of Robert Adam, like a fortress. It is his only surviving building in the city and is basically a tower with Gothic windows. He planned it in 1776 but it was not completed until much later – in 1792.

Nearby is the New Observatory, Roman Doric and in the shape of a cross, begun in 1818 and designed by William Playfair. There is also a monument in Grecian Doric form to his uncle, John Playfair, who was also president of the Astronomical Institution.

William Playfair was also responsible for the monument to Dugald Stewart, another Grecian-style construction like a small circular temple. Stewart succeeded Adam Ferguson as professor of moral philosophy at the university in 1785. Both his memorial and that to Burns on the lower slope of the hill near Regent Road, designed by Thomas Hamilton (1830), were copied from the monument of Lysicrates in Athens.

Above them rises the column of Nelson's Monument, a rather Gothic design by Robert Burn

The glories of Calton Hill. **Far left**: The neo-classical memorial to the philosopher Dugald Stewart by William Playfair (1822). **Near left** Nelson's Monument (1807) by Robert Burn. **Below** The ribs of the intended National Monument, started in 1822 and never completed because of lack of funds.

The steady expansion of the New
Town over the years is marked by
distinctly separate stages of
development.

The First New Town

The Second New Town

Moray Estate

Stockbridge and the Dean Valley

The West End

The East End and Calton Hill

Further Extensions

and supposed to represent an upturned telescope. On top of the 106-foot (31.8m) tower is a time ball which drops daily at 13.00, at the same time the Castle cannon is fired.

But the National Monument which stands on the summit is the one that grabs the eye. Funds with which to complete it were not forthcoming and it stands now not as a memorial to the Scottish soldiers and sailors who died in the Napoleonic Wars as was intended but to the hasty enthusiasm of those who conceived it.

It was supposed to be an exact copy of the Parthenon to be used as a grand memorial church with catacombs beneath, a sort of 'Scottish Valhalla'. C. R. Cockerell designed it originally but Playfair was ultimately responsible.

In 1822, when part of the money had been collected, the foundation stone was laid with great ceremony but only the base and 12 columns were built – at the cost of £1000 each. Ever since, the structure has been called all sorts of names: Scotland's Pride and Poverty, Edinburgh's Disgrace and Edinburgh's Folly.

Waterloo Place, which leads from Princes Street to the hill, was conceived to give access to the new prison on the south slope. In 1815, the year of Wellington's victory, Robert Stevenson started work on the street. Old houses had to be cleared, a gorge crossed and tons of rock removed from the hill. Now all that is left of the jail is the little 'fortress' of the governor's residence and the underworks that support St. Andrew's House.

Further east is the old Royal High School. The school was founded in 1128 and originally supervised by the abbots of Holyrood. But by the early nineteenth century, when a new building was considered, it was the responsibility of the city fathers. The site at Calton Hill was chosen in 1825 after much discussion. Thomas Hamilton, a former pupil, was asked to plan it and he kept the cost down to £24,000. Building was completed in 1829 and it is generally regarded as one of the best of the city's neo-classical edifices.

The New Town to the east was mooted as far back as 1811 on ground belonging largely to Heriot's and Trinity Hospitals, and Mr. Allan of Hillside. Once again Playfair took over a project, this time from his master William Stark, who had stressed the importance of trees and landscape in his discussions. Stark died in 1818 and the following year Playfair completed his design. It is very spacious and Royal Terrace, on the north side of the hill, is the grandest part of the triangle. It is the longest continuous frontage in the city – very nearly a quarter of a mile – and was built between 1821 and 1860.

Regent Terrace, which looks south over the Old Town, is an impressive continuous block which climbs to make a grand sweep around the end of the hill. It is decorated with a wrought-iron balcony which runs the whole length.

In between, the triangular garden was designed for the proprietors' use by Joseph Paxton with the idea that it would be more attractive than the scheme at the West End.

The West End

The story of this area, bordered by Queensferry Road and Haymarket Terrace, Belford Road and Atholl Crescent, is spread over many years. James Gillespie Graham produced a master plan in 1813 but progress was confused by the feudal rights of landowners and an enormous number of architects. Building in the area went on until 1907.

Robert Brown designed most of the area from Melville Street to Coates Crescent for the Walker family in 1813. In the middle of the street, where it is crossed by Walker Street, is Melville Crescent, laid out by John Lessels in 1855 with a grandoise statue of the 2nd Viscount Melville in the centre.

At one end of the street is St. Mary's Episcopal Cathedral, designed by Sir George Gilbert Scott in 1879, a solid soaring edifice to Victoriana. It is the largest ecclesiastical building erected in Scotland since the Reformation.

The Misses Walker of Easter Coates were largely responsible for the creation of the massive cathedral. They left their grand old manor house – and the fortune they made by letting off the bulk of their estate during the latter stages of the building of the New Town – to the Church. The result was the cathedral with its two western towers, finished in 1917, named Barbara and Mary after them.

Atholl Crescent, by Thomas Bonnar (1824), was the home of William Gladstone's father, Sir John, who lived at Number 11. Across the road, in Coates Crescent, an earlier block by Robert Brown built between 1813 and 1823, is the W. E. Gladstone Memorial, moved there from its original site in St. Andrew's Square in 1955. Atholl Crescent is interrupted by Canning House, the last of the office towers to be built in Edinburgh's centre before they were banned in 1974.

The two crescents lead into Shandwick Place where Sir Walter Scott lived for two years at Number 6. He left when he gave up his post as clerk of session in 1830.

Scott was instrumental in helping his literary neighbour in Manor Place, Mrs. Grant of Laggan, acquire a pension of £100 a year from George IV. The lady, who wrote *Letters from the Mountains*, held many parties for celebrities of her time and the profits from her writing, together with bequests from deceased friends and the pension paid through the Civil Establishment of Scotland, made her later years comfortable. She died in Manor Place in 1838 at the age of 84.

Manor Place leads into Rothesay Place, built by John Watherston between 1876 and 1907. There were strange disturbances reported by one owner who had brought home a piece of wood from a friend's cottage in the north of Scotland. Drawers opened and closed of their own accord, teapots fell off the table, and a pervading smell of tobacco lingered. It was all blamed on a sailor called Merry Jack Tar who was supposed to be haunting the flat above the old Theatre Royal (now the Post Office).

In the theatre itself ghosts apparently re-enacted plays on stage after the manager and his family had retired to their upstairs flat. This story, also linked with Tar, was mentioned in a pamphlet marking the closure of the theatre in 1859.

The Moray Estate

In 1822, the same year work began on Royal Circus, Lord Moray advertised his estate for a development. It had been bought 40 years before by the previous Earl of Moray to use as the family's suburban home. It was an odd-shaped piece of land, north of Charlotte Square, bounded by the deep gorge of the Water of Leith on its further side.

The Earl, in the conditions he set for the sale of his grounds, had determined to make the new area of the highest quality. He had, in the architect's words, done 'everything in his power, consistent with his own interest, to render the plan ornamental to the City and convenient for the inhabitants'. He had ensured, equally, that none of the

expense of streets, sewers, boundary walls or pleasure gardens would fall on him but, proportionately, would be the purchasers' responsibility.

The plans for the new estate were drawn by James Gillespie Graham. For a fee of five guineas he supplied drawings of each house front, including full-size details, which would grace the newest part of the New Town. He even designed the railings which had to be of a standard pattern – a distinctive double rail with wreaths in between – for the price.

Gillespie Graham shied away from the grid-iron pattern of Craig and created instead the majestic curves of Randolph Crescent, Ainslie Place and the many-sided Moray Place, connected with short avenues to the streets of Craig, Reid and Sibbald.

All the building that was going on was quite a surprise to many of the townspeople. An anonymous diarist wrote, in March 1823, that the sale of the Earl's grounds 'which commenced last year, is likely to lead to the formation of a third grand division of our new town. The addition of from 700 to 800 new dwelling-houses in Edinburgh every year for some years past, one would think, must through time over-stock the market and lower the rents, but this state of matters has not yet taken place.'

In October he was still astonished at the progress: 'The most remarkable increase as to buildings of expensive architecture are those on Lord Moray's ground .... Now a great part of three or four sides of the Octagon are visible.'

Moray Place, the grandest of circuses, is, in fact, 12-sided. Only two sides can be seen at a time and each has a Tuscan portico, alternatively plain and pedimented. Lord Moray took one of the houses, Number 28, for his own home.

Most of the house-plots had been sold by 1827 although a few plots on the south side of Great Stuart Street and Ainslie Place remained undeveloped until the middle of the century.

On the steep, wooded slope that led from the houses to the Water of Leith, the land was planted with shrubs and pathways were made. It became known as Lord Moray's pleasure-ground. It, too, was paid for by the householders who enjoyed it and who contributed to its upkeep. Their successors still use the gardens for a stroll along the cliff whose retaining walls are now ivy-decked.

Stockbridge and the Dean Valley

Across the Water of Leith, beyond the city boundary, there was building too. The villages that had existed for centuries were swallowed up by new streets but they were not digested and still remain – black, old and incongruous in the middle of the grey eighteenth- and nineteenth-century serenity.

The earliest development of these outlying villages began in 1813 when the portrait painter Sir Henry Raeburn began to sell house-building plots in the street that he had given to his wife Ann, and named after her. It is rather grand in the middle but the houses at the two ends of the street have a doll-house charm with long front gardens, a rare thing in Georgian streets. Tradition maintains that Raeburn designed it himself but it may have been the work of the architect James Milne.

In nearby Henderson Row on July 1, 1823, the foundation stone of the new Edinburgh Academy was laid despite the opposition of the Town Council. The Council maintained that distinctions of wealth would be introduced if there were a rival to the high school where children from all walks of life had studied together. But Sir Walter Scott was behind the new school, together with other powerful voices like the judge, Henry, Lord Cockburn. Both men joined the first board of 16 directors, whose chairman was Robert Dundas of Arniston.

The Council were furious but could do nothing. There was a rumour, though, that the Council deliberately chose the site for William Playfair's massive St. Stephen's Church to block the view of the new academy which could be seen from the whole length of Howe Street.

Where Henderson Row meets Hamilton Place is the district of Silvermills. In 1607 quantities of silver were found at Linlithgow, 15 miles away from the city, and ore was refined on the banks of the Water of Leith. Traces of the mills, bought by James IV with the mines, remain on both sides of West Silvermills Lane.

In 1824 the Lord Provost Learmonth proposed a new bridge to his newly acquired estate of Dean, north of the river near the west end of town. He had ideas of development too and employed Thomas Telford to build Dean Bridge, begun in 1829, which was one of the highest of its era. But a recession had set in and it was another 20 or 30 years before the streets like Oxford and Eton Terraces were built – in Victorian style.

The old village of Dean, west of the bridge, has partly survived almost hidden in the gorge of the Water. It was, in the sixteenth and seventeenth centuries, a very busy milling centre where there were 11 mills and many 'baxters' (bakers) of Edinburgh.

City Life

The most extraordinary thing about all the energetic, speculative building and investment that went on in the whole of the New Town was that the common people were starving.

At the turn of the nineteenth century the city streets were infested with beggars, there was widespread unemployment and famine – and ugly violence followed.

War with France and poor harvest made food scarce and dear. The 'meal mobs' – famished townspeople – attacked shops to provide grain for their malnourished families. In 1800 Parliament was forced to allow the town's authorities to raise £10,000 to give food to the impoverished but it wasn't enough and further riots, in the Grassmarket and Cowgate, followed. Permanent soup kitchens and cash handouts had to be made for those in need.

In 1811 Hogmanay was, in the words of diarist W.M. Gilbert, 'disgraced by a series of riots, outrages and robberies'. Two people died in the riot and a reward of 100 guineas was offered for the arrest of the murderers. Three youths, all under 18, were hanged.

There was also the problem of professional beggars and those who refused to work in a House of Industry (the work house) were sent to Bridewell Prison and the special society formed to deal with beggars heard 622 cases in its first year of operation.

The Committee for the Relief of Workmen out of Employment helped a few with work on the roads project, costing £10,000 at Calton, and on the Union Canal to Glasgow.

Properly trained police were brought in to replace the much-criticized town guard and they were certainly well occupied by those, not finding work, who fought and looted in the streets.

Despite the problems of the city, the poverty and lack of public funds, the New Town grew to be acclaimed as a huge architectural and town planning success, much admired throughout the Europe of the era and still renowned today.

Unusual in the New Town is the rural feeling that has been captured in the pleasant development of Ann Street. The artist Sir Henry Raeburn, whose wife was called Ann, started laying out the land in 1813 with unusually long gardens in front of the rather formal Georgian houses.

The Georgian House

An English tradition brought style and quality to Edinburgh living

Towards the end of the eighteenth century the building of the Edinburgh New Town with its terraces of spacious Georgian residences permitted a style and quality of living previously unthought of in Scotland. The new residents of this extension to the city were consciously Anglophile in their admiration of all things English and wished to reproduce the high standard of living they glimpsed on their very occasional visits to London. Some of the grandest of their private dwellings stood on Charlotte Square at the west end of James Craig's New Town plan.

The north side of this square was designed by Robert Adam and its building begun before

his death in 1792. It is a masterpiece in the Georgian neoclassical style. Under the influence of ancient Roman architecture Adam created an impressive 'palace' façade to dominate the handsome square. Heavily rusticated at the base and decorated with a variety of light ornament on the upper levels, this symmetrical façade embraces separate houses, all of which underwent drastic interior alteration during the Victorian period. Now, one of them – No.7 – has been completely restored to the style of the late eighteenth century.

Its owners and keepers, the National Trust for Scotland, went to enormous lengths to guarantee the authenticity of the restoration. Appropriate furniture and fittings were acquired from all over the country; suitable paintings either given or borrowed; layers of paint removed from walls and woodwork in an attempt to discover the original colour scheme; floor-boards dry-scrubbed in the original style; and eighteenth-century pattern fabrics specially woven for curtains and coverings. The result for the visitor is a genuine experience of the life-style of such a house around 1800.

In every room there is a fascinating array of artefacts. The dining room, its table prepared for dinner with Wedgwood dinner service and Sheffield plate; the adjoining bedchamber (reconstructed here, as it would have been in the late eighteenth century, on the ground floor) with its wonderful four-poster bed dominating the room; and, perhaps most magnificent, the formally arranged drawing room stretching the entire width of the house. Do not miss the kitchen in the basement, and try to imagine a small army of servants needed to run such a grand, sophisticated house.

Two other features make a visit to No.7 Charlotte Square an extraordinary pleasure. The first is the absence of ropes cordoning off the valuable 'exhibits'. You can stroll freely around the house. Touching of the furniture is, of course, forbidden but the lack of obvious restrictions makes for a more relaxed atmosphere.

Right The contents of the dining room date mainly from the last quarter of the eighteenth century. Note especially the harlequin set of chairs.
Left This Wedgwood dinner service was made around 1830.

Above No kitchen was complete without a mortar and pestle. This large specimen is made from marble.
Right The kitchen was painted blue as it was believed that this colour contained something to ward off flies.

Viewpoints

Enjoying Scotland's capital city from the summits of seven hills

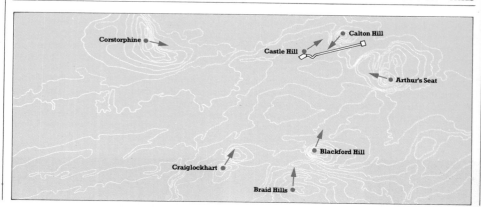

Calton Hill

$\mathcal{E}$dinburgh was described by her native son Robert Louis Stevenson as a 'precipitous city'. Like Rome, she is built upon seven hills, though perhaps without the craggy magnificence of her southern counterpart. Nevertheless, Edinburgh's 'mountains' do provide an amazingly variegated panorama of street and building, close and park.

The hills are all named:

Blackford	539ft (164m)
Braid	675ft (206m)
Castle	435ft (133m)
West Craiglockhart	575ft (175m)
Arthur's Seat	823ft (251m)
Calton	328ft (100m)
Corstorphine	531ft (162m)

The highest is Arthur's Seat, named in the fifteenth century with the revival of interest in the Arthurian romances. An extinct volcano of red igneous rock, Arthur's Seat offers panoramic views over the city to the Pentland Hills and the Firth of Forth.

Calton Hill, as Stevenson noted, is the best place from which to view both the Castle and Arthur's Seat. The views along Princes Street and of the Old Town are truly magnificent. It slopes rather abruptly on the northwestern ridge.

Blackford Hill was described by Scott as the spot where Marmion stood gazing with rapt wonder and delight on the scene below. Overlooking the gentle southern suburbs of the city, it is located in a park with a pond and assorted birdlife. It is also the home of the Royal Observatory

Craiglockhart Hill, of hard basalt, overlooks the southwestern part of the city. The village of Swanston is still much as it was when Stevenson described it.

Braid Hill gives fine views of Ben Lomond to the northwest and the slopes of the Pentlands to the south.

Corstorphine Hill offers a wide panorama of the city. The Clemiston Tower was built to celebrate the centenary of the birth of Sir Walter Scott (1771). The crest of the hill figures in Stevenson's *Kidnapped* and is the site of the Edinburgh Zoo.

Castle Hill is perhaps the most commanding spot in Edinburgh. Since it was the starting point for the city, almost the whole of both the Old and New Towns are visible, and the parapets make for an infinite variety of overlooks.

For the energetic, fit and trim, the hills can be mounted over the course of a couple of days. Transport is easily arranged by bus, foot or car.

Edinburgh Castle   General Post Office   Scott Monument   St. Mary's Cathedral   West Register House

Outlook
Tower   Greenside Village   Register House   King James Hotel

Bank of   North British   Caledonian
Scotland   Hotel   Hotel

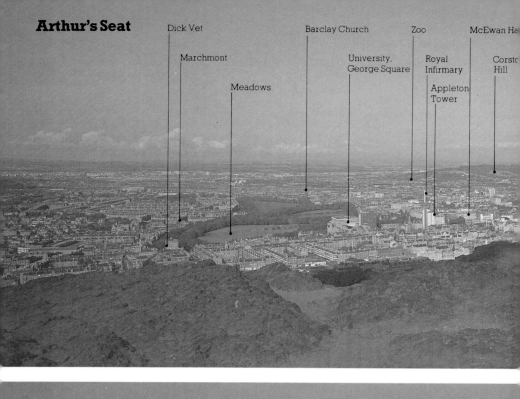

Arthur's Seat

Dick Vet

Marchmont

Meadows

Barclay Church

University,
George Square

Zoo

Royal
Infirmary

Appleton
Tower

McEwan Ha

Corsto
Hill

Blackford Hill

Granton

West Register House

St. G

Astley Ainslie Hospital

Edinburgh Castle

Royal Infirmary

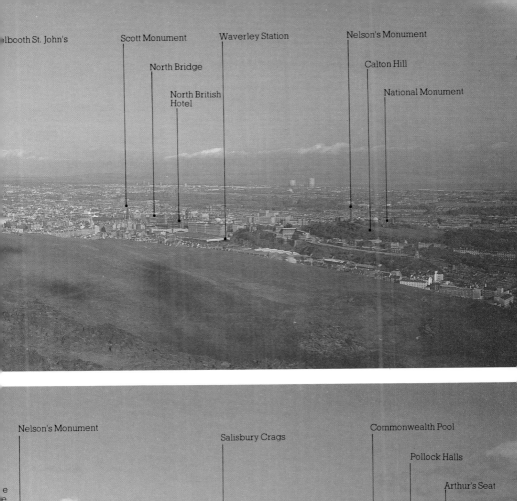

lbooth St. John's

Scott Monument

Waverley Station

Nelson's Monument

North Bridge

Calton Hill

North British
Hotel

National Monument

Nelson's Monument

Salisbury Crags

Commonwealth Pool

Pollock Halls

Arthur's Seat

Braid Hills

Forth Bridges

Corstorphine Hill

Granton

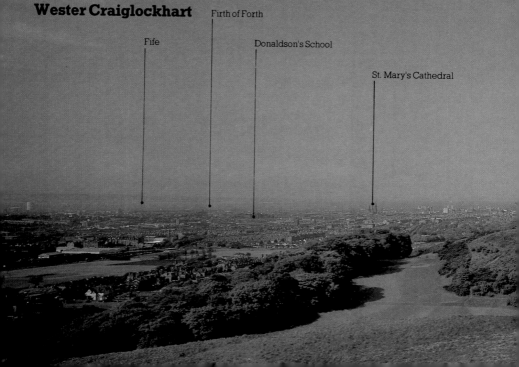

Wester Craiglockhart

Firth of Forth

Fife

Donaldson's School

St. Mary's Cathedral

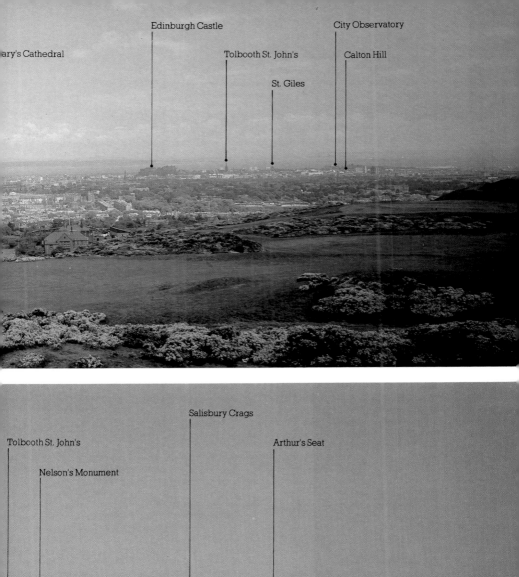

ary's Cathedral

Edinburgh Castle

Tolbooth St. John's

St. Giles

City Observatory

Calton Hill

Salisbury Crags

Arthur's Seat

Tolbooth St. John's

Nelson's Monument

Corstorphine

STB Offices

National Monument

Calton Hill

North British Hotel

Edinburgh Castle

Arthur's Seat

Castle Hill

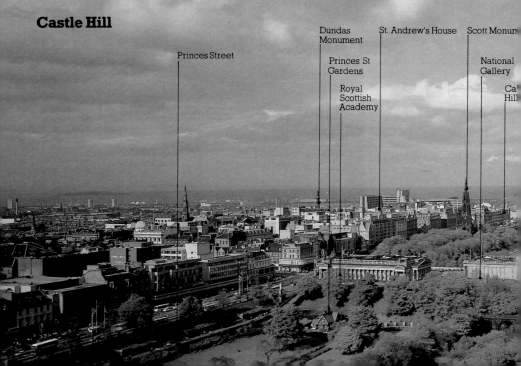

Princes Street

Dundas Monument

Princes St Gardens

Royal Scottish Academy

St. Andrew's House

Scott Monument

National Gallery

Ca' Hill

National
Monument

Nelson's
Monument

Waverley Station

Royal High
School

North
Bridge

The Mound

Bank of Scotland

Assembly Hall

Ramsay Lodge

St. Giles

Section of Castle

Tolbooth
St. John's

Villages of Edinburgh

The other Edinburgh: a patchwork of rural life, history and tradition

To most visitors, historic Edinburgh consists of the Castle and Holyrood Palace with the Royal Mile in between and the New Town to the north. Such a view does no justice to the other sections and deceives the people who hold it.

In the first half of the eighteenth century, there were as many as 46 villages spread out over the area which Edinburgh now covers. Although over the next two centuries, the boundaries gradually melted away, there are still many semi-rural communities with independent histories and traditions in existence today. Dean Village, with its riverside tranquillity, is very much a country town, while the coastline villages have a completely different character, and could be miles away. It is this blending patchwork of communities which has to be understood for Edinburgh to be fully appreciated. And without the villages Edinburgh would lack much of her charm.

Dean Village

The romantic informality of Dean Village contrasts vividly with the classic regular style of its neighbour, the New Town. Set in a valley with steep wooded slopes on either side, the distinctive red pantiled roofs of the village buildings may be seen clearly from many vantage points around it. The apparent uniformity of the bright rooftops is deceptive however and a closer inspection reveals an eclectic architectural approach to building with varied wall finishes and a diversity of period, style and condition. This is not surprising. It is natural that a village which has existed for 800 years or so has some changes.

Accessibility to the Water of Leith resulted in a milling community being established here as far back as the twelfth century and, for a long time, the city and the Incorporation of Baxters (Baker's Union) operated 11 watermills and two granaries in the area. Numerous relics of those times remain today.

Bell's Brae House, originally built as an inn in 1640, was the Baxters' meeting place and in the northeastern wall is the bakers' stone with symbolic wheat sheaves, the ripening sun and bakers' shovels.

At the bottom of Bell's Brae stands the Baxters' Tollbooth, built in the same century and the official headquarters and granary of the incorporation. It is typical of Scottish domestic architecture of the time, with stair towers and cut-away corners over the window lintels and on a wall adjoining Dean Bridge parapet is a stone with the inscription: 'Blessed be God for all his gifts' This came from Lindsay's Mill of which only three grindstones remain on its site by the riverside path formerly called Miller's Row. Jericho Mill, almost completely destroyed by a fire in 1956, is being restored as offices.

Before the building of Telford's Dean Bridge in 1832, the village was also important as a crossing point, for Bell's Brae was the main road out to Queensferry and the north. In 1751, the road was turnpiked with a toll bar at the top of the hill and some distance down it were the stables and coach houses. Both have now been restored as offices.

Many other buildings, including some houses in Dean Path and a seventeenth-century building near Dean Bridge, have also been sympathetically modernized. Others have gone completely but have been replaced by suitable worthwhile structures. Well Court, a great square of red stone buildings, designed by Sydney Mitchell in 1884, was built on the site of some old cottages to provide community housing in a highly experimental way. Dean House has also gone. In its place stands the cemetery, where Lord Cockburn and other great personalities rest.

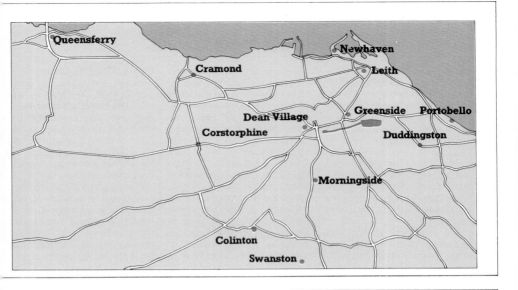

Baxters' mills of yesteryear in Dean Village by the Water of Leith

Corstorphine

Despite rapid expansion in the twentieth century, bringing modern office blocks, shops and houses in its wake, the spirit of old Corstorphine lingers on. Situated on the southwest side of the city, Corstorphine today is clearly a residential area, surrounded and interspersed by parks and wide open spaces. But it has, like other villages, a main street and several historic features of interest.

For centuries farming was the mainstay of the local economy – mostly wheat and potatoes in the eighteenth century, then market gardening some time later. Owing to the presence of a spring of 'weak sulphurous water' reputed to have medicinal properties until it became polluted as a result of reclamation of the loch which once existed here, Corstorphine also had its day as a fashionable spa with its round of balls and concerts for the wealthy families of Edinburgh.

In 1910, an important craft industry was set up by the son of William Morris, making 'dovecot tapestries'. In 1946, it became the Edinburgh Tapestry Company and still continues in business today.

Of Corstorphine Castle, once lived in by Adam Forrester to whom the estate belonged, little remains, except a few relics found by local houseowners through the years, and an ancient stone dovecot, circular in shape, still has some 1060 nests to provide 'fresh food for the laird' and 'fertilizer for his crops' had he been there.

Not far away and probably part of an avenue of trees once leading to the castle is an old sycamore tree, 55 feet (16.7 m) high and 12½ feet (3.8 m) girth, always veiled with beautiful foliage in summer. Legend has it that the ghost of Christian Nimmo, who stabbed her lover, James Lord Forrester, by the tree in 1679, still haunts it.

Dover House in St. Margaret's Park was built in the mid-seventeenth century and displays characteristically Scottish crow-stepped gables. The ornamental gate pillars at the east High Street entrance to the park were probably once the entrance to the castle.

Corstorphine Kirk, another relic of the Forrester reign, contains some interesting early tombs of the family, with carved stone effigies and heraldic panels. A lamp, high on the building, placed there to guide travellers coming along the marsh or along the loch late at night in days of yore, has now been replaced by a symbolic electric light. In 1905, the church was successfully modernized to harmonize with some of the earlier structures and now, considered to be the 'Corstorphine Heirloom', is a source of pride to the community-conscious inhabitants.

Morningside

Traditionally a salubrious part of Edinburgh (the accent is said to have derived from Irish elocutionist, Thomas Sheridan, father of the famous playwright), Morningside actually had its origins in agriculture and it was only the advent of the railways at the end of the nineteenth century that brought about its considerable change in status.

Many years ago, the village was centred on the small area now occupied by the Public Library and the Merlin pub. The Old Tollhouse was built on the lawn surrounding Braid Church on Morningside Road and has now been rebuilt as a gatehouse at the entrance to the Hermitage of Braid Drive. Number 259, its original number, can be seen on a lintel at the rear of the building.

Later, the nineteenth century influx of wealthy people brought with it a great 'growth' in the building of beautiful villas in the district of Cluny, Hermitage and Braid. Each villa had resident servants, usually spinster ladies, and at that time the population ratio of Morningside was two females to one male.

Of these buildings not many remain, although Number 6 Morningside Place, home of the Misses Balfour, aunts of Robert Louis Stevenson, still stands complete with the author's initials which he himself carved on a cupboard door. Of the humbler and older residences, a group of old stone cottages in Springvalley Terrace remain, as do some cottages at 160 Morningside Road, one of which has an outside stone staircase. Two large square stones with holes to support gibbets in Braid Road were the scene of public executions.

Monumental stones in the churchyard

This old dovecot houses 1060 nests

The residents also knew how to enjoy themselves, however, and Carter's Parade, on the first Friday in April, was the excuse for great festivity, usually ending up in the Volunteer's Rest (now Volunteer's Arms or the Canny Man). This pub, standing at the corner of Canaan and Morningside Lanes, has a complete range of copper whisky blending jugs and measures as well as an accounts book (dated 1892-93) in which regular customers were each allocated a page and there are such entries as 'George the joiner – glass of whisky – 4d'. One of the customers, the painter Sam Bough, presented the inn with a two-sided oil painting for use as a sign board today displayed in-

Morningside serenity

side the pub. Perhaps he did not want to see his name entered in the book. Today, Morningside is a spacious suburb which in many ways still retains the well-to-do air of the turn-of-the-century. The wide streets and well-preserved buildings reflect the comfortable standing of the residents. Trees and wide open spaces, many of them hospital and school grounds, break up the unfolding vista.

Not only does Morningside preserve this atmosphere; people also still demonstrate many of the characteristics that have made their village celebrated. The Morningside accent, for instance, with its 'refained' vowels, is still a city landmark.

Colinton

Today, the affluent 'village' of Colinton, with its beautiful villas surrounded on all sides by the serenity of the unspoilt countryside, makes it hard to believe that at the turn of the nineteenth century it seemed to be in decline. Although agriculture was the main source of employment, many people depended on the distillery, skinnery and water mills powered by the Water of Leith as a means of livelihood. The former two died a natural death, while the latter was no competition for the steam-operated machines now being used elsewhere.

The coming of the railways in 1875 turned the course of events. Now that Colinton was within commutable distance of the city centre, wealthy people started building villas here. This was not surprising. The rural beauty of the area still survives today. The Pentland Hills, the starting point of the Water of Leith, and Colinton and Craiglockhart Dells, with ivy-entwined sycamore trees, wild hyacinths and pink hedgerows

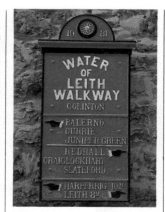

Walking by the waters

of dog rose, have always been outstandingly beautiful

Despite its expansion, many relics of Colinton's past remain, emphasizing the village spirit of the area. Colinton Brig, the main road into the village, retains much of its character, and the ruins of Colinton Castle may still be seen in Merchiston Castle School. The Parish Church, first erected in 1771 on the site of an earlier building and mod-

ernized in 1968, has many features of historic interest. An old mort safe, to prevent bodies from being dug up for medical research in bygone days still stands to the left of the entrance gates, while ancient tombstones in the churchyard provide material for perusal. James Gillespie, millowner and public benefactor, lies buried here, as does Reverend Dr. Lewis Balfour – maternal grandfather of Robert Louis Stevenson and once minister of the church. Indeed, the novelist spent much time in Colinton and his grandfather's manse and old yew tree (seen from Dell Road, over the wall and across the graveyard) are mentioned in *Kidnapped*.

Many other buildings of note are to be found throughout the village, some of them designed by Sir Robert Lorimer. Glenlyon and Almora in Pentland Avenue, distinguishable by their semi-circular towers, are two such examples. Across the road, built in 1898 but Scottish seventeenth century in style are the 'Sir William Fraser

Swanston

Separated from the rest of Edinburgh by half a mile of farmland, Swanston, nestling on the lower slopes of the Pentlands, with fields or golf courses on all sides, is in truly splendid rural isolation.

This unspoilt hamlet remains much the same as when Robert Louis Stevenson and later Edwin Muir knew it. The T-shaped wood behind Swanston, planted by a Trotter as a memorial to a descendant of the house who fell in battle, is still

green and lush. The village centre with its old-world charm has also not altered much in the last century or so.

A group of seventeenth-century white-washed cottages, with blue paintwork, black chimney pots and thatched roofs have been sympathetically restored and modernized. The old farmhouse, the heart of the village, now being used as a bothy, and the White House, the old school, are still there.

A later addition, was some

stone cottages with slated roofs, around a square. Some distance away is Swanston Cottage, described as a 'rambling infinitesimal cathedral' by Stevenson in *St Ives*. It was used as a summer cottage by the Stevenson family from 1867 to 1880 and the house on the left of the drive leading to the cottage belonged to Alison Cunningham, known as 'Cummy' to the novelist, his 'first wife and second mother'. John Todd, a Swanston shepherd provided

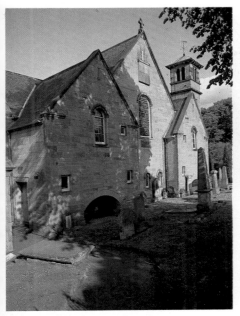

The parish church dating back to 1771

Rural glades surround the village

Homes', originally founded by a wealthy merchant for the rent-free use of retired ladies.

Of the humbler abodes, several small cottages are still in evidence. Those at the foot of the long steps near the church have unusual porches, rough-finished façades and moss-covered pantiles. Others of a similar ilk are on Spylaw Bank Road which also has the old station master's cottage connected by wooden steps (Jacob's Ladder) to the platform of a former station. Redhall Mill is still in use today and the Old Boag's Mill which produced bank notes in 1735, later turning to the grinding of oatmeal and barley, also still stands.

Seventeenth-century cottages in Swanston

the writer with many anecdotes of his working life and some of these stories are also depicted in the author's book, *St. Ives.*

Apart from Swanston Golf Club and the new Swanston Farm, there is little else of the village. It truly earns its reputation of being tiny and unspoilt and, now classified as a Conservation Area, it will probably remain so. Within the village, the small white houses stand out against the lush green background, while from the outside, screened on all sides by high trees, it is an oasis of quiet retreat and a delightful contrast to the vital beat of the city centre.

Duddingston

Located between Duddingston Loch and Arthur's Seat, with Holyrood Park to the west, is the village where a sense of enclosure prevails. The high walls, tall trees and remains of the old stone boundary all contribute to the intimacy of the old village centre.

At the beginning of the eighteenth century, the cottage weaving industry was the main

Duddingston Loch and the village

Portobello

It was a battle in Panama's Puerto Bello in 1739 which gave rise to the name and possibly the development of this village. A returning sailor built a house called Porto Bello in a spot where the Baptist Church in High Street now stands. He or his successor in the house dabbled in saddlery and coach repairing and the last pottery works, in Bridge Street, was moved to Crieff in 1972.

In order to attract more custom in 1753, he advertised that a horse race would be run 'at Porto Bello, in the midst of the Freegate Whins'. Thus began the growth of a community.

By the end of the eighteenth century, the village was developing in two ways. William Jameson 'Father of Portobello' started an important pottery industry using the extensive beds of clay lying on its beaches. The site soon became a service station for itinerants.

The bracing air and miles of golden sands had the potential of attracting another market which John Cairns was quick to spot. He acted promptly and, in 1795, advertised 'bathing machines on the sands'. These proved most popular and brought about the spread of the many simple Georgian houses,

Greenside

Because of its miniscule size, it is hard to believe that Greenside was ever a village, much less such an interesting one. Lying below Calton Hill's western slope and Leith Walk, and including today's Blenheim Place and Greenside Row, it was given to the sporting fraternity by James II to practise the art of mimic warfare. Thus it became a Tilting Ground and, later, in the nineteenth century was the place for holding open-air plays and revels. Until 1769, it was also a popular site for the burning and hanging of criminals and witches. Indeed, there are records showing that in 1717, a certain Robert Irvine had both hands cut off *before* he was executed here. His body was then flung unceremoniously into a quarry hole at the east end of Royal Terrace.

In the mid-sixteenth century a Carmelite monastery is said to have existed here and still to this day an official in the Convent of the Carmelites in Rome bears the inimitable title 'Il Padre Priore di Greenside'.

A hospital for lepers was established in the building left unoccupied by the nuns.

Greenside has changed much since those days and even since the 1960s a lot has

means of support for most people living in the area, when the manufacture of a flaxen cloth – Duddingston Hardings – was at its peak. By 1845, severe competition had brought this to a halt and gradually the old weavers cottages on the Causeway (the main road) were also demolished. Later the pits, breweries and the mills provided jobs for the men, and where Duddingston Road crosses Braid Burn, some of the latter may still be seen, although only brewing still thrives.

The Sheep's Heid Inn, said to be the oldest licensed premises in Scotland is in the Causeway. It is said that James VI frequented the inn and in 1580 presented the landlord with an embellished ram's head. By the inn is an old skittle alley and the Sheep Heid Trotters (celebrating their centenary in 1982) meet here

Duddingston Kirk, built in Norman style, is the oldest building in the village. A watch tower, to guard against body snatchers, stands in the churchyard, and at the gate are some old jougs – iron collar and chain, to punish evil-doers – and a loupin-on-stone – to help old or obese horsemen mount.

There is a seventeenth-century building where Bonnie Prince Charlie is said to have slept before the Battle of Prestonpans. Duddingston House, designed in the eighteenth century by Sir William Chambers and surrounded by a 200-acre (81 ha) park is now Mansion House Motel and golfers make use of the grounds while famous Duddingston Loch is now a bird sanctuary.

---

usually used as summer homes for visitors. Between the High Street and the sea and especially at the east end of Bath Street, many of these may still be seen.

The Victorians also found Portobello a relief and they too built villas – this time large baroque ones – and also established parks and bandstands and erected a wide promenade along the sea front to 'take the airs'. Later, numerous 'amusements' were added to the existing features and so Portobello became known as the 'fun place' of Edinburgh.

Personalities of note visited or lived here too: Sir Walter Scott came to stay with friends in what is now known as Bellfield Street and it was in Portobello that he completed the first canto of *The Lay of the Last Minstrel*. The Scots comedian, Harry Lauder, lived at 3 Bridge Street for a time and the King's Road was named after George IV when he rode down the street to review his troops.

Despite its past glory, by 1967, it was evident that much had to be done to aid Portobello's deteriorating condition. The Victorian mansions had fallen into disrepair and the miles of golden sand, such an attraction in former days.

By the beginning of the 1970s, the Beach Nourishment Scheme had taken effect and tons of sand from a nearby beach were poured onto Portobello's shores. This not only improved the appearance of the beach but also protected the promenade wall and sea front. Many buildings such as the George Cinema were listed for preservation, while others were at least refurbished.

---

been demolished. On the site of the Tabernacle, a baptist church of some repute, stands the Playhouse, first built in 1929 for use as a cinema and now a popular theatre.

Of other places and events only historic and literary records remain to fill in gaps from the past. James Nasmyth, inventor of the steam hammer, as a small boy often accompanied the servants to the bleaching green on Calton Hill and in his writings he mentions the 'blacksmiths, coppersmiths and brassfounders busy in the

'Church on the Hill'

Greenside workshops'.

Robert Louis Stevenson was also a frequent visitor. His paternal grandfather, an elder at Greenside Parish Church, the 'Church on the Hill' still standing today, once occupied the house at Number 1 Baxter's Place – of which the novelist writes in picturesque terms of its 'great size, infinity of cellars, garrets and apple lofts'. On the death of the grandfather, Robert Stevenson, his three sons bequeathed a section of their garden to the church, on which was later built chapel.

Queensferry

Situated at the narrowest point of the Forth, nine miles (14.4 km) west of the city centre, Queensferry (often erroneously known as South Queensferry) still has the feel of a Scottish east coast town with a small, tightly-knit community.

The name has ancient associations with Queen Margaret, for it was just west of the town at Brinks Rock that she disembarked in 1067 as the bride of King Malcolm. Legend has it that her footprint may still be seen on the rock on which she landed. The scene has been commemorated in the Burgh Arms.

Queensferry has been an important crossing point for many years and the friars of the Carmelite Monastery were the first ferrymen. To the north of the Church of St. Mary of Mount Carmel, built over 500 years ago and one of the oldest Carmelite Houses in Great Britain still used for Christian worship, there is a line of rocks stretching to the Firth, showing traces of cutting to form landing stages for the ferry boats. The first ferry service was not officially opened until the time of King David I in 1129, however, and Queen Elizabeth II and Prince Phillip were the last to use it in 1964, just prior to the opening of the New Forth Bridge. The Ferry Fair, which still held in the second week in August, features the Bury Man, who is completely covered in burs from the burdock plant and visits householders for donations.

A feature of Queensferry has always been its terraces and it is in East Terrace that the oldest house in the town, the Black Castle, built in 1626, still stands. Typically Scottish in character, it has crow-stepped gables and ornamental dormer windows and the narrow staircase in the east gable is reputed to be a smugglers' stair. Next door is the Forth Bridge Hotel, also dating from the seventeenth century, which was much modernized after a fire in 1910.

The Burgh Chambers, which was. once a hotel, is now the Burgh Museum.

The Tollbooth, with its pointed steeple and outside staircase was originally a prison. The four-faced clock was added to commemorate Queen Victoria's Jubilee.

The other main church in

Cramond

Cramond's view of the River Almond

Nestled around the estuary of the River Almond 4½ miles (7.2 km) northeast of the city centre and backed by an attractive rural hinterland, Cramond is one of the prettiest villages lying along Edinburgh's 9 miles (14.4 km) of coastline.

Conclusions drawn from archaeological digs in the area point to beginnings as far back as AD 142 when Antonius Pius established a fort here to be used as a base for his men when building the 'Antonine Wall' stretching from the Forth to the Clyde. A plan of the fort can be found next to the Kirk, itself partially constructed from Roman stones, while various Roman artefacts are at the Huntly Museum in the city centre. The latest find, a chance discovery in 1976 on the site of a proposed car park, has brought to light an exceptionally well-preserved Roman building, one of its walls standing 5 feet (1.5 m) high.

Despite these relics of a Roman heritage and even the ghost of a Roman centurion which supposedly roams the bottom of the village steps frightening local dogs, the village is predominantly eighteenth century in character. The Industrial Revolution did not pass it by. Water-driven iron-mills were put in harness for the production of iron implements such as nails and shovels, to be gradually replaced by paper

Queensferry, the Kirk, completed in 1635 but renovated in the nineteenth century, also still stands today. It had great influence within the community and parishoners were actually fined for being absent from worship or for taking a boat across the ferry on the Sabbath.

Despite the strict religious background, a distillery flourished here at the beginning of the nineteenth century. It was situated near the pier, between the present Stag Head Hotel and the Queensferry Arms Hotel, and parts of the original building still remain.

Because of Queensferry's attractive location on the Forth, it is ideally situated for pleasant walks and rambles. To the east lies Cramond, to the west, Hopetoun House, while Dalmeny, a planned estate village with great grass verges and a very fine medieval church, is only a mile away.

The old buildings of East Terrace

Newly restored house

and furniture some years later in the mid-nineteenth century. Some of these original mills still stand, as do many of the workers' white-washed cottages which, although much modernized, still retain their old-world charms.

Other buildings date from earlier times. Cramond Kirk and Cramond Tower are both medieval in origin, the latter having once been the property of the Bishops of Dunkeld when it was used as the basic part of the earliest house.

Cramond Inn, is a popular watering hole, reputed to have connections with Stevenson's *St. Ives*, while Cramond House is said to have provided the setting for his *House of Shaws*.

The bridge crossing the River Almond carried traffic between Edinburgh and nearby Queensferry and one of the old tollhouses still stands today. Legend has it that King James V was once being attacked by gypsies on the bridge when a local miller, Jock Howieson, came to his aid. Howieson's reward was the land of Braehead, on condition that his descendants would wash the hands

and feet of all new sovereigns on their first visit to Scotland. In 1952 Elizabeth II was the last to have been the recipient of this quaint gesture.

Interesting though the history is, it is the scenery which first catches the eye and there is a wide variety of walks in the area made all the more enjoyable by the bracing sea air. Northwards towards Hound's Point (so called because of the dog which supposedly haunts it) and Queensferry, a walk passes several interesting features en route, one of which is the first Gothic Revival building in Scotland – Dalmeny House. At low tide one can walk to Cramond Island, inhabited only by birds and mammals. A wide, open promenade leads to Granton and Silverknowes, while a delightful route through leafy glades along the river goes to Barnton.

Newhaven

To many people Newhaven still conjures up images of traditional fish-wives, clad in colourful costumes, their cry of 'Caller Ou' resounding through the streets. Unfortunately, these ladies, immortalized in Sir Walter Scott's *The Antiquary* are no longer there, the last one having retired in 1977 at the sprightly age of 89. The village, undergoing extensive re-development, survives, however, and much has been preserved for the appreciation and enjoyment of many generations to come.

Newhaven was originally established at the beginning of the sixteenth century when James IV, at war with England, decided to build a Scottish navy of his own. Its flagship, to be called the *Great Michael*, could not be constructed in Leith owing to insufficient depth of water and so new dockyards were laid out at 'Novus Portus de Leith' (Newhaven) and

Vessels in harbour

Flemish, Dutch and French workers brought in to build the ship. The death of James at the Battle of Flodden brought an end to the ship-building industry which had started to flourish here but soon afterwards the Society of Free Fishermen was founded, adding fuel to Newhaven's increasingly significant

standing as a fishing village.

As an offshoot of this industry, a reputation for the preparation of sea food was established in the eighteenth century and in 1767, a wine merchant, Thomas Peacock, petitioned Edinburgh for a few of the links and cottages where the food was prepared. The Peacock Hotel, named after him, still stands.

For a short time in the late 1700s, Newhaven also became the most important ferry and packing station in Scotland, although competition from nearby Granton, established in 1835, soon put this to an end.

Fishing again came to the rescue, this time in the unlikely form of oysters. A bowl of them cost 6d – 2½p – and that included the bowl. Newhaven Fish Market came into being in 1896 and the stalwart Newhaven Fisherwomen's Choir was established during the First World War.

Today, the tramlines and old

Leith

Despite its proximity to the city centre, Leith has always been entirely distinct from it and some animosity has prevailed between the two. Today, many locals bemoan the changes which have taken place here, but it's vital – if chequered – history more than compensates for the steps it has taken under the name of progress.

In the fourteenth century, Logan of Restalrig was allowed to establish the little village of Leith as a burgh of the barony, with fewer privileges than a royal burgh, but holding the

right to have incorporations (trade guilds). Even then, trade rivalry between Leith and the city existed and was not improved when, desperate for money, the laird finally sold the superiority of the shore and harbour to Edinburgh. The powerful Leith incorporations were not recognized by the city and friction prevailed until 1833 when Leith gained its independence only to lose it again just after World War I.

Because of its standing as a port and nearness to the city centre, Leith was often the first glimpse of Scotland many royal

visitors ever had. It was here that George IV landed with such pomp and ceremony. Mary of Gueldres, Queen Madeleine, Mary of Guise and of course Mary Queen of Scots also arrived on its shores and it was in Lamb's House (now used as a centre by the Edinburgh and Leith Old People's Welfare Council) that the latter rested. The royal procession would go through Kirkgate, the main street, passing the Church of St. Mary (today, South Leith Church in the churchyard of which are recorded the names of Leith's merchant princes and

Fisherfolk's cottages in the old port

towering lamp-posts which were still in the Main Street in 1948 are no longer there, and most of the buildings have either been restored or completely demolished and new ones put in their place. This on the whole has been done with taste and the cottages on the north side of the Main Street have been restored to retain many of their original Flemish features, with red pantiled roofs and external staircases. Other restored areas include Lamb's Court, Fishmarket Square, Peacock Court and the fishermens' burial ground.

Victoria School, not much altered since 1875 when it was built, has twisting stairs and meandering corridors, as well as an interesting museum of Old Newhaven. Among its exhibits is a copy of the 'Newhaven Sculptured Stone' dated 1588. Local legend has it that this commemorates the part played by the village in the defeat of the Armada. Few would have thought that such a tiny place could have been so influential in its day.

mariners in great days of sail). Some stayed for a time and Charles I played golf in what is now known as Leith Links.

Leith was once a popular bathing resort with a bathing machine on the sands as early as 1750. Shipbuilding was also important and *Sirius*, the first British steamship to cross the Atlantic, was built here in 1837.

Trinity House, belonging to the guild of the sea-faring community still stands today. Part of it is a Maritime Museum and a Raeburn portrait of a famous Leith admiral hangs on one of its walls. The original Custom House in Commercial Street is also still there as is the Boundary Bar, halfway up Leith Walk, complete with brass plate

Leith's Custom House

marking the boundary between Leith and Edinburgh, before 1920.

Indeed, many old buildings have been restored. The Old Leith Bank at the corner of Bernard Street and Constitution Street; King's Wark, an early eighteenth-century tenement building nearby.

Much has also disappeared. The Auld Gaiety, a music hall, is no longer there and neither are the fiddlers, organ-grinders and beggars, including Commodore O'Brien who sat daily on the east side of Leith Walk, in a little masted boat given him by order of George IV.

Perhaps mistakes have been made in the past, but interest has been recently revitalized in preserving that which remains and the tarnished gems of historic Leith are at last being polished for posterity.

The National Gallery of Scotland

Scotland's premier collection of Old Masters and indigenous artists

*I*n contrast to immense galleries like the Louvre in Paris and the National Gallery in London, with their labyrinth of rooms and endless corridors, the National Gallery of Scotland, designed by W.H. Playfair, is entirely accessible and human in scale.

The collection of paintings is not enormous although it contains the most important group of Old Masters in Great Britain outside London and is studded with rarities and masterpieces from almost every major period in Western art. The collection was begun in the 1830s by the old Royal Institution and given its international significance in

1946 by the loan of the Duke of Sutherland's collection – one of the finest collections in Great Britain – containing major works by Raphael, Titian and Rembrandt. In recent years the quality of the collection has been further augmented by the gallery's well-conceived and perspicacious buying policy which has recently enabled it to acquire major works.

A new wing on a lower level houses a Scottish collection which may well surprise the visitor. It has its fair share of curiosities but also includes the work of Scottish painters of international interest: Ramsay, Raeburn and Wilkie.

The following selective tour through the gallery traces the major European artistic movements illuminated by the most important and interesting pictures in the gallery. The easiest and most logical way to gain a good overall impression of the collection is to make your way to the rear of the ground floor after turning left through the entrance. Beginning in Room 7, walk in an anti-clockwise direction around the main floor and then mount the staircase at the rear of the gallery to view the nineteenth-century and Impressionist collections. The comprehensive Scottish wing is downstairs.

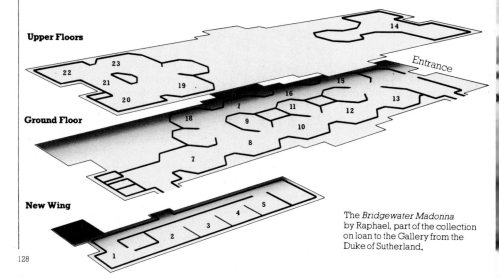

Upper Floors

Ground Floor

New Wing

The *Bridgewater Madonna* by Raphael, part of the collection on loan to the Gallery from the Duke of Sutherland.

Room 7

This room houses some of the earliest paintings in the gallery. If they all look very different from one another it is because they were painted during the Renaissance, one of the most revolutionary periods in the history of art.

The Renaissance was a dramatic cultural upheaval – literally a rebirth of learning – and affected every sphere of Europe's creative life. In the great city-states of Italy – Florence, Rome, Sienna – scholars rediscovered the literature of ancient Greece and Rome. The Christian ethos of the medieval world was gradually replaced by a new confidence in man's ability to organize his own cosmos. The repercussions on painting were enormous. The flat, decorative late medieval style was abandoned as artists struggled to represent mankind in a believable, naturalistic way. To this end they studied anatomy and practised drawing from life. By 1500 an artist's ability was judged by his skill in painting the figure. A new discovery, scientific perspective, was used to create the illusion of three-dimensional settings.

The medieval tradition of artist as craftsman is exemplified by the thirteenth-century *Tuscan Triptych* displayed in this room. Painting was only one of the artist's skills. His aim was to create a valuable and awe-inspiring object of worship. In this case a large amount of gold-leaf has been employed; the small figure scenes stand out like jewels against the rich background. An altarpiece like this was meant to be closely observed – the scenes of Christ's Passion on the side-panels, for example, are clear

Verrocchio's *Madonna and Child*

and very detailed.

The small late fifteenth-century panel fragment depicting the *Death of St. Ephraim* attributed to Giuliano *Amedei* presents an interesting stylistic contrast with the much earlier triptych. By the time this small panel was painted, artists were studying their environment far more closely. The painter of the triptych made no attempt to place his small figure groups in naturalistic settings but, here, the artist has surrounded his group of mourners with a believable, if stylized, landscape. The figures interact one with another; one can almost hear the murmur of conversation. Unlike the consistently stylized drapery in the triptych, their

robes fall into natural folds.

The stylistic contradictions of Lorenzo Monaco's *Madonna and Child* are the result of an incomplete assimilation of Renaissance ideas. The Madonna herself is of an older tradition – rather like a Byzantine icon – but the child is much more believable. The artist attempts to model the faces and hands but he treats the Madonna's robe in the stylized medieval way. Incidentally, the strange colouring of the Madonna's face was not intentional. Centuries of kissing by the devout has worn away the surface to reveal the green underpaint.

There is no painting here by the greatest Renaissance genius, Leonardo da Vinci.

However, a *Madonna and Child* by his teacher, Andrea del Verrochio, is a particularly tender treatment of this subject. The Madonna gazes down at a very life-like baby fidgeting and sucking his finger. Behind her, Verrochio displays his knowledge of the new perspective in his depiction of an ornate Roman ruin. The drawing of the Madonna's hands for which Verrochio was particularly noted is beautiful. This kind of sweet Italian painting was especially appreciated in Victorian England and this example was owned by John Ruskin.

The background of Raphael's *Bridgewater Madonna* has been overpainted at some time, but the figures show why Raphael was considered one of the greatest Renaissance painters. Not only are they beautifully drawn but they are juxtaposed in perfectly harmonious balance.

The only non-religious work in this room is a portrait by a Florentine contemporary of Raphael, Andrea del Sarto. Raphael and Leonardo had exploited all the subtle effects of oil paint to make the portrait into a penetrating study of the sitter's personality. Following their example, del Sarto employs sensitive brushwork and a restrained tonality to create a very intimate portrait.

Room 8

The main centres of the Renaissance in Italy were Florence, Rome and Venice. Michaelangelo, Leonardo and Raphael worked mostly in Florence and Rome where accurate observation and fine drawing were valued above all else. However, in Venice there was a greater emphasis on colour and the free handling of paint. Absorbing the achievements of Florence and Rome, the Venetians used them to create a far more sensuous style of painting

and the great master of the sixteenth century was Titian. He dominated the scene for most of the century, and no major painter could escape his influence. The five Titians which hang in this room are on loan from the Duke of Sutherland and span the artist's long career.

The Three Ages of Man was painted when Titian was in his early twenties. It is typically Venetian in concept – a poetic work in which landscape is combined with figure painting. A master of the nude, he painted the male figure with an absolute sureness of touch. Titian also invented a new type of female nude exemplified by the *Venus Anadyomene*. Voluptuous and potentially erotic, she recurs in the work of every painter to specialize in the nude from Rubens to Renoir.

In the 1570s Philip II of Spain commissioned Titian to paint a series of mythological subjects. Well aware of his patron's erotic tastes, Titian took the opportunity to show off his mastery of the female nude. The two pictures from that series which hang here represent scenes

from the legend of Diana the huntress. In *Diana and Actaeon* the youthful Actaeon accidentally interrupts the goddess while she is bathing at a fountain in a forest glade. It is an essentially voyeuristic scene. The intruder strides in from the left plunging Diana's naked attendants into disarray while the goddess herself raises a cloth in a gesture indicating anger rather than modesty. Through the arch on the distant horizon a little hunting scene foreshadows Actaeon's fate – Diana turned him into a stag and his own dogs tore him to pieces.

Vengeance is once more the theme in *Diana and Calisto* where the goddess chastises her pregnant handmaiden for her carnality. Here Titian has evolved in style from the smooth finish of *The Three Ages of Man* towards a much more impressionistic and free approach. Paint is applied unevenly over the picture – in some places it is just skimmed over the canvas while in others it is applied densely. The movement and drama are underlined by the immediacy of the technique.

Diana and Actaeon by Titian

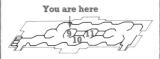
Room 9

Scotland lost nearly all of its religious art during the Reformation and the *Trinity Altarpiece* is almost unique in its survival. Nobody is sure of the original function of the two remaining panels though they were once thought to be organ shutters. More likely, they are the flanking wings of a triptych, the central section of which was destroyed. We do know that they were specifically painted for the Collegiate Church of the Holy Trinity, which stood, until the railway came, on the present site of Waverley Station. We also know that they were not painted by a Scottish artist but by the fifteenth-century Netherlandish painter Hugo van der Goes. He was greatly esteemed for his draughtsmanship and fluid use of oil paint, a technique which had recently been refined in Flanders. The commissioning of such a work by a major artist says a great deal about the cosmopolitanism of fifteenth-century Scotland.

The panels are painted on both sides and mounted on a mechanism which turns them at 30-minute intervals. In their closed position, Sir Edward Bonkil, first provost of the Collegiate Church, is depicted kneeling in front of the patron saint of music, St. Cecilia, conventionally portrayed at the organ. The Bonkil portrait is astonishingly realistic and full of character, and was probably painted from life when he travelled to Ghent to arrange the commission.

The panels open to reveal King James III of Scotland and his wife Margaret of Denmark kneeling in front of their country's respective patron saints – St. Andrew and St. Canute. The fine painting of fabrics and the rich opulence of the backgrounds are typical of Flemish painting though the execution of the royal portrait heads suggests that they were inserted by a local artist after the paintings were shipped to Scotland. It was undoubtedly because of the royal portraits that the panels survived the Reformation. The subject of the missing centrepiece remains a mystery and one can only guess at its splendour.

Room 10

Typical Venetian works by Titian's younger contemporaries are hung in this room.

The recent cleaning of Jacopo Bassano's *Adoration of the Kings* has revealed its brilliance – real Venetian colour. Its exuberance is also typical of Venice – the nativity is just an excuse for a full-scale costume pageant. Everything – colours, patterns, texture – conspires to produce a gorgeous spectacle, but don't be too dazzled. The young Bassano also excelled in portraiture and there are a number of fine portrait heads set into the tumult of robes and accessories. Bassano's attempt at an architectural setting is little more than a caprice.

Tintoretto is most famous for his large-scale mural decorations in which he attempted to combine the drawing of Michaelangelo with the colour of Titian. His *Deposition of Christ* really belongs in the dark of a chapel in the Venetian church of St. Francesco della Vigna. There the candlelight in which the scene takes place would have appeared even more eerie. Tintoretto has managed to give Christ's limp body a real feeling of weight and one can sense the struggle involved in manoeuvering it down from the Cross. The two crouching figures in the foreground are derived from Michaelangelo's sybils from the ceiling in the Sistine Chapel.

Spanish painting is poorly represented in the collection.

Of the works by El Greco only *The Saviour of the World* truly shows his visionary power. But even this has a certain sweetness which detracts from the potency of the image. Christ has the hieratic appearance of the icons from El Greco's native Crete, combined with the elongated and mannered drawing style of Tintoretto whose work influenced the young Greek when he was studying in Venice. By the time he executed these paintings El Greco had been settled for

El Greco's *The Saviour of the World* painted in the 1590s

many years in Spain where his heightened emotionalism was sympathetic to the religious fervour of the Spanish people.

Velazquez painted *An Old Woman Cooking Eggs* when he was only 19 years old. He was to become one of the greatest portrait painters of all time and, although this picture is a genre piece, the realism of the head painting is quite remarkable. Spanish tradition was essentially realist and Spanish painters excelled at the depiction of surface textures. The still-life in the foreground rivals the best Dutch still-lifes.

Bassano's *The Adoration of the Kings*

Room 11

Painting north of the Alps was always quite distinct from Italy. Painters in Germany and the Low Countries were more pragmatic and their figures are individual, not generalized, types. They were less inclined to experiment than the Italians and medieval traditions persisted longer. But by the beginning of the fifteenth century, Renaissance ideas began filtering through.

Bernard van Orley was a Brussels painter who did his best to imitate the new southern style. He may have visited Italy and certainly saw Raphael's tapestry cartoons which came to Brussels to be woven. His work may not look much like Raphael to today's viewer, but in his day he was known as 'The Raphael of the Netherlands'. The bulky figure of Christ in *Before the Crucifixion* is similar to Michaelangelo's male on the Sistine ceiling and it fits awkwardly with the grieving women who are still treated in the nothern manner.

Quentin Massays, a leading Antwerp portrait painter, obviously knew about Raphael's and Leonardo's accomplishments. *Portrait of a Man* has an intimate naturalistic air to it. The notary (if that is what he is, for nobody has explained his halo) sits in front of an arcaded window behind which recedes a beautiful rocky landscape similar to Leonardo's in the *Mona Lisa*.

Hans Holbein the younger is also best known for his portraits, especially those of the court of Henry VIII. The unusual *Allegory of the Old and the New Testaments* is a small-scale work executed before he left his native Basle to settle in England. Although it is propagandist in nature – it proclaims the superiority of the new Protestant religion over the old order – the figures are treated with the same realism as his portraits.

Massys' *Portrait of a Notary*

Room 12

Here are works by the two greatest Flemish painters of the seventeenth century: master and pupil – Sir Peter Paul Rubens and Sir Anthony van Dyck. Both worked in England for the ill-fated Charles I and were knighted for their services.

Rubens was a multi-talented genius: diplomat, courtier and linguist, he is one of the most attractive personalities in art history. As a young man he travelled throughout Europe, and he thoroughly absorbed the grand Venetian decorative manner, imbuing it with his own passionate temperament. The result was a colourful ebullient style – full of energy and movement. Rubens satisfied the demands for his work by organizing his workshop on factory lines. Though he was responsible for the overall design of the pictures much of the work was carried out by assistants.

The *Reconciliation of Jacob and Esau* is the sort of small oil sketch Rubens always made for a larger painting. The colour and brushwork is fresh and spontaneous and his composition is full of exotic detail – note the camels in the top right-hand corner.

The full-size *Feast of Herod* is a hugely enjoyable banquetting scene. Rubens has converted one of the most horrific of biblical tales into a brilliant costume piece. Salome sweeps across the picture carrying the head of John the Baptist. After his assistants had completed their tasks it is likely that Rubens himself worked over his canvas, for the bravura brushwork bears his unmistakable stamp.

Van Dyck's *St. Sebastian*

Rubens' *Feast of Herod*

Bound for Martyrdom is an early work painted in the exuberant baroque manner of his master. However, his reputation was made in England as a portrait painter to Charles I and his court. The painting of the Genoese Lomellini family was done in Italy before he settled in England. He was never averse to flattering his subjects and they look down on us with amused disdain.

If you are acquainted with the work of the Dutch painter Vermeer, *Christ in the House of Martha and Mary* may come as a surprise. It is the earliest of his

The Lomellini Family by van Dyck

known works and its biblical theme and large scale make it quite unlike the tranquil domestic interiors for which he

is so famous. The existence of one religious picture caused art historians to presume that Vermeer had done others which have since been lost. This prompted the famous Dutch forger van Meegren to produce a number of fake Vermeers in the style of the Edinburgh picture. The sombre tonality of the picture is characteristic of a group of Dutch painters who imitated the dramatic contrasts of light and shade of the Italian painter Caravaggio. A more typical example of this school's work is Hendrik Terbrugghen's *Beheading of John the Baptist* – possibly the most depressing picture in the gallery.

Room 13

This room is devoted to seventeenth-century artists working in Rome.

It is dominated by *Landscape with Apollo and the Muses*, the largest landscape ever painted by the French-born artist Claude Lorraine. Claude worshipped classical Rome and at an early age decided to spend his life among her ruins. His pictures are not depictions of actual places but idyllic dreams of perfect landscapes peopled by mythological figures. But the figures are

Il Contento by Elsheimer

almost incidental to the composition, and Claude can be seen as the father of pure landscape painting. His work had an enormous influence on succeeding generations of artists.

Two of the smallest and rarest pictures in the gallery are the work of a German expatriot living in Rome, Adam Elsheimer. Elsheimer worked in oil paint on a copper surface – a technique which gives his colours a striking luminosity. In *The Stoning of St. Stephen* the shiny metal underneath makes the bloody gash on the martyr's forehead horribly vivid. *Il Contento* is his masterpiece. An agitated crowd is trying to prevent Zeus abducting the goddess of happiness, unaware that he has replaced her with the goddess of discontent. The picture is filled with movement and dramatic contrast. In spite of the miniature scale of his work and his early death at the age of 32, the vitality and atmosphere of Elsheimer's style inspired a

Elsheimer's *The Stoning of St. Stephen*

host of younger painters from Rubens to Rembrandt.

Even as early as the seventeenth century, Italian artists were looking back to the achievements of the High Renaissance. Domenichino, Guido Reni and Poussin aspired to the calm of Raphael.

The effectiveness of Domenichino's design in his *Nativity* relies on the clear surface pattern formed by the arrangement of his figures. In this he was an important influence on Poussin.

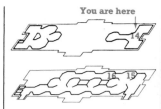

Rooms 14 and 15

Both these rooms are closed temporarily at the time of writing (Spring 1987), but will reopen in due course, possibly with a display of pictures of academic and historical interest.

Room 16

A Frenchman, Nicholas Poussin spent his working life in Rome where he was influenced by antique friezes and the figure style of Raphael. He dedicated his life to developing a detached unemotional style through which he could express his deep religious and philosophical convictions.

The Seven Sacraments is a second version of this unusual subject. By freezing all action and subduing the colour, he aimed to induce a quiet, contemplative response. The meaning of each of the sacraments is emphasized by the symmetrical composition

Detail of Poussin's *Baptism*

Detail of Poussin's *Mystic Marriage of St. Catherine*

which focuses attention on the central action – in the Baptism for example, the pouring of the water onto Christ's head.

Sixteenth-century Holland was a thriving trading nation and the art of the period reflects the Dutch bourgeois preoccupation with everyday life.

Dutch landscapists were the first artists to paint naturalistic landscapes. Avercamp's atmospheric *Winter Landscape* is thronged not with classical figures, but with ice-skaters. There are no antique ruins in *The Banks of a River* by Jacob van Ruisdael, only a real Dutch town in the distance.

Peter de Hoogh shared Vermeer's interest in the depiction of ordinary rooms and objects. His simple picture of a *Courtyard with an Arbour* (in the corridor leading to Room 17) would have been unthinkable to the Italians.

Frans Hals of Haarlem was almost exclusively a portrait painter. The pair of *Portraits of a Gentleman and His Wife* are extremely fine examples of his mature work, the figures clearly proclaiming in confident poses their wealth and security.

Hals' deftness of touch was second only to Rembrandt's. Rembrandt's earlier portraits are very tightly painted – *Portrait of a Young Woman with Flowers in Her Hair*, wearing a minutely detailed lace collar, shows how precise he could be. However, he was not satisfied only to represent the surface appearance of things and his later work – particularly his self-portraits – shows his obsession with inner character at the expense of expected standards of finish. The *Self-Portrait* is alive with his brushwork.

But Rembrandt was also much moved by biblical stories and often used them as subjects for his paintings. The sentiment of *Hannah and Samuel* is touching because of the tender relationship between the old woman and the boy – the more convincing because the model was probably the painter's own son. The picture on the easel, *Woman in Bed*, was probably meant as part of a larger biblical composition. The model is thought to be Geertje Dircx, who lived with the artist.

At the height of his fame Rembrandt had many pupils, not all of whom were to develop the same free technique as their master. Gerrit Dou was intrigued by light and reflections and painted exquisitely detailed little pictures such as *Interior with a Young Violinist*. Very different from Rembrandt's later work, this is obviously a young man's painting, carefully detailing the usual paraphernalia associated with students. Books are strewn around and there is an upturned beer tankard lying on the floor – things haven't changed much in 350 years.

Self-Portrait from 1657, one of several painted by Rembrandt

Achilles Lamenting the Death of Patroclus by Hamilton, 1763
(temporarily out on loan, Spring 1987)

El Medico (The Doctor) by Goya

Room 17

Back to Italy again, this room is mainly dedicated to the eighteenth-century painters who worked there. At that time no gentleman's education was considered complete unless he went on the 'Grand Tour' and visited the artistic centres of Europe. Rome was the highlight of the trip and the painters resident there profited from the lucrative tourist trade. It was the height of fashion to have one's portrait painted while in Rome – often with a typical Roman background such as the Colosseum. Pompeo Batoni's portrait of *Princess Benedetto Guistiani* lacks the fashionable landscape backdrop, but in the strong characterization and delicacy of handling you can see why he was the most popular portrait painter in the city.

The Scots painter Gavin Hamilton worked on a grandiose scale and one cannot imagine even the most enthusiastic tourist carrying home his *Achilles Lamenting the Death of Patroclus.* Hamilton was a dealer in antiquities who spent most of his life digging up Rome. His unparalleled knowledge of ancient Roman art was the main influence on his painting, though his figure style owes a great deal to Poussin.

In complete contrast to the academicism of Hamilton is *The Finding of Moses* by the Venetian painter Giovanni Battista Tiepolo. There is nothing pedantic about this bravura romp by one of the greatest decorators of the eighteenth century. Tiepolo makes absolutely no attempt at historical accuracy. Although this scene is sup-

posed to have taken place in ancient Egypt, he has dressed Pharaoh's daughter in sixteenth-century finery and her attendants – especially the dwarf – are straight out of a Renaissance court.

The style of the Spanish painter Francisco de. Goya also owes something to Tiepolo although he lacks the Italian's frivolity. Indeed his later work was exceedingly dark and pessimistic. *El Medico* is an unusually light-hearted picture of a doctor on his rounds warming himself over a brazier and is a tapestry design meant for a decorative scheme in one of the Spanish royal palaces.

Room 18

During the eighteenth century the English aristocracy de-

veloped a passion for portraiture, and many gifted painters specialized in giving the public what it wanted. Perhaps the greatest was Thomas Gainsborough who gave his clients good value for money.

The Honourable Mrs. Graham was only 18 when she sat for Gainsborough, so we can be sure that her youthful bloom had nothing to do with flattery. But young faces present even the finest painter with a difficult problem – they can so easily appear bland and characterless. Gainsborough has coped by making a great play of the costume – a dazzling piece of work. Mrs. Graham was shown at the Academy in 1777 and we can be sure that she outshone her rivals.

Gainsborough's chief rival

Detail of Gainsborough's *The Hon. Mrs. Graham*

Chardin's *Still Life*

Constable's *The Vale of Dedham*

was Sir Joshua Reynolds, first President of the Royal Academy and one of the most respected figures in English art.

In matters of theory Reynolds was the most erudite man in the country, but when it came to painting portraits he lacked Gainsborough's vitality though his pictures of women and children have an attractive sweetness. The *Ladies Waldegrave* – three fashionable sisters – are portrayed with an appropriately flattering eye.

In France, J.B.S. Chardin is distinguished from his contemporaries by this unaffected and direct approach to subject matter as can be seen in his *Still Life: The Kitchen Table*. Neither could anything be simpler than *Vase of Flowers*, his only surviving flowerpiece. It is a minor masterpiece.

In contrast fellow Frenchman Antoine Watteau has painted supremely artificial works. His imaginary scenes of costumed ladies and gentlemen cavorting in prettified pastoral settings are really *bon-bons*. This is not to belittle his talent, for Watteau was a fine draughtsman and kept albums of his beautiful drawings from which he selected the figures for his compositions. *Fêtes Venitiennes* is not only one of his finest pictures, it is also one of the best preserved.

Rooms 19 and 20
The room to the left at the top of the stairs is mostly dedicated to early nineteenth-century English painting, so Frederick Edwin Church's *Niagara Falls from the American Side* is decidedly out of place. Church was one of the leading lights of the emergent nineteenth-century American landscape school which sought to celebrate the natural wonders of the New World. He could hardly have found a more awe-inspiring subject than Niagara and represents the full force of its torrents on a suitably enormous canvas.

John Constable's *Vale of Dedham* is positively serene by comparison. It is based on a classical composition by Claude Lorraine though it does contain precise features of Constable's local landscape such as the tower of Dedham Church and the meandering River Stour. This is a highly finished exhibition picture worked on at length in the studio and quite different from the loosely treated little sketch *On the Stour* which was probably executed in a few minutes direct from nature.

However, the most magnetic picture in the room, far outshining Church's bombastic Niagra, is J.M.W. Turner's *Dream of Italy*, the paint surface of which seems almost dissolved in light. Unlike Constable who adored the English landscape, Turner was besotted by Italy. His pair of Roman views, *Modern Rome* and *Rome from the Aventine*, are full of topographical details such as the Colosseum, yet they remain poetic evocations of a golden Mediterranean world.

In the early nineteenth century pure landscape was considered a minor art and Turner was obliged to include mythological or historical figures to make his pictures acceptable to the Royal Academy. Constable refused to compromise his authentic view of rural England and, unlike the successful Turner, he gained little official recognition. Despite these differences, in Turner's and Constable's freedom of handling and preoccupation with light effects they can be seen as precursors of the Impressionists.

Eugene Delacroix, the greatest romantic painter of nineteenth-century France, admired both Constable and Turner although he was preoccupied with monumental figure composition rather than pure landscape. Like all romantics, he was intrigued by exotic Eastern subject matter and *The Chessplayers* gives us a hint of the opulence of his colour and technique.

Upper Rooms 21, 22, 23.

All the paintings hanging in these rooms are the work of men who, in one way or another, rejected the authority of the French Salon. Their experiments and investigations were to transform people's ideas about painting and sow the seeds of an aesthetic revolution they could have scarcely foreseen.

Gustave Courbet's small canvases, *View of Ornans with Church Tower, River in Mountain Gorge* and *The Wave* may look harmless enough – even conventional to modern eyes. But in the 1850s their painter represented all that was revolutionary in French art. Courbet waged war against the Academy and all it stood for. When his works were accepted for exhibition in the annual Salon, they incurred bitter criticism on account of what was seen as their vulgarity. If his work failed to be accepted he characteristically set up an alternative show – erecting a tent and charging admission! Courbet offended against official taste both in his choice of subjects and the way in which he painted them. He chose 'down to earth' things – a local burial or men breaking stones for example. Not for him historical or mythological subjects, false sentimentality or overt moralizing. Something of this direct approach can be seen in these three small pictures; especially in the simplicity of his sea composition with its broad use of palette-knife. The unprettified, sober townscape is a view of Ornans – the artist's hometown. Courbet's attitude to his art was influenced in no small way by his political idealism. A convinced socialist,

perhaps the most bizarre episode of his extrovert career occurred in 1871 when he was held responsible for the destruction of the Vendome Column during the Paris Commune of that year. His last years were spent in exile in Switzerland.

The other small landscapes hanging here alongside the work of Courbet represent another – less violent – anti-Academic trend in mid-nineteenth-century painting. *Soleil Couchant* and *Cottages at Barbizon: Evening* by Charles Daubigny and *Pool in the Forest* by Narcisse Diaz are both typical, in their freshness and intimacy, of the pictures produced by a group of landscapists working in the Fontainbleau woods south of Paris. Centred on the village of Barbizon, they have become known as the Barbizon School and anticipate the Impressionists in their dedication to working directly from nature out of doors.

They admired Dutch seventeenth-century landscape painting and the work of John Constable and the spontaneity of many of their small pictures recalls that of the English artist. The charming picture *Entrance to a Wood* was painted by the group's chief mentor, Camille Corot, and is a fine example of the subtle, poetic type of landscape which made him the most popular and influential landscape painter of his generation. Building up a picture with small areas of soft tone, Corot produced a very indistinct romantic effect, paying scant attention to precise line-drawing and concentrating on the atmosphere of a subject. This aspect of his work not only endeared him to the Impressionists but also made him a favourite with generations of forgers who made sure that Corots continued to come onto the market long after his death in 1875.

Pictures by the Impressionists are so often reproduced

that the shocking effect they must have had on the public in the 1870s can easily be forgotten. But, even here, where they rub shoulders with the pictures of the Barbizon school, their brightness – the high pitch of their colours – produces a shattering contrast.

The spirit of the group is epitomized by Auguste Renoir's *La Promenade*. Such a delightfully casual subject would have been unthinkable earlier in the century. The naturalism of the picture is a result of Renoir's acute observation of the effect of light filtering through the trees and dappling the strolling couple. And it was light and the difficult technical problem of rendering its transitory effects that obsessed the Impressionists. Claude Monet spent his whole life grappling with the problem. In the 1890s he painted entire series of works – almost scientific studies – of the same subject seen at different times of day and in different weather conditions. *Poplars on the Epte* and *Haystacks: Snow Effect* are from two such series. The picture of haystacks is a very good example of the Impressionist belief that the shadows of objects are tinged by the object's complimentary colour.

In the painting of poplar trees the form of the trees is broken up by the shimmering light rendered with small agitated brushstrokes. These small dabby brushstrokes became a hallmark of Impressionist pictures. Alfred Sisley produced some of the prettiest of them. *Mosley Weir: Hampton Court* was painted when, along with several other of the Impressionists, he fled to England during the 1870s in order to escape the political turmoil of France.

Together with Monet, Camille Pissarro was to become one of the most dedicated and consistent practitioners of Impressionism, but his large *River*

The Wave by Courbet

Haystacks by Monet

Landscape hanging here was executed before he had fully developed his ideas. *The Kitchen Garden at the Hermitage, Pontoise* is a more typical work.

Edgar Degas' *Portrait of Diego Martelli* displays all the characteristics which set him

Degas' *Diego Martelli*

apart from other Impressionists.

The picture's greatest strength is the superb drawing of Diego Martelli (note the delineation of the crumpled trousers). Degas was a magnificent draughtsman, traditionally trained, and this love of drawing always tended to make him antipathetic towards the Impressionists' overwhelming preoccupation with light. For Degas light was a dramatic tool with which to compose arresting pictures in the quiet of his studio and not something to be slavishly copied out of doors. But in spite of his more conventional attitude towards picture-making, he was in many respects an innovator. One of the first painters to use the camera extensively in his work, he became fascinated by the unusual appearances of things seen from unexpected angles. Extending the Impressionist range of modern subjects, he painted the races, women in hat shops, laundresses. The ballet, in particular, gave him endless scope to compose interesting groups of contorted figures and the artificial theatre lights prompted him to explore exciting, unnatural combinations of colours. Note how deftly Degas is able to contrive a composition like *Group of Dancers* from a severely limited palette of greens and oranges. While some of the Impressionists

Gauguin's *The Vision of the Sermon (Jacob Wrestling with the Angel)*

escaped to England to avoid the deprivations of Paris under seige by the Prussians in 1870-1871, Degas stayed on, enduring dreadful hardships. As a result he soon began to lose his sight. *Nude Study for 14 Year Old Dancer, Dressed* is a bronze taken from one of the sensitive wax models he made when his almost total blindness prevented him from painting.

A comparison between Paul Gauguin's *Vision of the Sermon: Jacob and the Angel* and the previously discussed Impressionist pictures will give some idea of the extreme reaction against Impressionist naturalism which occurred in the 1880s. Before he found his very personal voice Gauguin worked in an Impressionist style, exhibiting with the group in their later exhibitions. *The Vision* is his first overwhelming anti-naturalistic picture – an imaginary subject painted in flat brilliant colours. The convoluted

shapes of the Breton women's headdresses are silhouetted against a field of strident vermillion. The diagonal thrust of the tree across the picture plane is inspired by similar compositions found in the Japanese prints popular in France at this time. The overall effect of Gauguin's picture is closer to that of medieval stained glass than the work of the Impressionists and it was, indeed, the emotional impact found in medieval work with which Gauguin wanted to imbue his picture. Gauguin continued his visionary painting in the South Seas. The serene mood of a picture like *Three Tahitians* gives no indication of the inconveniences and hardships he suffered there.

Gauguin eventually abandoned the small brushstrokes of the Impressionists to paint in flat areas of vivid colour but van Gogh chose to develop them into a violent personalized calligraphy. *Olive Trees* vibrates with the artist's disturbed personality. The brushstrokes of colour writhe over the surface of the canvas. What might have been a rather charming scene in the hands of one of the Impressionists has become an emotional expression of the artist's state of mind. Like Gauguin who fled from the bourgeois life of a stockbroker to dedicate himself to art, van Gogh came to painting late in life. For a very short period in 1888 the two painters even tried applying paint, Seurat's art is in almost every other respect alien to that of the Impressionists. Unlike them he had no interest in capturing the fleeting moment but wanted to compose harmonious classical pictures. The small study hanging underlying forms of nature – the solidity of an apple or a mountain. In his later years he lived a hermit's life near Aix en Provence, constantly analysing a very narrow range of subjects. The underlying structure and shape of *Mont St. Victoire* was a

Van Gogh's *Olive Trees*

living together but this experiment was not a success. .

The Impressionist method of building up an image with small strokes of paint of precisely the right tone and colour had always been a more or less instinctive process. George Seurat investigated the actual scientific basis for the theories vaguely espoused by Monet and the other Impressionists. Under the influence of various optical theories current in the 1880s, he developed a way of placing small dashes of pure colour alongside one another, intending them to fuse into correct areas of tone to the eye.

Apart from the similar way of

here is a free sketch for the monumental depiction of a contemporary bathing scene in the National Gallery, London.

Whatever the virtues of Impressionist painting, it could never really defend itself against the criticism that it was lacking in form. Impressionist pictures were painted quickly in an effort to capture a particular moment – the transitory effects of light on things. The structure of things was more or less irrelevant. Paul Cezanne began by painting in a more formless manner than any of the Impressionists but gradually became obsessed by the problem of describing the simple

source of constant fascination for him. Using the natural brush-strokes and a limited palette, he repeatedly tried to find some equation for its form on canvas. Many of these attempts are unfinished, like our example here, almost, as if the task was too daunting to be successfully accomplished. Cezanne's single-minded dedication to solving this problem influenced a generation of artists. The first great movement of the twentieth century, Cubism, developed as a result of his research and he is now generally regarded as one of the most influential artists of the last 100 years.

1   2   3   4   5

The Scottish Collection

The new downstairs extension houses the gallery's Scottish collection. These few rooms offer a quick survey of eighteenth- and nineteenth-century Scottish painting which should not be missed. It is an uneven group of paintings but the best pictures certainly rank alongside many of the masterpieces of European painting upstairs.

Keeping company amidst a number of undistinguished early portraits we meet with the haunting eyes of the French philosopher *Jean-Jacques Rousseau*. The painting is by Rousseau's friend Allan Ramsay who exemplifies the sophisticated, cosmopolitan, eighteenth-century Scot. Ramsay made a considerable reputation in London, eventually becoming court painter to George III. This was an appointment much resented by Reynolds whom contemporary critics considered superior in male portraiture. Reynolds never produced anything quite so perceptive as this characterization of the quicksilver Rousseau. Rousseau was upset that Ramsay had made him look too 'shifty'. Reynolds' admirers, however, conceded that Ramsay was without equal in the portrayal of female beauty.

The other great eighteenth-century Scottish portraitist, Sir Henry Raeburn, made his reputation entirely in Scotland, immortalizing the leading lights of the eighteenth-century cultural revival. Had he shown more in London perhaps his international reputation might now stand higher, for at his best he has the freshness and fluidity of Goya. A portrait like *Sir Patrick Inglis* shows Raeburn at his most natural. Executed quickly and simply in broad brushstrokes of fresh colour without fussing over unnecessary detail, in it he has captured the whole character of his sitter.

In contrast his magnificent portrait of *Colonel Alastair McDonnel of Glengarry* in full highland dress seems rather over-worked. But it is a costume piece and must have looked very dramatic high on the wall of some dark baronial hall.

On a less serious note, who can fail to be charmed by Raeburn's portrait of *The Rev. Robert Walker Skating on Duddingston Loch*. The ludicrous sight of this dour minister skating is one of the most memorable images in the gallery.

Sir David Wilkie's reputation was made in London where he became a member of the Royal Academy. The honest realism of his early work comes straight from Dutch art. The narrative and attention to detail in such story pictures as *The Letter of Introduction* and *Distraining for Rent* made him enormously popular in his own day. However, in later life after suffering a breakdown of health he visited Spain where he came under the influence of Spanish painting. These last pictures are the antithesis of all his early work – large in scale and loosely painted. Unfortunately, he

mixed bitumen with his paint to make his dark colours richer and this has caused these pictures to crack dreadfully.

The remaining rooms are filled with a plethora of lochs, beasties and elders of the Church. Enjoy wandering through for they are great fun, if not exactly high art. Marvel at Noel Paton's enamelled fairy paintings crammed with hundreds of tiny female nudes – in reality, Victorian soft pornography. Thrill to the drama of James Drummond's costume pieces, starring the ill-fated Mary, Queen of Scots. Do not miss the tiny tempera panels of William Dyce whose exact technique and sincere approach to religious subject matter influenced the English Pre-Raphaelites.

Finally, as you are leaving, note the large Impressionistic pictures of the West Coast of Scotland by Sir William McTaggart. He understood the Impressionist's theories before any other British painter and his brushwork and fresh colour points the direction of modern Scottish painting.

Far left *The Quarrel of Oberon and Titania* by Paton, 1849.
Above *Rev. Robert Walker Skating* by Raeburn.
Below *The Storm* by McTaggart, dated 1890.

National Gallery of Modern Art

Masterpieces of twentieth-century painting, sculpture and graphic art

In the Summer of 1984 the Gallery moved to much larger premises in Belford road. It is now housed in the former John Watsons School, a neo-classical building designed by William Burns in the 1820s. It is set in spacious grounds which the Gallery intend to landscape gradually over the next few years to incorporate some of its sculpture collection.

Now that the Gallery has a new home, it can show much more of its permanent collection at any one time. In spite of the inflated price of modern art, the Scottish National Gallery of Modern Art has succeeded in building up a very respectable collection since its founding in 1960.

The core of its collection is a small group of works by the pioneer artists of the twentieth century. 'Candlestick' by George Braque is a very good example of the work of the cubist movement he developed along with Picasso in the years leading up to World War I. There are pictures from the various phases of the career of Pablo Picasso, probably the most universally acclaimed artist in history; a tiny canvas 'Mother and Child' from his famous 'Blue Period', a cubist still-life of 1912/13 called 'Guitar, Bottle and Gas Jet' and two still-lifes, 'La Table de Musicien and 'The Soles', both painted in later contrasting styles. Do not miss 'La Leçon de Peinture' by Henry Matisse. It is an uncharacteristically sombre picture by an artist famed for his bright colours, a picture composed of simplified decorative shapes. There are a number of fascinating surrealist works: pictures by Rene Magrite, Joan Miró, Max Ernst and Giaconetti. The works of German and Russian artists – often greatly influenced by avant-garde French developments in the early years of the century – are displayed alongside the French work. Note the chilling nude by Otto Dix.

The gallery is also famous for its comprehensive selection of British Twentieth Century painting. All major figures are

Artistic tradition in Scotland

The long traditions of Scottish art are linked with those of Europe in certain respects, but, in others, they are unique. The national tradition of painting really begins with the Renaissance – or, rather, the lack of it, for the Renaissance spirit of artistic independence totally failed to spread to Scotland at the time. Unlike England, where itinerant Continental painters such as Holbein and Van Dyck took the place of the monkish artists expelled by the Reformation, Scotland had little such imput. The chief reason for this was the sheer distance from the centres of European art, though the climate and the dour Scottish character may have had something to do with it as well.

Thrown back on their own resources, the Scots developed their own native art style. Mostly, Scottish painters worked in portrait – a tradition that was to expand and flower until it reached its peak in the work of the eighteenth-century artists Allan Ramsay and Henry Raeburn. These were the painters of the first great Celtic revival, even though Ramsay made his reputation in London and eventually became Court Painter to George III.

As this tradition reached its peak with Raeburn, another tradition was being founded with the work of the young David Wilkie. His development marks the beginning of a new movement in art which was not just of Scottish, but also of European, importance. Wilkie's adoration of the Dutch and Flemish schools led him to adopt the genre style in his painting. This, sometimes in a slightly debased form, became a cult in Victorian times. Wilkie was described by Millais as the greatest Scottish painter; he became so fashionable that, when his painting showing the return of the veterans from Waterloo was exhibited at the Royal Academy, London, barriers had to be erected to keep back the crowds.

The style became part of the

represented from Matthew Smith, with his very personal interpretation of French Fauvism, to David Hockney, one of the most popular artists in Britain today.

A unique feature of the Scottish National Gallery of Modern Art collection is its group of works by Scottish painters. Relatively unknown in the rest of Britain, painters in Scotland at the beginning of this century were often closer to continental developments than their counterparts in England. They form a specifically Scottish school known as the Colourists. Their brightly coloured work is often on view. Look out for paintings by Peploe, Cadell Hunter and Fergusson.

Reclining Figure 1951, in bronze, is one of two by Henry Moore in the grounds.

Scottish Academy tradition, together with good portraiture, following Raeburn's example. By the mid-nineteenth century, the former was becoming steadily more romantic – subjects included scenes from Scott's novels, border ballads and the like – and centred on landscape.

It was at this time that yet another tradition started, which has deeply influenced Scottish art down to the present day. This was a painterly version of the Auld Alliance, demonstrating the continuing Scottish love of things French and of French culture in particular.

In reaction to the conservatism of the Scottish Academy, a group of young painters started looking to France and, in particular, to the work of the Impressionists. Gradually, the link grew. Sir William McTaggart, for instance, was the first notable painter in Britain to work in the Impressionist tradition.

McTaggart was joined by a group known as the Colourists. This group was Glasgow- and Edinburgh-based (the first Academy rebels had been from Glasgow). Scotland's painters today still show the influence; it is notable, for instance, in the work of Joan Eardly, one of Scotland's most important painters.

The story of Scottish art is made up of many strands and themes. Some Scottish artists took the prosperous road south; others, like Raeburn, have been neglected in Britain, though acclaimed on the Continent and in the USA. One factor remains constant – the fact that individuality has been preserved in Scottish art. Its great flowering was almost as much a reaction to external circumstances as the result of the gifts of the painters themselves. The guiding light, in art as in much else since the Union of Parliaments, has been the determination to make painting an integral part of an independent national heritage. In pictorial form, this shows itself in the free handling of paint; in attitude, it shows itself in a spirit of fierce independence which has persisted to the present day.

National Museums of Scotland

Royal Scottish Museum

A celebration of the skills that powered the Industrial Revolution

As might be expected of the capital of a proud and ancient nation, Edinburgh's many museums are treasure-houses of national, as well as local, importance.

The Royal Scottish Museum, Chambers Street, has many claims to distinction. First, it is the only national museum in the UK to house its main collections under one roof. Second, it is housed in one of the finest Victorian buildings in the country; its light, spacious galleries,

molluscs, birds, scientific instruments, geology and so on. There is also an emphasis on industry, invention and technology.

Such emphasis is natural enough, for many of the leading lights of the great days of the

Because of very extensive repairs to the roof which are planned over the six year period 1986-1992, at any one time a few of the display rooms will be closed. Do not worry, there will still be plenty to see.

host of Scottish inventors and entrepreneurs, many of whom are now forgotten but whose achievements played a major part in the shaping of our modern industrial world.

On the ground floor, the sheer scale of the Hall of Power and the exhibits within it aptly set off the importance of its chief theme – the development of steam as the power source which set the wheels of industry turning. Here, Scottish ingenuity combined with Scottish pragmatism to major effect; it is often forgotten that James Watt's first backer, John Roebuck, was Scottish and that it was only after the latter ran into financial difficulties that his share in Watt's patents was sold to Matthew Boulton.

Dominating one end of the Hall of Power is a giant industrial waterwheel, made in Manchester in 1826 for a firm of millers in Aberdeen. Close by it stands another major exhibit, the locomotive *Wylam Dilly*. This dates from 1813 and, with its twin, *Puffing Billy*, is the oldest locomotive in existence. Next to the locomotive is a working model. Scale models are a major feature of the Royal Scottish's engineering and scientific collections; in many instances, recorded push-button commentaries are also available.

The huge natural history section displays elephants, the skeleton of a blue whale (**left**) and the dodo of the Indian Ocean (**above**). The attractive iron galleries of the Main Hall are shown on the opposite page.

arranged around a striking main hall, make an ideal setting for the varied collections. These range from celebrated mammal and bird exhibitions through practically every artistic and scientific field.

There is a splendid Hall of Evolution, there is a Hall of Minerals, there are excellent displays of mammals, fish,

Industrial Revolution were Scots themselves, or had links with Scotland. James Watt, whose skill and ingenuity made the steam engine into a practical proposition, was born in Scotland; Robert Stephenson, with his father, George, a pioneer of the railway age, was educated at Edinburgh University. These are only two examples from the

In the southeast corner of the hall is the enormous black cylinder of the Boulton and Watt Double-Acting Beam Engine

(1786). This is an early example of Watt's work. Contrary to popular belief, Watt did not invent the steam engine; he took the existing Newcomen model and vastly improved it, making it far more efficient, as well as cutting down on fuel consumption. The resulting engine was the work-horse of the Industrial Revolution. It was long-lasting, reliable and, with appropriate modification, could be used in mines, iron works, mills, pumping stations and breweries. Many Watt engines continued in service until the end of the nineteenth century; the museum's engine worked for 99 years before being replaced.

Like many great ideas, Watt's was simple in concept. While repairing a Newcomen-type model, he realized that it was extremely wasteful to first heat the cylinder to produce the steam and then to cool the cylinder to condense it. On a Sunday afternoon walk, it came to him that a separate condenser and air pump was the answer. The latter was the key part of the invention. It sucked the air out of the condenser to produce a partial vacuum. The steam from the cylinder rushed into this vacuum, where it was immediately condensed. The surrounding steam at atmospheric pressure then moved the engine's piston.

The size of the Boulton and Watt engine is in keeping with its importance in the annals of the Industrial Revolution. To the north of *Wylam Dilly*, however, is another exhibit, which, though far smaller in scale, was just as important to the world of agriculture as the work of Watt was to the growth of industry.

In 1750 the Scottish millwright Andrew Meikle produced his version of the 'fan-tail' gear for automatically keeping a mill facing the wind. This was one of the greatest advances in windmill engineering ever recorded, for it meant that the miller no longer had to alter the position of the mill's sails manually when the wind changed direction. Meikle went on to apply his inventiveness to adapt the windmill as a 'wind-engine' for the driving of farm machinery as well as the grinding of corn. The museum's model may have been an inventor's model, or it may have been made to demonstrate advances in windmill design.

Agriculture, however, was rapidly overhauled by industry as the prime source of the nation's wealth and a host of new inventions flooded onto the market to make that industry more efficient and productive. As always, Scottish pioneers led the way. James Nasmyth's

Museum floor plan

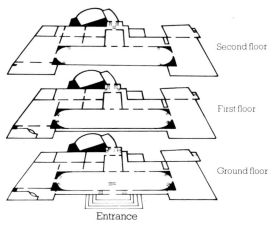

Second floor

First floor

Ground floor

Entrance

Some of the fascinating encounters that await the visitor to the Royal Scottish Museum are pictured here. They are representatives from the four main departments of the museum – art and archaeology, geology, natural history and technology
The departments generally are not restricted to one area but have exhibits on several floors.

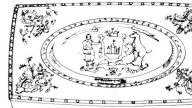

Scottish silver box 1736

Fish fossils, 350 million years old

Relief of Pharoah Akhenaten
1365-1348 BC

Model of Bell Rock
lighthouse 1833

Locomotive *Wylam Dilly* 1813

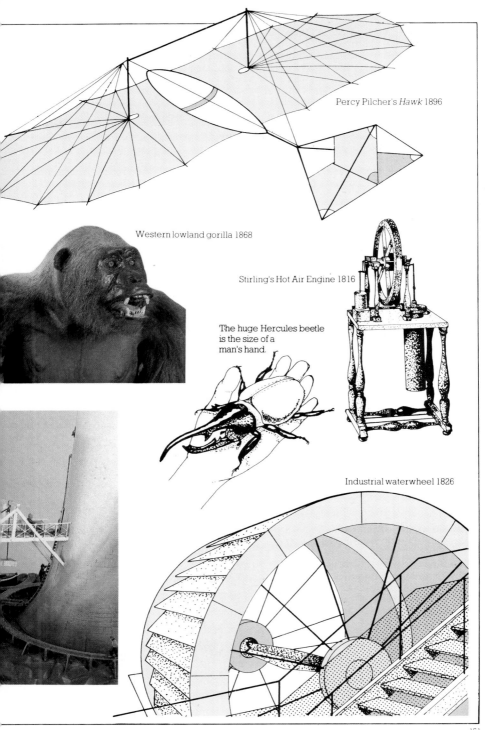

Percy Pilcher's *Hawk* 1896

Western lowland gorilla 1868

Stirling's Hot Air Engine 1816

The huge Hercules beetle is the size of a man's hand.

Industrial waterwheel 1826

steam hammer (1842) – a model by the west wall – made it possible to forge large pieces of iron. Nasmyth was also a pioneer of machine tools, the life blood of modern industry. His fertile mind encompassed many fields, including an intriguing anti-invasion floating mortar, designed to destroy 'by one masterly blow, the largest ship of an invading enemy'.

Scottish inventiveness was not confined to the large or monumental. Hanging in the Hall of Power is Percy Pilcher's 'Hawk' glider, dating from 1896. This is the oldest flying machine in Britain and, though its inventor was born in Bath, it was built and flown in Scotland. Pilcher was working on a powered airplane when he crashed to his death in 1899; had he survived, it is an open question whether Scotland, rather than the USA, might not have given birth to the flying machine.

A last intriguing exhibit is the Stirling Hot Air Engine (1816), directly across from the Pilcher glider. Invented by Robert Stirling, a Perthshire minister, the engine used hot air, rather than steam, as its driving force. Its special feature was a regenerator to absorb and store heat that would otherwise have been wasted. A similar type of engine is being used in space experiments today.

Through the south door of the Hall of Power is the Hall of Shipping. During the nineteenth and early twentieth centuries, Scotland was the centre of the world's finest shipbuilding industry and its Clydeside yards produced literally thousands of ships for all nations, ranging from humble tugs to sleek warships and vast ocean liners. The museum's shipping exhibits are divided between this hall and the Hall of Victorian Engineering, but here note the models of the armed merchantman *Yellow Carvel* (1480) and the warship *Great Michael* (1511). These demonstrate that the Scottish maritime tradition stretches back over centuries.

There is yet another example of Scottish invention. By the middle of the south wall is the screw propeller invented by Robert Wilson of Dunbar in 1826. Though there is fierce dispute – as there was in Wilson's own lifetime – as to whether he was first in the field, his screw is very similar to modern design.

Directly above the Hall of Shipping on the first floor is the gallery of Lighthouses and Bridges. Both of these were among the principal Scottish achievements in the nineteenth century; in the Edinburgh area alone, there are the Dean

Bridge and the Forth Rail Bridge, the latter being joined today by its road equivalent. Leith Docks were another major civil engineering achievement.

Just in front of the east entrance is a model of the Bell Rock lighthouse. This was designed by Robert Stevenson, grandfather of the author Robert Louis and the principal lighthouse engineer of his day. It was completed in 1811. The model not only shows details of the lighthouse itself, but of how the men who built it went about the task.

The Stevenson family influenced Scottish lighthouse design for several generations. Near the Bell Rock exhibit, in a case against the east wall, is an elaborate oil lamp of considerable candlepower, designed in 1842 by Alan Stevenson, eldest son of Robert.

However, the chief glory of Scottish civil engineering in the nineteenth century was undoubtedly the construction of the Forth Rail Bridge. On a pillar beside the open well looking down to the Hall of Shipping is a series of photographs showing the construction of the bridge. Work on it began in January 1883 and the opening ceremony was on March 4, 1890. During the intervening

Scotland's Oil – 1851

Say 'Scotland's oil' to the man in the street and he will immediately associate the statement with the towering oil platforms of the North Sea. Yet the true story of Scottish oil begins in 1851, years before the first US oil well was drilled.

The Scottish oil industry was founded by one man, James 'Paraffin' Young. He discovered the secret of extracting oil from a special coal, called Torbanite, found in West Lothian, and in 1851 he established the

James 'Paraffin' Young, founding father of the modern oil industry, and the chemist Robert Angus Smith.

world's first commercial oil works. With the exhaustion of Torbanite supplies, he found a subsitute in oil-shale and the Scottish oil-boom began.

By 1865, some 120 companies were in the field, though the number soon dwindled. Nevertheless, even with the growth of the giant oil industries of the USA and the Middle East, Scottish shale oil survived until 1962, when the price of it finally became economically exorbitant and the last shale working closed.

Dunlop's first pneumatic bicycle tyres, made in 1888. The Royal Scottish has the front wheel and tyre.

years up to 4600 men worked on it at any one time, while the bridge cost approximately £3 million to build. Nearby, the stages of building the Forth Road Bridge (1964) are shown. This cost considerably more than its Victorian predecessor, even allowing for the changing value of money.

The pick of the Victorian engineering collections is now housed in the Hall of Victorian Engineering. Here, the exhibits cover every aspect of Victorian endeavour. Compare the presentation models of notable locomotives – note in particular the early Stephenson-type *Edina* (1840) – with that of the cruiser *HMS Terrible*, built on Clydeside in 1898. It was the most powerful warship of its type in its day, its 48 boilers

driving it at a top speed of 22 knots. Its builders, J & G Thomson, gave the model just as much attention as the ship itself.

Yet another controversy has raged over two juxtaposed exhibits in the hall – an interesting reminder of how jealous our business-like Victorian forefathers could be. The dispute over who developed the first pneumatic tyre was bitterly contended at the time and the exhibits here demonstrate the work of the two Scots who laid claim to the invention – John Boyd Dunlop and R. W. Thomson. Today, it is clear that Thomson invented the principle of the pneumatic tyre in 1845 at the staggeringly early age of 23 – it is shown here fitted to an 1845 Brougham – but, because of practical difficulties, the idea languished until 1887. Then Dunlop married his skill to new techniques to produce the first durable pneumatic tyre.

Thomson, however, was ac-

tive in many other fields. As well as being a pioneer of steam road traction, he contributed greatly to the development of the gas industry, as his rotary exhauster, used to pump gas, shows. Gas lighting itself was pioneered by yet another Scot, William Murdock, in 1798. The importance of the Scottish contribution to the gas industry is commemorated by the Royal Scottish at its outstation at Biggar, 29 miles (47km) southwest of Edinburgh.

Naturally, the Royal Scottish contains much else of absorbing interest to the visitor, whether tourist or resident. This brief glimpse of one aspect of its contents, however, should serve to demonstrate how much we owe today to the extraordinary breed of men produced by Scotland, who combined the willingness to experiment with practical sagacity and a stubborn belief that nothing was impossible.

The National Museum of Antiquities

The gift of an eccentric Earl preserves Scotland's national heritage

Edinburgh's other notable museum is the National Museum of Antiquities of Scotland, in Queen Street, which, unlike the Royal Scottish, restricts its exhibits to those of Scottish origin. The emphasis has always been on archaeology – it is Scotland's premier archaeological museum, housing an internationally important collection – but other exhibits cover almost every aspect of Scottish life from earliest times to the present century.

The museum was founded by the 11th Earl of Buchan (1742-1829). Buchan was one of the great eccentrics of his day, free with his advice on practically every issue. Amongst those he bombarded with correspondence were George III and George Washington, both of whom he rather surprisingly addressed as 'cousin'.

Though the Earl's eccentricity and vanity undoubtedly put some people off – one letter reads simply 'I beg you will send me no more intimations respecting the meetings of the Antiquarian Society' – his creation flourished. It moved to its present home, which it shares with the Scottish National Portrait Gallery, in 1891.

Today, the exhibits are arranged on three floors, with temporary exhibitions on the stairs from time to time. Many of the major displays have been redesigned recently, while alterations and additions are constantly being made. There is always something new to see, particularly at the entrances to the various galleries, where new discoveries and recent acquisitions are put on special display.

The ground floor is devoted to exhibits of sculptured stones, medieval and later antiquities. The sculptured stones are in their own gallery and represent a unique collection of sculpture, dating from the Roman withdrawal from Britain to AD 1050. They are a surviving memorial to the great and dramatic changes which swept Scotland during this period; on one hand, the collapse of Pictish society in northern Scotland and the decline of Romano-British culture on the Scottish border and, on the other, the growing influence of waves of invaders who sought to conquer. Chief among these were the Angles, of Saxon origin, the Irish, particularly that group known as the Scots, and the Vikings, otherwise referred to as the Norse. The stones also mark the great change from paganism to Christianity, which eventually served to link all the various artistic styles and produce one of the greatest artistic flowerings Scotland has ever seen.

There are also permanent exhibitions in the main gallery, including, towards the back, a display of Scottish costume. Although small, the collection shows the dress of both the grand and the humble. The late seventeenth century and early eighteenth century male suits look particularly rough and uncomfortable to wear; they are in interesting contrast to the adjacent silks and satins.

However, for many the chief interest of the ground floor lies in the fascinating juxtaposition of objects in the various areas of

This museum has permanent displays on three floors and temporary displays may be found on the stairs. The ground floor gallery contains a variety of material ranging from sculptured stones to silver and costumes. The first floor gallery is largely devoted to archaeology and the second to the Romans.

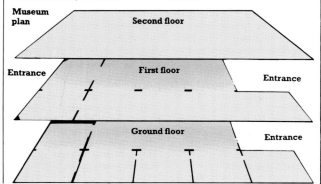

Museum plan

Second floor

Entrance

First floor

Entrance

Ground floor

Entrance

1

2

On this page are some of the interesting treasures to be found in the Museum.

1 Two beakers 2000-1600 AD

2 Two silver-gilt chapes, part of the St. Ninian's treasure

3 The Hunterstone Brooch circa AD 700

4 Roman iron helmet mask with traces of silver plating, late 1st century AD

5 Pictish symbol stone 7th-8th century AD

6 Three carved stone balls and a macehead circa 2000 BC

7 Gold collar and earring circa 2000-1700 BC

3

4

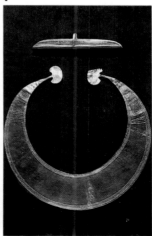

5

6

7

the main collection. The silver and plate exhibits – both religious and secular – are of outstanding national importance. So, too, are the displays of weapons, including pistols and swords. Though the former were largely made in Scotland, the blades of the latter, in the majority of instances, came from southern Germany.

Situated towards the rear of the gallery is the grim structure of the Maiden, a Scottish precursor of the guillotine. This example was made in 1564 and continued in use in Edinburgh until 1710, being used for public executions on Castle Hill, in St. Giles and the Lawnmarket. Among its notable victims was Regent Morton, executed in 1581, who is said to have helped to design it.

Scottish life had its cultured side, however, during even the grimmest periods of its history. At the time the Maiden was claiming its victims, Edinburgh's goldsmiths and clockmakers were creating some of the best examples of their work. Though many of the best craftsmen, such as Heriot and Ramsay, moved to London with the Scottish court after the Union of Crowns, others continued the tradition.

Look for the copy of the National League and Covenant, and for the priceless Lewish Chessmen, part of a set of exquisitely carved walrus ivory chess pieces. Particularly on the ground floor, the exhibits are changed quite often. A new and interesting exhibit appears and something else which was on display returns to the vaults.

The first floor gallery contains the museum's great hoard of prehistoric and Viking antiquities. The word 'hoard' is a literal description of quite a few of the treasures, many of which came from burial sites located throughout Scotland. The exhibits relate to the period from the first appearance of man in Scotland to the Norse settlements in the late Dark Ages.

Among the earliest exhibits on show are a collection of Neolithic polished axes. These stone axes date from between 4000 BC and 2500 BC. They were not just functional tools; the examples here demonstrate that such axes could rise to the status of minor works of art in their own right. They were made of specially selected stone and some even came from as far away as the Alps. They probably did not reach Scotland directly; it is thought that they were passed from tribe to tribe as gifts until they eventually reached their northern home.

In the centre of the gallery, there is a reconstruction and linked exhibits from one of the most important late Neolithic village sites in the world – Skara Brae, Orkney. The museum's links with this site are extremely close; not only does it house the material found in the celebrated 1920 excavations, but it has also mounted a subsequent expedition there.

Note also the elaborate jet necklaces that are on display. This easily worked stone was frequently used to make objects for personal adornment in the late Neolithic and early Bronze Ages; as well as necklaces, buttons and toggles were carved in it. From the same period come the carved stone balls, which are a prominent feature. Modern research has succeeded in dating them, but it is still not clear what they were used for.

Gold is also an important part of the collections. The two most significant displays show a variety of ornaments made in the Bronze Age; these include the recently discovered hoard of late Bronze Age armlets and bracelets from Easter Ross.

The gift of craftsmanship persisted over the centuries. In later times, the Celtic metalworkers became renowned for the skill with which they worked and decorated their products, particularly those made of bronze.

The Hunterston Brooch is one of the finest examples of Celtic jewellery to survive. It bears a Norse inscription and dates from the eighth century AD.

The Vikings were jewellery-makers too, though they preferred silver to gold. As it was Viking custom to bury the dead with their earthly riches, the museum has amassed a large collection of Viking jewellery. Among the most striking – and certainly the largest – examples are the Thistle brooches, so-called because of the decoratio at the end of the pin.

The most spectacular treasure of recent years, however, is undoubtedly the hoard of late Pictish silver, found on St. Ninian's Isle, Shetland, in 1958. The carefully decorated objects had been placed in a wooden box and hidden beneath the floor of the church in about AD 800, probably to protect them from being stolen in a Viking raid. The artistic motifs displayed on the hoard are similar to those seen on the sculptured stones in the ground floor gallery.

On the second floor, the gallery is devoted totally to exhibits demonstrating the Roman presence in' Scotland. From the first century to the fourth century AD, southern Scotland was a buffer zone between the hostile tribes north of the Forth and the rich Roman province to the south of Hadrian's Wall. Thus, Scotland never knew the full benefits of the Pax Romana, but, in purely military terms, the Romans left a wealth of material behind.

The exhibits here record the military facts of the Roman presence – from the building of the

Antonine Wall to scenes of the domestic life of the legions – and the native reaction to it. The Bridgeness slab came from the eastern end of the Antonine Wall at Bridgeness, West Lothian, and dates to approximately AD 140. The left-hand panel forms one of the most remarkable images of Roman Scotland to survive. Roman parade armour, from the principal fortress in southern Scotland, is also on display, plus a collection of military tools. Examine the tools in particular, for it is interesting to note how the basic shapes of some of them have remained virtually unchanged up to the present day.

Another interesting Roman survival is the huge collection of iron nails that were apparently buried deliberately at Inchtuthill, Perthshire. The fort there was abandoned even before it was completed, as the troops intended to make up its garrison were needed elsewhere.

A reconstruction of a Celtic chariot provides an interesting insight into the type of weapon the Celts used to oppose the deadly legion. But the gallery's greatest treasure is the hoard of Roman silver known as the Treasure of Traprain, discovered in 1919 during the excavation of Traprain Law, Scotland's largest hill fort and capital of a tribe known as the Votadini.

The hoard largely consists of silver plate, but the four coins which were found indicate that it was buried between AD 410 and AD 425. The objects are of particularly fine quality and come from a table service, a lady's dressing table, an army officer's uniform and possibly a church, as some of the objects are stamped with Christian symbols.

Most of the objects, however, are crushed or cut into pieces. The mystery is how such a treasure found its way into a native settlement in the first place. The first theory is that the hoard represents loot captured on a raid south of Hadrian's Wall, which was subsequently cut up so that the spoil could be divided. The second is that the silver was given to the leader of the tribe as a bribe to stop him raiding into Roman territory.

These are only some of the treasures of the museum and, although, as has been said, the collections are rotated regularly, there is much of interest that there is simply not room to display.

On the opposite side of the road there is another gallery used for special or visiting exhibitions, which usually are arranged each Summer.

Scottish National Portrait Gallery

This gallery is in Queen Street in the same building as the National Museum of Antiquities. It is a very good collection of portraits of famous Scots and of others connected with Scottish History. Amongst many others, there are portraits of Robert Burns, Flora Macdonald, Prince Charles Edward Stewart at Age 12 and in old age, David Hume the philosopher, James Watt the Engineer, Sir Walter Scott, Lord Byron, Thomas Carlyle and Robert Louis Stevenson. On the second floor there is a gallery of twentieth century portraits, including Winston Churchill, Ramsay MacDonald, Sir Compton Mackenzie, Hugh McDiarmid, a recent portrait of Sir Alexander Gibson the conductor by John Houston, and a very new portrait by John Wonnacott of Sir Adam Thomson in British Caledonian's Hanger 3. He is the founder and present chairman of the airline.

Statues and Monuments

A miscellany of the many memorials Edinburgh has raised to heroes

The Gothic fantasy of Sir Walter Scott's monument dominates east Princes Street, towering over the gardens at the foot of St. David's Street.

Designed by George Meikle Kemp, a joiner and draftsman, and with a twice-life-sized statue of the seated Sir Walter by the sculptor Sir John Steell, it is a legacy to the romantic Gothic Revival popularized by Scott.

The competition for the design of the monument, announced in 1836, caused enormous controversy over the design and the winner: Kemp was accused of plagiarism – and he was an unknown from the lower classes. But his monument was inaugurated after interminable squabbles and delays on August 15, 1846, and immediately became one of the major attractions of the city.

Kemp designed the monument, inspired by Melrose Abbey and Gothic memorial crosses, in only five days and it was chosen by the Memorial Committee despite designs submitted by illustrious architects like William Playfair

The monument is 200½ feet (601.5m) high, and the 55-square-feet (5m^2) base rests on a foundation of solid rock 52 feet (15.6m) below street level.

Above the foundations, rising seven steps on each side, is a quadrangular platform where the statue of Scott and his dog, Maida, rests. It is carved from a solid block of Carrara marble that originally weighed 30 tons and was, in fact, the first marble statue in Scotland.

At each corner of the platform, four massive piers of clustered shafts are joined by pointed arches and the space above is vaulted over with ribbed arches. The vaults are supported by four external buttresses, rising 90 feet (27m). A gallery surmounts the four principal arches and contains a central room, the Museum Room, completed in the 1870s.

Above the gallery the main tower rises steeply and contains a further three galleries with connecting stairs. The uppermost gallery is a climb of 287 steps but the view from the top is spectacular.

The exterior is highly decorated with 64 characters from Scott's novels and a further 16 statuettes are of Scottish poets.

Extensive restoration was undertaken in the mid-1970s at a massive cost of £154,000 – a sharp contrast to the original cost of the monument of £16,000.

David Livingstone

At the Waverley Bridge entrance to East Princes Street Gardens stands this statue to David Livingstone, the nineteenth-century explorer and missionary. After discovering the Zambezi River and Victoria Falls, he was awarded the Gold Medal by the Royal Geographical Society, shortly after which he was made an honorary burgess of Edinburgh. Livingstone died in 1873 while searching for the source of the Nile, and his body was returned to Britain to be buried in Westminster Abbey. Three years later this bronze statue was erected. It is the only statue in the gardens sculpted by a woman, Amelia Robertson Hill. Although it was said to be an 'admirable likeness', many present at its inauguration thought this statue to be too small for the open air and more suitable for the interior of a building.

Allan Ramsay

The marble statue, showing this eighteenth-century wigmaker turned poet wearing a silk nightcap, was sculpted by Sir John Steell, who carved it from a solid block that weighed 18 tons. Ramsay, who moved to Edinburgh from his native Lanarkshire, became a great success in the capital through

his writing and bookshop and was among the pioneers of lending libraries, opening one in the High Street in 1725. This, and his involvement with the theatre which he fought to have legalized in Scotland, made him very unpopular with the Presbyterian Church.

The statue, erected in Princes Street Gardens West in 1865, was commissioned by one of his descendants, Lord Murray, who appears on one of four medallions on the plinth. General Ramsay, the poet's grandson, the poet's wife and two great-granddaughters are depicted on the others.

Charles II

In Parliament Square the Merry Monarch, Charles II, prances near the grave of the Gloomy Reformer, John Knox, whose remains were buried here when it was St. Giles graveyard. Charles's statue is the oldest in Edinburgh and the oldest equestrian statue, dated 1685, in Britain. It is thought to be of Dutch origin but the sculptor is unknown. No one knows quite how much it weighs but when it was built no supporting struts were inserted. As a result the horse is buckling at the knees and has to be repaired frequently, the last time in 1972 when it was injected with a specially prepared plastic resin.

The statue was removed during the nineteenth-century renovations to St. Giles and was put back again in 1835 when Robert Mylne, the King's Master Mason in Scotland, added the plinth.

John Knox

An ironic memorial to the reformer of the Scottish church, John Knox, stands against the wall of St. Giles in Parliament Square. 'He sleeps,' wrote Robert Louis Stevenson, 'within the call of the church that so often echoed to his preaching.' The bronze statue of Knox, who campaigned tumultuously against 'graven images' in churches, was designed by Pittendrigh MacGillivray in 1902 and cast in 1906. The statue marks the approximate site of the dour man's grave (this area used to be St. Giles graveyard) and seems to look accusingly at the nearby statue of the Merry Monarch, the libertine King Charles II.

George IV

Designed by Chantrey in 1831 to commemorate the King's glorious visit in 1822, this statue stands in Hanover Street. George's visit was very popular and he was rapturously welcomed, even though he wore pink silk tights under his kilt. The royal tour, the first since the Scottish defeat at Culloden, was seen as a recognition of Scottish participation in the union as a partner rather than a vanquished nation.

Melville Monument

This 150-feet-high (45.7 m) stone column, topped with a statue of Henry Dundas, 1st Viscount Melville, has a rather turgid history. Building began on the column, a copy of Trajan's Column in Rome, in 1821. The money, £3,500, was raised by officers, petty officers, seamen and marines who served Melville during his time as First Lord of the Admiralty, but it ran out before completion, and the city was forced to help out financially. However, it is still not certain that building debts have been cleared.

There was also a squabble over the siting – first it was to be at Calton Hill then its present site in St. Andrew Square was chosen; followed in 1823 by hot debate whether or not it should be completed at all. Others suggested it should be rededicated to William Pitt. Finally, in 1837 after 14 years of argument, Melville, so powerful in his day that he was nicknamed King Harry the Ninth, triumphed and a statue was designed by Sir Francis Chantrey and carved by Robert Forrest.

Dundas, a man of indefatigable industry, was Solicitor General for Scotland at the age of 24, Lord Advocate between 1775 and 1783, Treasurer to the Navy, under William Pitt, from 1784-1800 and then First Lord of the Admiralty.

Scottish American War Memorial

The Scottish American War Memorial Committee dedicated this statue to 'the Scottish effort in the Great War' in 1927. The bronze cast had taken the designer, Professor R. Tait Mackenzie, of Philadelphia, three years to complete and it is entitled 'The Call'. It shows a kilted soldier on a plinth looking at a frieze where volunteers from all walks of life are represented. Above the frieze are two interwined wreaths, one with a shield of the Stars and Stripes and the other with the shield of St. Andrew's Cross.

At the beginning of World War II the statue, in Princes Street Gardens West, was covered in sandbags to preserve it. The bags were ceremoniously removed during a memorial service on May 30, 1942.

Alexander and Bucephalus

Sir John Steell first modelled this huge statue 50 years before it was finally cast in bronze – the first cast in Scotland – in 1883, the cost paid for by subscribers. It shows the Macedonian king Alexander taming his warhorse Bucephalus as a representation of 'mind over brute force' and was unveiled in 1884 on the west side of St. Andrew Square. In 1916 it was moved to its present position outside the City Chambers in High Street, because it was a traffic hazard. The Gladstone Memorial Committee paid the cost of the move as they replaced it with a statue of Gladstone but this, too, had to be moved in time.

Earl Haig Memorial

A Bombay parsee, Sir Dhumjibhoy Bomanzi, commissioned this bronze statue of Earl Haig and his horse 'in admiration of the services rendered to the British Empire by the Field Marshal'. Haig was Commander in Chief of the British Army in World War I. The statue was designed by George Wade and unveiled in 1923 on the northern edge of the Castle Esplanade, alongside a parade of memorials to Scottish soldiers and regiments.

Adam Black

The politician and publisher was Lord Provost of Edinburgh from 1843 to 1848 and is depicted by John Hutchison, the sculptor, in his robes of office. Black, who also represented the city as a Liberal Member of Parliament, refused the knighthood normally offered to retiring Lord Provosts, with the words, 'I have no need of a title for my wife to be called "my lady" (she was already a Lady) and I have enough heirs to do without airs and graces.' He was one of the city's most prominent publishers, founder of A & C Black, and had acquired the copyright for some of the early editions of the *Encylopaedia Britannica* and Scott's Waverley Novels. The statue, cast in bronze, was erected in Princes Street Gardens East in 1877.

Duke of Wellington

This statue, outside Register House in Princes Street, so pleased the Duke of Wellington that he wanted a copy for his London home. But as the complete equestrian sculpture weighed 12 tons, he had only the bust cast.

Known as the 'Iron Duke in bronze by Steell', it was among the first successful models of a

prancing horse, cleverly using the tail as means of support. The Duke's war horse, Copenhagen, was unavailable as a model for the sculptor, Sir John Steell, so he borrowed a horse of a similar breed from the Duke of Buccleuch's stables at Dalkeith Palace, to which he again resorted for models for the Albert Statue in Charlotte Square.

Sir William Chambers

When the Town Council commissioned a statue of their former Lord Provost William Chambers there was heated argument about the suitability of the design – a recumbent figure that was to have lain in St. Giles Kirk. But the Kirk authorities objected and the council were forced to find an alternative site. A competition for a new design was launched and the sculptor John Rhind won with his model of Chambers, brother of the publisher, standing in his Provost's robes. The bronze statue was erected by the Town Council in 1891 and unveiled by the then Lord Provost John Boyd in Chambers Street at a cost of £1400.

The Royal Botanic Garden

The largest section of the Royal Botanic Garden is the Arboretum, where visitors can wander or rest in the shade of trees and shrubs from all over the world. Some of the most brilliant flowering is in the nearby Rhododendron Walk.

Labels on map: Demonstration Garden, Alpine House, Copse, Rhododendron Walk, Azalea Lawn, Tea Room, Inverleith House, West Gate, Arboretum Road, Arboretum, Peat Garden, Woodland Garden, Inverleith Terrace

*F*ew cities in the world can boast a park or garden of over 70 acres (28 ha) only a 10-minute bus ride from the centre. As you pass through the East Gate, Inverleith Row, you can see what makes Edinburgh's Royal Botanic Garden different; the emphasis on woodland and wild areas contrasts completely with the formality of mansion gardens.

The quiet sanctuary of the Royal Botanic Garden contains exotic orchids, Amazon lilies, a fossilized tree from thousands of centuries ago, an excellent collection of Scotland's heathers and five giant beds of all types of azaleas which from the beginning of June are a blaze of colour.

The Botanic Garden is best known for its collection of rhododendrons and as a scientific establishment. In 1980 the garden, the second oldest botanic garden in Britain, was voted the best garden in Europe, for its collections and contribution to science and education.

The magnificent gardens are the result of two Edinburgh physicians establishing a physic garden in 1670. Medicine at the time relied largely upon herbs and, from the Dark Ages to the early Middle Ages, upon the work of monks. The use of plants until about the beginning of the nineteenth century was central to medicine and, until the creation and development of physic gardens in the sixteenth and seventeenth centuries, it was the monastic communities that maintained interest in herbs and their healing potential. Even today plants are used as starting materials for semi-synthetic drugs or, indeed, as pure drugs.

Physic gardens were always associated with universities where medicine was taught because medicine relied upon plant life and its study. Dr.

Robert Sibbald, the first Professor of Medicine at Edinburgh University, and Dr. Robert Balfour, an eminent physician, recognizing the unsatisfactory state of medicine in the city, decided to establish a physic garden for the cultivation of medicinal and other plants.

The site the two doctors secured was just 40 feet (12 m) square, a small plot of land not far from Holyrood Abbey. The venture was successful, with the assistance of James Sutherland, the first Intendant of the Garden, but they could not have dreamed that such humble beginnings would result in today's renowned Botanic Garden of

some 70 acres (28 ha).

In 1676 Balfour and Sibbald realized that more land was required and they took over the garden attached to Trinity Hospital — on the site of which Waverley Station stands today. James Sutherland was responsible for both gardens and in 1695 was appointed Professor of Botany at the university and in the same year took control of part of the Royal Garden at Holyrood. Four years later Sutherland was appointed King's Botanist and in 1710 he became Regius Professor of Botany.

The Royal Botanic Garden was extremely fortunate both in

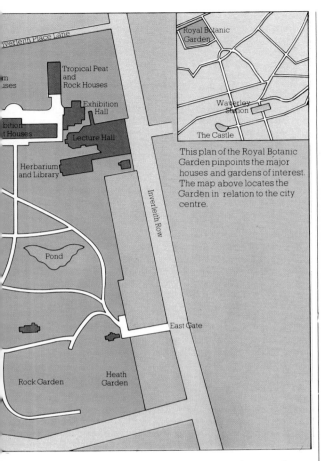

This plan of the Royal Botanic Garden pinpoints the major houses and gardens of interest. The map above locates the Garden in relation to the city centre.

Sutherland and, later, John Hope. Sutherland's reputation for skill and learning coupled with exceptional energy earned him the monopoly on botanical teaching in the city.

It is to Hope's eternal credit that he was able to restore and develop the Botanic Garden afterwards. Hope had originally entered the University of Edinburgh as a medical student but his interest in botany took him over. He went to Paris to study under Bernard de Jussieu (1699-1777), Professor of Botany at the Royal Garden in Paris, one of the strongest supporters of the Linnaean system of plant classification. It is today a uni-

versal system of nomenclature and classification.

In 1763 Hope carried out his greatest achievement from the point of view of the garden's history. The Trinity Hospital Garden was in 1763 moved to a larger site of about five acres (2 ha) off Leith Walk, to a site where Haddington Place now stands. At the same time, Professor John Hope, the Regius Keeper, obtained a permanent income for the new garden from the Crown, from which time the Gardens came under the Commissioners of Her Majesty's Works and Public Buildings.

John Hope's period as Super-

intendent of the Garden was one of great activity. His two great interests were plant physiology and systematic botany and these studies and his teaching contributed greatly to the science. He encouraged his students to research in the field and it is now acknowledged that he and his pupils were the pioneer investigators of Scottish plant life, collecting not only from the mainland but from Arran, Mull, Orkney, Shetland and Skye as well. His name has been commemorated for all time in the genus of trees from South China, South-east Asia and Indonesia and Malaysia – *Hopea*.

Hope was succeeded in 1786 by Daniel Rutherford who, as a chemist, was more interested in plants as objects for his experiments in determining the chemistry of the atmosphere. Of his six principal gardeners during his 33 years as Professor and Keeper of the Royal Garden, John Tweedie was notable. Tweedie had worked at Dalkeith Palace Gardens, and later, in 1825 at the age of 50, left to explore the reported botanical splendour of South America. Tweedie introduced several species of *Verbena*, the Chilean Jasmine and a number of other exotic and colourful plants which can be seen in the herbarium at the Gardens.

Rutherford was responsible too for appointing John McKay of Edinburgh as Principal Gardener in 1800. He removed old trees, exchanged plants with the Gardens at Kew, London, and embarked on botanical excursions with a number of dedicated students. McKay died in 1802 but in 1810 Rutherford was again lucky in his gardeners; this time he appointed William McNab, a leading horticulturalist from Kew.

McNab showed immense enthusiasm in his task of developing the Botanic Garden. He introduced many new and rare plants and carried out the culture of aquatic plants such as Egyptian water lilies and other water-living plants from Bengal, south and east Asia, the United States and India.

McNab was the organizer for the move to Inverleith, the home of the gardens today. Transporting and transplanting well-established trees and shrubs has never been easy and the collection was a considerable one. McNab invented a transplanting machine to allow the removal of mature trees. The operation took over two years and it is McNab who should be credited for the fact that virtually nothing died.

Up until this time specimens from abroad had been introduced in a rather haphazard way; most of the botanical excursions were concentrated on native Scottish plant life.

Naturalists had accompanied expeditions: the group of monkey puzzle trees between the Pond and the Azalea Lawn, for example, were introduced in 1795 by Archibald Menzies, a student under Professor John Hope. He had accompanied Captain Vancouver in the *Discovery* in 1790 and returned with the specimens from Chile. Later expeditions included that of Captain James Clark Ross's *Erebus* to the Antarctic in 1839. Many specimens were introduced, however, by an informal system of exchange with other gardens, notably Kew.

The Universities (Scotland) Act of 1889 proposed that the Botanic Garden should be transferred to the University of Edinburgh. Balfour resisted for a number of reasons. As a result the gardens were handed over by the Treasury to the First Commissioner of Works and the gardens had to be open on Sundays. The public showed their approval: 27,000 visited over four Sundays while the Free Church Presbytery denounced the arrangement as 'a most wanton desecration.

The following year, 1890, the Right Hon. the Lords Commissioners of HM Treasury set up an enquiry to consider the role of the Keeper and the outlay for the gardens in the future. The beginning of the Royal Botanic Garden as it is today at last began to take form.

Towards the end of the 1830s more formal transactions on a large scale were contemplated, and by 1844 the first volume of *Transactions* had been published. But the scheme was on a small scale until the period from 1905 to 1925 which was especially rich in the introduction of foreign species – in particular the collections of George Forrest from western China. Their classification by botanists on the university and garden staffs resulted in botanical papers on Asiatic rhododendrons, primulas, gentians, lilies, conifers and other groups of plants which were to completely transform the gardens. Exchanges of seeds are now made with gardens all over the world, and trust funds, such as the Rock Plant Trust Fund, sponsor botanists on collecting trips.

But to return to the last century: in 1864 the Experimental Garden of the Royal Caledonian Horticultural Society was transferred to the Botanic Garden and in 1876 a further 30 acres (12 ha) of ground surrounding Inverleith House were added. The gardens were at this time under the supervision of Isaac Bayley Balfour, who had succeeded his father John Hutton Balfour.

New accommodation for botanical research and teaching was built, laying out of the Rock Garden started and new glasshouses were constructed – some of which survived until 1966. Edinburgh became an important centre for taxonomic research, especially on the plants of China and the Himalayas which included the famous rhododendrons. This work owed much to the naturalists who accompanied expeditions of exploration, and in particular to the plant collector, George Forrest, who brought from China many important horticultural plants and over 40,000 dried and living specimens for scientific research.

Isaac Bayley Balfour quickly realized the need for extensive modernization and reorganization of the gardens themselves and the way in which they were controlled. Up until 1889 the Botanic Garden was under the dual control of the Treasury and the Commissioner of Works. Balfour saw that dual control led to inefficiency, more money was needed for maintenance and development and research should be furthered.

The Winter Palace in the late nineteenth century

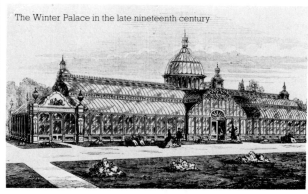

A walk through the gardens

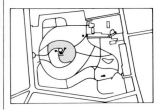

The Rhododendron Walk

Edinburgh's Royal Botanic Garden now contains the largest collection of rhododendrons in Britain. The most beautiful display is in the Rhododendron Walk which extends from the West Gate entrance, and many others are dotted around.

Thickets of the largest leaved of the hardy bamboos provide shade and protection for other plants, which include specimens of *Bergenia*, mainly Himalayan and Chinese, and plantain lilies.

Shrubs from New Zealand have found the protection from wind and frost and the full sun they need on the south and west facing walls of Inverleith House. These include *Sophora tetraptera*, the kowhai, with its curious golden yellow flowers that appear in June and *Hoheria sexstylosa* which flowers profusely in July and August.

To the north of Inverleith House and along one side of the *Rhododendron x praecox* hedge is a collection of *Enkianthus* species. Their clusters of white, pink or reddish flowers appear in spring, and in autumn their foliage turns magnificent hues of orange and crimson.

Near the *Enkianthus* are several plants which would be considered delicate when grown on the east coast of Scotland: the evergreen *Desfontainea spinosa* from Chile produces yellow-lobed scarlet flowers during the summer and *Mahonia lomariifolia* blossoms yellow flowers in November.

Several plants in the Rhododendron Walk produce either fruits or flowers as late as November and, in the case of the hellebores, in December and January. The spectacular Corsican hellebore, for example, produces pale green flowers from a mass of toothed foliage well after the New Year. On the east side of Inverleith House is a collection of magnolias which, as well as producing large, attractive flowers in spring, also contribute to autumn colour.

The Arboretum

Much of the original planting in the Arboretum, south of the Rhododendron Walk, was carried out on the basis of assembling all the species of a single genus as near together as possible. The introduction of new species, especially from the Himalayas, western China and North America, and the need to plant some species to give shelter to others, has made it impossible to adhere strictly to the plan. The main collection of oaks, for example, is on the lawn to the north of Inverleith House, but some fine specimens are found near the pond, to the east, as well.

The Arboretum, the Latin name for a botanic garden of trees, has been added to continually since its founding in 1877. The lawns include a varied sampling of trees of the rose family, such as the flowering crabs and rowans, hawthorns, and of the maple and lime families. There are also willows, poplars, silver birches and alders. The extensive collection of barberries is located principally on the lawn between the conifers and the main collection of oaks.

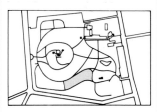

The Peat Garden

It was under the direction of William Wright Smith that the Peat Garden, the first in Britain, was constructed in 1939 at the north entrance of the Woodland Garden. A series of raised borders, rich in peat, has allowed the successful cultivation of plants like dwarf rhododendrons, primulas, gentians, lilies. An immense variety of creeping shrubs and dwarf shrubs provide winter cover so that ground penetration by frost is reduced. The dwarf lilies and the terrestrial orchids, notably the North African *Dactylorhiza elata* and the Madeiran *D. maderensis* are particularly interesting. *Primula whitei* and *P. gracilipes* are two of the primulas that attract visitors in such numbers, from spring onwards, that the surrounding turf is often worn bare. Ferns, such as the native Adder's Tongue, thrive in the peaty conditions.

The Woodland Garden

The Woodland (or wild) Garden is the least formal of the sections: the illusion of remoteness is achieved by introducing large masses of evergreen shrubs which shut off the surrounding buildings, and by

Spring

Summer

Autumn

Winter

trees which provide partial overhead shade.

Grassy paths wind through the woodland and the area is enlivened with evergreen shrubs to provide a leafy background and masses of colour in season.

Shade and shelter for the woodland vegetation is given in part by conifers such as cypress, thuja, fir and pine. Owing to atmospheric pollution, unfortunately, none of these is really splendid but at least they help the survival of other plants.

As well as an abundance of rhododendrons, the shrubs include hydrangeas, viburnums, eucryphias, camellias, magnolias and cotoneasters – as well as many others. Shade-loving plants include the striking may lily, with its heart-shaped leaves and small, white flowers, the wood anemone, greater celandine, the North American bleeding heart or Dutchman's breeches, the plantain lily of Japan, with its beautiful foliage, and, not least, bluebells and poppies.

The Rock Garden
To the east of the conifers in the Woodland Garden, lies the Rock Garden with plants from Europe, India, China, Japan, Australia, New Zealand and the Americas.

James McNab, as principal gardener, conceived and constructed the Rock Garden in 1871. He used the well-worn steps and landing of the old School of Arts in Adam Square, carried stones from the old Bank of Scotland buildings, basalts from Giant's Causeway and Staffa, and large masses of

granite and quartz, black hecla or lava stones. Isaac Bayley Balfour, however, wished to make improvements and the reconstruction work, which took until 1914, produced a rock garden that is fundamentally the one you see today. Large pieces of conglomerate from the slopes of Ben Ledi in Perthshire and red sandstone from Dumfries were used.

The spaces between the rocks harbour plants from many mountainous parts of the world – which are sometimes incorrectly thought to provide all rock garden plants. High mountain, or alpine, plants are found in great numbers in the Rock Garden, together with species from the varied environments of the warm Mediterranean shores and the cold permafrost regions of the Arctic.

There is a collection of mainly Scottish alpine plants in the centre of the Rock Garden; there are saxifrages, campanulas, alliums, gentians from Europe, America, Asia Minor, the Himalayas, China, Turkestan; a variety of species from Spain, Portugal, North Africa and the Americas; and the plants with white flowers from New Zealand include the celmisias with silvery, often sword-shaped, leaves and great daisy-like flowers and *Ranunculus lyallii*, probably the most beautiful buttercup in the world.

Miniature waterfalls and pools give the area added interest as well as ensuring sufficient moisture. Much of the rock is covered by prostrate or creeping shrubs. Species of *Cotoneaster* from the Himalayas, southeast Tibet and western China, for example, carpet the rocks and provide decorative fruits as well. The cotoneasters are best seen in the autumn, while shrubby potentillas and several species of broom provide bright colour during the summer. The dwarf rho-

dodendrons are invaluable for colour and cover and vary from the carpeting *Rhododendron forrestii* var. *repens* (named after its collector, George Forrest) and the taller species such as *R. lapponicum* which may reach three feet (about 1 m) in height and flower profusely in May.

Apart from the many creeping shrubs and the mats of herbaceous plants, conifers such as juniper help to hide the slabs of rock with the evergreen dwarf conifers adding colour and interest during the winter.

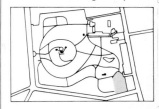

The Heath Garden
In the southeast corner of the gardens is the Heath Garden. There are over 30 varieties of heather which flower at different times from the beginning of June until the end of October. With colours ranging through gold, dark red and mauve and the varying colours of foliage, the heath garden is attractive at any time of the year.

In the 1830s, in the time of William McNab, a spendid collection of heathers from South Africa was cultivated. By the 1930s, however, heathers had become less popular with the public and only a few of McNab's specialities remained. Heaths from all over Britain and continental Europe gradually became more popular and so in 1935 a new Heath Garden was laid with thousands of plants being propogated. Species included the many forms of the variable ling or heather *Calluna vulgaris,* and the bell-heather *Erica cinerea,* from the Scottish highlands and other parts of Great Britain and

Europe; the many forms of *Erica carnea* from the mountains of central and southern Europe together with many other species of *Erica* from southern Europe, the Mediterranean and North Africa.

Thousands of these plants were introduced and planted informally with junipers, pernettyas and brooms as well as crocuses and squills to provide colour in every month of the year.

The Pond

North of the Rock Garden, past the East Gate, is the area where the Pond is the focal point. Several hardy aquatic and marsh plants can be seen here: the yellow water lily, *Nuphar lutea*, and the American species *N. advena*; groups of reed mace, also known as bullrushes, are especially conspicuous after the appearance of their cylindrical brown fruiting heads. Emerging well above the surface of the water in summer and autumn is the marestail, *Hippuris vulgaris*; the Cape pond weed, with its curiously branched white flowers, floats all over the surface; and during the summer the water lilac, native to Scotland, can be seen.

The first glimpse of colour around the Pond in spring is the Himalayan primula and in summer the most conspicuous plant is *Gunnera manicata*. This plant is the largest leaved plant hardy in Britain and resembles giant rhubarb – in a good season its leaves will grow to more than five feet (1.5m) across. Moisture-loving plants such as primulas, irises and astilbes flower in summer and the bright scarlet flowers of species of *Lobelia* continue into the autumn. Winter colour is provided by the royal fern, *Osmunda,* and the leaves and fruiting heads of reed mace.

Trees framing and overhanging the pond area include the golden weeping willow, the Austrian pine, a weeping ash and a group of Japanese maples to the west. The Pond is the main source of water for the Rock Garden and for the animal life seen in the gardens. Two families of foxes, grey squirrels, birds and smaller creatures all inhabit the gardens.

The Azalea Lawn

Northwest of the Pond, in the centre of the gardens, is the lawn devoted to azaleas – part of the genus *Rhododendron* which start to flower in May. Azaleas are among the most popular of flowering shrubs with an astonishing variety of flower form, colour and perfume.

The Lawn includes both deciduous types from eastern Europe, the Caucasus and Belgium and evergreen types from Japan. *Rhododendron x albicans* yield an exceptional scent from their white, pale pink or pale yellow flowers. They are the last to bloom, extending the season into July.

The Lawn is dominated by beeches and there are also numerous birches which include the two North American species, the canoe birch and the river birch.

At the foot of the Lawn there are rhododendron hybrids and several beautiful examples of the rose family. The hybrid crab-apple of the family *Rosaceae*, for example, produces bronze leaves and an abundance of purplish crimson flowers.

Plant Exhibition Houses

The glass houses today at Edinburgh's Royal Botanic Garden are, it is to be hoped, the last in a long line. The first was opened in 1834, restored in 1858, the buildings reconstructed in 1893, another range added in 1898 and in 1965 all were demolished, the new complex being opened in 1967. The houses are constructed with no internal supports, but are suspended on external pylons.

Cactus and Succulent House – No 1

Cacti come from deserts and survive with very little water. They show special adaptations, such as waxy coatings on leaf or stem and small leaves to minimize evaporation.

The plants have been arranged geographically to show convergent, or parallel, evolution: plants develop similar characteristics in similar climates although they are geographically separated and are not related to each other. Examples of this phenomenon are the African *Euphorbia*, with its characteristic shape of tall, ribbed columns, and the similar American cacti, *Echinocereus.*

Adaptation for survival is shown, too, by the stone plants of the *Lithops* genus. These small plants avoid detection by grazing animals, which frequently resort to succulent plants as the only source of water, by resembling pebbles.

The many glorious trees, flowers, shrubs and plants found in the Royal Botanic Garden are represented on the left-hand page by *Trillium sessile*, which prefers to live in the shade (**top left**); *Trillium grandiflora* in the Peat Garden (**middle left**); the 150-year old palm *Sabal blackburniana* from Bermuda (**main picture**); a mauve dwarf rhododendron (**bottom left**); and the immaculately kept pond near Inverleith House.

On this page are Himalayan poppies, also found in the Peat Garden (**top left**); exotica in the Cactus and Succulent House (**top right**); the tranquillity and miniature plants of the Rock Garden (**middle left**), a hybrid orchid of the *Odontonia* genus (**middle right**); and, near the Palm House, the delights of the Heath Garden where one bush or another flowers in every season.

Not only are they the right colour, but they are speckled as well so that they merge with their background.

The window succulents are unusual in that their leaves are normally buried in the sand. Only the flattened tips are exposed and these act as converging lenses to transmit light to the leaf. It is here that chlorophyll is stored for photosynthesis, which takes place when sufficient light is received.

The Warm Temperate Aquatic House – No 2

The pool and several water-living plants dominate this house, but there are also some succulents which require a moister atmosphere than that of the Cactus and Succulent House. Specially interesting are the species of *Selenicereus* and *Hylocereus* which in summer produce huge flowers of great beauty and an attractive scent.

The East Indian waterlilies, sacred in India and China, have bright pink flowers which are associated with the Buddha. Their leaves are held high out of the water.

The blue dawn flower, *Pharbitis learii*, blooms for the longest time of the plants in this house. Like most of the morning glories, to which group it belongs, it is best seen early in the day since the flowers which open in the morning lose their brilliance in the afternoon and fall in the evening. There are also large growths of sugar cane and species of *Hibiscus* and *Cinchona*. Quinine was isloated from *Cinchona* in 1820.

Tropical fish have been put in the pool to create as natural an environment as possible – and these are paid for by visitors who drop in coins from the bridge. After every weekend, the coins are collected – with just a few left to stimulate further contributions – and used to buy more fish.

Temperate Plant House – No 3

Here are plants from the warm temperate regions of the world, in particular those which would not do well in Scotland's climate, arranged geographically. Many of the trees are from Australia and include several species of *Acacia*, colourful in early spring, and *Eucalyptus. Callistemon,* also from Australia, has small flowers and dramatic scarlet 'bottle-brushes' made up of numerous brightly coloured stamens. Species from the cooler regions of Africa, the Canaries, China and Japan are also grown.

Cobaea scandens, growing over the railing, is a climber which gives off a smell of rotting fruit. The odour attracts fruit-eating bats who, in the wild, are deceived into pollinating it.

The locust tree (*Ceratonia siligua)* has long pods which are used as animal fodder in Mediterranean countries. Its seeds were used as the original carat weights by goldsmiths.

At the west end of the house the Tropical Aquatic House pool can be seen from below from a special chamber and there is a collection of aquatic plants and many species of tropical and cold-water fish.

Tropical Aquatic House – No 4

The gigantic leaves of the Victoria waterlilies from tropical South America are the main attraction here. In their native habitat they would grow to about 15 feet (4.5m) in diameter, but as this would be impracticable to allow in the plant house, they are removed each year and regrown from seed. Even so, they grow to such a size and strength that it is possible for one to support a baby. The base and sides of the lilies are covered in spikes, nature's solution to the threat of hungry fish. The sides are raised as an adaptation against turbulent

water which would overflow the leaf. The leaf structure of these plants is one of nature's wonders: as it cannot be seen properly from above, there is an underground viewing chamber beneath the pool, entrance to which is in the Temperate Plant House.

The strongly scented flowers of the Amazon lilies are as impressive as the plant itself and are produced from June to October, each one lasting just two days. When they first open in the late afternoon, they are a creamy white but by the second evening they change to a deep purplish-rose. They then become submerged and after the fruit ripens the seeds fall to the bottom of the pond.

Marsh plants include the Egyptian paper-reed, *Cyperus papyrus,* from which the ancient Egyptians made paper, and rice, *Oryza sativa.*

The southeast corner of the house is devoted to a group of plants which live for their mutual benefit with ants

One example of this phenomenon is seen in the trumpet tree (*Cecropia peltata*). The ants pierce the hollow stem and live in the internal cavity, and in return for shelter the ants, which tend to bite or sting on sight, protect the plant from insects.

The Fern House – No 5

Over 300 species of tree ferns create the illusion of a forest. In nature many grow on tropical mountains, up to an altitude of 1000 feet (300m), while others have come from temperate regions such as New Zealand, Australia and South Africa. The tallest in the house, *Cyathea australis,* can grow to nearly 66 feet (20m) in the wild.

As well as the collection of tree ferns, there are many other low-growing varieties and fern allies, such as *Selanginellas,* which are grown here for ground cover.

Cycad and Orchid House – No 6

The cycads with their huge, palm-like leaves dominate the house, and some are thought to be almost 200 years old. Cycads are not related to palms but to a family which is thought to link the ferns and the flowering plants.

Some of the 20,000 species of the orchid family are the other central feature. These most exotic of flowers are found in all parts of the world and are most abundant in the tropics.

Orchids vary enormously in shape – and for a purpose. The flower of each species resembles one kind of insect, so that insects may be drawn to the plant where they will unwittingly pollinate it. The unsuspecting insect, perhaps a bee or a fly, is attracted both by colour and scent whose resemblance is close enough for inexperienced male insects to attempt copulation with the flower.

Tropical Peat and Rock Houses

This is a separate house, divided into two sections, and shows some of the research activities carried out by the Royal Botanic Garden. One of the three main families under study is the *Ericaceae*, which includes heathers and rhododendrons, but there are also a number of unfamiliar genera. The other two families, *Gesneriaceae* and Zingiberaceae, are principally tropical, the former including rock garden plants. Many of the plants have been collected only recently, while others are in cultivation for the first time.

Exhibition Hall

To the east of the Plant Exhibition Houses lies the Exhibition Hall where more detailed information can be presented than in the rest of the garden. The Hall opened in 1970. Various aspects of plant biology are shown by text, audiovisual units and plants and the displays are changed at regular intervals.

The Palm Houses

The Tropical Palm House was opened in 1834 and in 1858 the larger Temperate Palm House was opened. A minimum night temperature of 46°F (8°C) is maintained in the Temperate House, while in the Tropical House it is never below 64°F (18°C).

The palms are of more economic importance than any other plant family, providing food, shelter and clothing for people all over the world.

There is an astonishing variety of species. The size of the stem and the structure of the leaves vary enormously, while some are altogether stemless. Their flowers are not usually particularly attractive, but the talipot palm from India and Ceylon, *Corypha umbraculifera*, has achieved distinction in producing an inflorescence about 33 feet (10m) long with about 60 million flowers.

The fruit of the palm varies much more than the flowers, ranging in size from a pea to the double coconut which can weigh over 30 pounds (13.6kg).

The outstanding palm in the Temperate House is *Livistona australis*, of which there are several specimens of different ages, one almost touching the roof. In the centre of the Tropical Palm House grows the remarkable *Sabal blackburneana*, the fan or thatch palm of the West Indies. This specimen was transplanted by William McNab's machine from Haddington Place in 1822. It is well over 170 years old and every May it produces an abundance of black pea-sized fruits.

Alpine House

This was designed to house some of the more tender species of alpine plant which would not find the conditions of the Rock Garden suitable. The plants in the house and its surrounds are constantly changing, but in spring there are crocuses, tulips, narcissi and fritillaries. There are always some dwarf primulas, and the saxifrages are usually found in flower for a long period. Some saxifrages form low cushions of foliage, so that water loss in the wild is reduced.

The Frames, adjoining the Alpine House, accommodate those species which would find conditions in the house itself too hot in the summer. Within the house, the floor is overlaid with moist sand in which the pots are plunged to avoid excess evaporation and to maintain a constant root temperature.

The Copse

West of the Alpine House, and the other Plant Exhibition Houses, is the delightfully informal Copse, similar in style to the Woodland Garden. Here in the Copse are birches, pine and eucalyptus, which are especially striking during the winter, while the *Acer palmatum* 'Senkaki' provides colour in spring and autumn.

Situated on a knoll overlooking the Palm Houses, the Copse is protected by belts of holly and pines. Winding grassy paths are lined with bushes of rhododendrons, magnolia, meconopsis, lily and many others. The collection of viburnums extends beyond the Copse on to a grassy slope. Of special note is the rapid growing Japanese *Magnolia obovata*, whose large creamy-white flowers are conspicuous in June not only on account of their size but also because of their heavy perfume which, on a still evening, is noticeable many yards away.

Northwards from the Copse is the most magnificent herbaceous border. The planting has been carried out with the aim of a succession of flowering, so that when one end has finished flowering the other is still in full bloom, making the border a constant attraction.

Near the western end of the herbaceous border is the Monterey cypress, one of the best specimens in Britain of this species native only to California. Continuing round to the West Gate entrance, outstanding among the trees are the maples and yews.

The Demonstration Garden

The informative role of the Royal Botanic Garden is served by the Exhibition Hall and the Demonstration Garden, as 'classrooms for the public'.

The display of annual plants shows the gardener what he can grow at home. The layout is changed each year, but it may include pansies, marigolds, wallflowers and dahlias. Hedges, too, are exhibited so that the intending gardener can select with a better idea of what he may expect.

There are a number of other informative displays. The display of plant family relationships shows the horticultural development of several popular plant groups – for example, species of the *Brassica* genus, such as cabbage, cauliflower and kale, are grouped to show their various relationships to one another.

Plantings include culinary and medicinal herbs, grasses including the South American pampas grass, while others illustrate aspects of plant biology.

A place of learning

Training the botanists of the future is an important part of the work carried out at Edinburgh's Royal Botanic Garden. Former students include today's head gardener at Tokyo Palace and the Director of the Botanic Garden in Ghana. Some 42 student gardeners are employed in the gardens, and they attend a three-year diploma course in amenity horticulture.

The primary function of a botanic garden is botanical and horticultural research, and in particular the accurate identification and classification of plants. The gardens, the glasshouses and the herbarium (a collection of preserved plant specimens from all over the world) house the plant material for such research. A comprehensive reference library with over 75,000 volumes, augmented by an extensive collection of prints, photographs and manuscripts, supplements the herbarium.

There is a ten-acre (4 ha) experimental ground which serves both for training and for grafting and experimental cultivation. Four students and one curator are employed here, with 100 people employed in the herbarium and 250 in the gardens.

It has been proposed, as part of the garden's commitment to the dissemination of knowledge and a concern for safety, to mount a permanent collection of plants that are poisonous. The two species of deadly nightshade, for example, are a particular hazard for the unwary as one can be confused with the cherry and the other with damson. Other common causes of child illness or fatality, laburnum pods and green potatoes among them, would be exhibited.

The Royal Botanic Garden, since its humble beginnings as a Physic garden under three inspired men, has achieved a major place in the botanic gardens of the world. In 1980 over 592,000 people enjoyed the results of the work of dedicated men for three centuries.

Zoological Park

A marvellous menagerie where education and research are paramount

The deceptively narrow entrance to Edinburgh Zoo gives way to the 80 acres (30 ha) which contain some of the world's rarest and most beautiful animals in an area of natural beauty which, at its northwestern tip, fades into the woodland of Corstorphine Hill.

Edinburgh Zoo is in a constant state of development with its energetic programmes of breeding from stock, the introduction of new species from other zoos and the continuous schedule of new buildings and enclosures on the areas acquired for development. With such activity, it is difficult for the zoo itself to keep pace with the location of each species. The map contained in their otherwise most informative booklet is therefore sometimes out of date. The map that appears on the opposite page, however, records the species to be seen in the zoo in the summer of 1981.

With so much to see in such sympathetic surroundings, it is wise to allow at least half a day if not more for a tour of the zoo. As you enter through the main gates, taking the path to the right, you will see the Californian sealions on your left. There are one male and two females, one bull being on loan to London Zoo for breeding purposes. The pool was cut from natural rock in 1914 and sealions have always been happy in it. Sealions can move very fast in water, achieving nearly 20 miles per hour (32 km/h) by planing across the surface. Feeding time, at 15.00 in the summer and

14.30 in the winter, sees them diving and leaping for fish.

Flightless birds are on the right, followed by the Brunton aviaries and the pheasants. Pheasants have been hunted so extensively in the wild that the group now numbers several of the world's most endangered birds among its 48 species. These rare and beautiful birds are high on Edinburgh Zoo's list for its commitment to breeding and reintroducing into the wild.

North of the aviaries is the Orchard Paddock, with its small pond and overhanging apple trees. The Paddock usually contains a collection of mammals, such as the South American capybaras and Australian wallabies, and large birds, such as cranes and peafowl.

As the path bends to the right, you will see the cassowaries, which are not unlike the emu in appearance. They can inflict extremely unpleasant wounds, however, and the male, whose responsibility it is to incubate the eggs and rear the chicks, can become ferocious during the breeding cycle.

Past the cassowaries to the right, you will come upon the Reptile House. Of the tortoises, turtles, snakes, lizards, crocodiles and frogs, toads, newts and salamanders in the Reptile House, the two dwarf broad fronted crocodiles should not be missed.
In the summer, some of the collection is moved outside to the Reptile Rock, where they can

be seen in a more natural environment.

One of the very small red eyed tree frogs cannot always be spotted because of its camouflage colouration. Tree frogs are much flatter than frogs which live on land. This gives them even distribution of weight over the whole body and enables them to balance and move with great agility on branches and leaves. The circular disks on the tips of their fingers and toes and the loose skin on the belly act as adhesive pads which enable them to climb up smooth surfaces.

The Parrot Garden houses several species of parrot, the Australian cockatoo and the South American macaw.

One aviary is devoted to the mynahs, whose powers of mimicry are undisputed but for which there appears to be no scientific explanation.

From the shrieks and whistles of the mynahs, you will find little respite in the Chimpanzee House. A constant display of screaming, clapping, gesticulating and hurtling down the slope to their enclosure to land, full face, against the 1¼-inch thick (32 mm) armoured glass is all part of a chimpanzee's fun. In fact, such displays indicate a continual competitiveness found in any group of chimpanzees, since their society is founded upon a dominance hierarchy.

There is a picnic area, which if you want to make a day of it is a perfect setting overlooking the rest of the zoo.

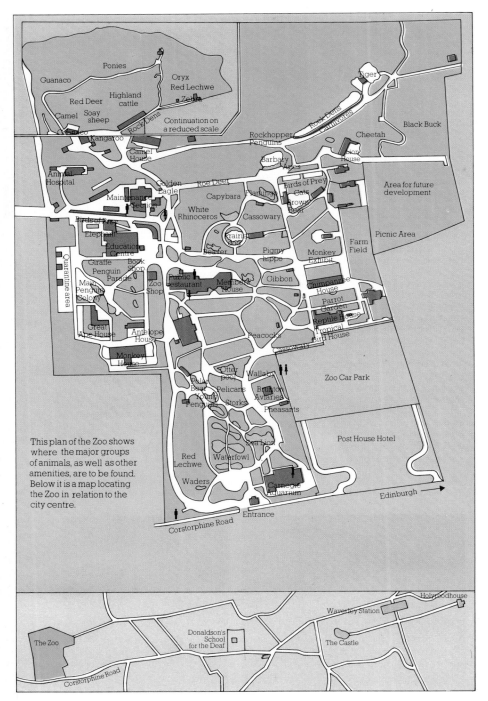

Ponies

Guanaco

Oryx
Red Lechwe

Tiger

Red Deer   Highland
            cattle

Zebra

Camel   Soay
         sheep   Continuation on
                  a reduced scale

Rock Dens   Rock Dens
             Carnivores

Black Buck

Guanaco   Kangaroo   Rockhopper   Cheetah
                                       Penguins
           Camel
           House   Sea Lion
                        Barbary   House
                        Apes
Animal
Hospital   Area for future
                                                      development
            Golden   Roe Deer   Birds of Prey   Cats
            Eagle
Maintenance   Capybara   Flamingo   Brown   Picnic Area
Depot   Shop
       Birds of Prey   White   Farm
                       Rhinoceros Cassowary Field
       Elephant
              Education   Prairie
              Centre   Dogs
       Giraffe   Beaver   Pigmy   Monkey
       Penguin   Book   hippo   Exhibit
Main   Parade   Shop
Penguin   Zoo   Public   Membra   Gibbon   Chimpanzee
Colony   Shop   restaurant House   House
                                                       Parrot
                                                       Garden
       Great   Reptile House
       Ape House   Tropical
              Antelope   Bird House
              House   Peacocks
       Monkey   Cassowary
       House
                                                       Zoo Car Park
                        Otter   Wallaby
                        pool
                  Polar   Pelicans   Brunton
                  Bear   Storks   Aviaries
                  Young   Pheasants
This plan of the Zoo shows   Penguins
where the major groups
of animals, as well as other   Sea Lion   Post House Hotel
amenities, are to be found. Red
Below it is a map locating   Lechwe   Waterfowl
the Zoo in relation to the
city centre.   Waders   Edinburgh
                                   Carnegie
                                   Aquarium
                              Entrance
            Corstorphine Road

Holyroodhouse

Waverley Station

Donaldson's
School
for the Deaf   The Castle
The Zoo

Corstorphine Road

181

West of the picnic area is the brown bear enclosure. Brown bears were once common in Scotland, but they have been extinct here for many hundreds of years. They are now found only in remote mountain ranges from Alaska to the Atlantic, across Europe and Asia. They are easier to breed than polar bears, which tend to be rather solitary animals. The species from Kodiak Island of Alaska can weigh as much as a ton and, when upright, measure an awesome eleven feet (3.3 m).

Next to the brown bear is the Scottish wildcat, which looks like an ordinary tabby at first sight. It has bolder markings, particularly on the club-shaped tail, however, to distinguish it from its more peaceable relative. Its predilection for small mammals and birds has provoked gamekeepers and crofters practically to eliminate it. It has been saved, however, by the replanting of Scotland's forests by the Forestry Commission.

Edinburgh Zoo is noted for its success in breeding Snowy owls, to be seen with buzzards, eagles and other owls in the Birds of Prey enclosures. In the wild, the Snowy owl is a winter visitor to northern Scotland and

A brown bear (**above**) takes a nap.

further north still. Its feathers are basically white with brownish-black markings. In its natural environment of snow-covered areas, it is camouflaged most effectively from a potential predator: if it were completely white, it would be far more noticeable.

The Birds of Prey enclosure leads you to the Barbary Rock which is a most impressive home for the Barbary macaques (of the monkey family). Steep layers have been hewn into the rock, which towers many feet above the path. Continuing eastwards, you will come upon the king of all

animals, the lion, who is happily located in a large enclosure interspersed with crags of old Midlothian farmhouse stone. On to the cheetah, which in the wild would be able to achieve speeds of 70 miles per hour (113 km/h) in short bursts. The cheetah's large enclosure slopes upwards into a mass of long grass and trees where the animal bounds about.

The uphill path past the cheetah's enclosure takes you to the tiger enclosure and the Rock Dens, which house several species of jaguar, leopard, and hyena.

The northwestern area of the

(**right**) a tiger sits brooding and a leopard either yawns or snarls. The leopard is the smallest of the 'big cats' and the most agile.

Edinburgh zoo simply does not look like a zoo. The eye moves over fields containing zebra, red lechwe, highland ponies, soay sheep, red deer and guanaco – each having the freedom and space to graze and move around in peace. Many theories have been advanced to explain the zebra's brilliant black and white stripes: one theory, which it would be difficult to justify when the animal is viewed in an enclosure, suggests that the stripes disrupt the form of the animal from a distance and at dusk, when predators in the wild would be hunting, merge together to form a uniform grey. The theory seems convincing when you see the zebras in Edinburgh's zoo, silhouetted in the dusk on the horizon.

It is known that there is a badger sett in the north of the zoo in the area of open country, but since they are nocturnal and, in any case, extremely retiring animals, you will not spot them.

A sense of freedom is not entirely lost when you leave the fields and the kangaroo enclosures as you wind your way down to the camels. They appear not to be enclosed at all – in fact their enclosure is surrounded by a dyke which is concealed by a slight rise in the ground. The Arabian camel or dromedary has one hump and is found only in a domesticated state. The Bactrian camel has two humps – so identification is simple. Camels can tolerate extreme heat and cold and can survive days without water.

The southern part of the northern zone of the zoo contains the European crane, the golden eagle and roe deer which roam in the Whitson Wood. The golden eagle is found throughout the Scottish highlands and is Britain's largest bird of prey. Although they are long-lived in captivity, breeding has only rarely been successful.

The white rhinoceroses, towards the centre of the zoo, are fascinating to watch as they indulge in mock battles. Their agility belies their great weight, as does their name their colour. It is thought that 'white' came from the Afrikaans *wijd* meaning wide.

Next to the white rhino is the Beaver Pool, which is another excellent example of how a zoo can exhibit animals in a happy and natural environment. Beavers are aquatic mammals which use their paddle-shaped tail as a rudder. It is also beaten on the ground or on the water to indicate alarm, and is used to flatten mud when they are building dams. The Beaver Pool is usually a scene of frenetic activity with the animals engaged in a continuous process of gnawing branches to suitable lengths, ferrying them across the pond and positioning them, using mud as their mortar.

The prairie dog builds enormous underground townships in the prairies of North America, consisting of intricate networks of fairly deep tunnels. The keepers have to be vigilant in preventing the prairie dogs emerging all over the zoo. The prairie dogs are social animals and co-operate in warning of approaching danger and 'console any animal that has been frightened by a would-be predator.

Edinburgh Zoo has four pairs of Chilean flamingoes, all of which have bred successfully. These graceful birds with rosy-pink plumage are particularly interesting to watch when they are performing courtship displays before mating: the elegant rose-peach tail feathers are raised in a fan as the male bird struts and circles.

From the Flamingo Pool, past another cassowary enclosure, the small and rare pygmy hippopotamus comes into sight.

Moving directly westwards you will find the western zone of the zoo, which houses the elephant, giraffe, tapir, apes, monkeys and, most important of all, the penguins.

Edinburgh Zoo is well known for its splendid collection of penguins, which is the largest and most successful group anywhere in captivity. A king penguin was first reared in 1919 as a result of the shipping company, Christian Salvesen, bringing back large numbers from South Georgia. The main breeding pool numbers about 40 king penguins and 90 of the smaller gentoo penguins.

Penguins are found mainly on the islands around the Antarctic and some in tropical waters – and so it is astonishing that they have bred so successfully in Edinburgh. Penguins cannot fly, but they more than compensate for this by using their wings as paddles so that they speed through the water at up to 25 miles per hour (40 km/h). They are able to emerge, bullet-like, from the sea and land on their feet on ledges or ice-floes as much as six feet (1.8 m) above the water.

King penguins have a slate grey back and white underside, with brilliant orange patches on the sides of the head, throat and upper part of the breast. Young birds are covered in a thick brown down. The king penguin does not make a nest but holds a single egg on the feet with a fold of the skin and feathers of the abdomen. Both males and females help to incubate the egg, which takes about eight weeks.

The gentoo, basically black and white, has distinctive white markings on the crown and sides of the head which resemble earphones. Gentoos lay two eggs, which in the wild would be protected in a nest of pebbles and twigs and other pieces of vegetation. In the zoo, they are presented with nesting rings filled with pebbles on

March 15 each year. Gentoo courtship involves the exchange of pebble 'gifts', as well as stealing pebble-nesting material from neighbours. By the end of March, 80 to 90 eggs will have appeared and by the end of April they will have hatched. Only one chick in every two is reared by the penguins, but the second chick is usually fostered with other birds with the result that gentoos are sent to zoos all over the world.

When the young penguins are about six to eight weeks old they are removed to a crèche or nursery pool for one year. They are then moved for a further year to an enclosure adjoining the main colony. When they are two, they are allowed to rejoin the flock.

At 14.30 every summer afternoon just before feeding time, the penguins embark on a voluntary parade around the paths of the central area of the zoo. The spectacle of the penguin parade began in the late 1940s, quite accidentally, when a keeper left the enclosure gate open. The inquisitive penguins – and they are of a generally inquiring disposition – followed by an equally curious keeper, walked down the drive and along the pavement of the main road until the keeper judged it wise to turn them.

The penguins are fed at 14.45, after the parade, and 14.15 in the winter. Just near the penguins, you can also see the grey seals fed.

The Monkey House, the largest of the animal buildings in the zoo, houses ten different species of monkey. The cages are fronted with armoured glass rather than bars, as the zoo has discovered this prevents the animals from begging and showing off and it prevents the public from disrupting a carefully controlled diet by indiscriminate feeding.

East of the Monkey House, in

King penguins in conference.

the southern zone, you will find the polar bears who are to be seen clambering in and out of the water and reclining upon rocky islands. It was not many years after the zoo was founded in 1909 that the water level enabled one of the polar bears to escape. He did return – after heavy persuasion – and the water level is now maintained with an eye to safety. Unlike other bears, the polar bear is mostly carnivorous, favouring seals. In its native habitat around the fringes of the Arctic icecaps, its off-white colouring affords effective camouflage so that it may sneak up on its unsuspecting prey.

The rest of the southern zone is devoted to red lechwe, pelicans, gannets (the emblem of the Royal Zoological Society of Scotland) and storks, which are all fed after the sealions; the shy and wary otter, an aquatic mammal that lives on fish; the raccoon, noted for its habit in captivity of washing all its food; the South American Maguari stork; the sealions (mentioned earlier); and a splendid series of shrub-covered terraces with three large pools and waterfalls for the collection of ducks from all over the world, swans, and wild birds such as the waterhen

The Zoological Society of

Scotland was founded in 1909 as a non-profit making organization devoted to the study and conservation of wildlife. It became increasingly disenchanted with its inheritance of undersized, old-fashioned cages, which are often the trademark of an urban zoo.

The zoo acquired royal patronage in 1948 and in the 1980s the dedication and energy demanded by a far-seeing programme of acquisition of land, new buildings and enclosures is clearly demonstrated.

New species are usually acquired from other zoos on the basis of exchange – the introduction of animals from the wild is something of the past. Breed–loan schemes are in operation with zoos all over the world, so that Edinburgh, for example, may send out a male sealion to another zoo that has only females and receive in return one of the species it needs to continue it own breeding programmes. These co-ordinated schemes are based on mutual co-operation – how, in any case, would it be possible to assess the financial worth of a male sealion versus a female gentoo?

Edinburgh Zoo now has red pandas, a smaller and more interesting relative of the giant panda. More than one zoologist has been heard to comment on the intrinsic dullness of the giant panda despite its great popularity with the public and continual exposure by the media.

The zoo's staff of 100 is supplemented by volunteers, who, in the summer, bring the number up to about 200. Much of the building work has been carried out as a result of the government's Job Creation Programme. The zoo, in this way, has been able to save thousands of pounds on labour, which would otherwise have substantially reduced the funds available for the development of the zoo, and at the same time is combating

Flamingoes and storks lend their own particular grace to the Zoo, and polar bears always draw the crowds as they clamber from the water and recline on rocky islands. The penguins – of three kinds – are the largest group in captivity.

unemployment with its resulting boredom.

The zoo is financed by admission fees, Society subscriptions
and by the Adoption Scheme.
The need to adopt zoo animals
resulted from the conditions of
war prevailing in 1940, when
food was scarce. Anyone can
now adopt, for example, a kangaroo for £90 a year, a tiger for
£1000 a year or a weaver bird
for £5 a year.

The zoo's philosophy has always centred on the need to
educate as well as to entertain.
Each enclosure is clearly label-
led, with a description of the
animal's habitat and its life and
behaviour in the wild. The
Education Centre, which in
1980 saw 47,000 children from
infant age upwards, runs properly structured programmes of
education as well as producing
the necessary topic sheets and
literature. The Centre contains
a well-stocked bookshop with
books on all aspects of natural
history.

A visit to the zoo is something
that should not be missed when
you are in Edinburgh. The tranquillity and beauty of this huge
park is rivalled only by its variety of animal life – a kaleido-
scope of diving sealions, talking
mynahs, chortling chimpanzees and stately king penguins.

The Californian sealion

THE
EDINBURGH
INTERNATIONAL FESTIVAL

It should not be assumed Edinburgh becomes culturally alive for only three weeks of the year in August/ September during the Festival.

There are concerts, galleries, opera, theatre, exhibitions and many other events throughout the year and the city itself is always visually exciting.

However, this section concentrates on the enormous range of events during the Festival in the late summer of each year.

There are sections on:-

The Official Festival
The Fringe
The Film Festival
Edinburgh Book Festival (bi-annual)
International Jazz Festival

Several hundred companies give thousands of performances of plays, concerts, reviews, dance, mime, recitals, and operas. Then there are the films and the jazz and the many exhibitions – and the book festival (every second year). Especially during the Festival, Edinburgh is an exciting place.

The Edinburgh Festival

For three weeks in August the festival city plays host to the world

For three weeks every year Edinburgh is besieged by the top talent of the world – yet the identity of the city remains impregnable. Seen in full Festival regalia, this Athens of the north might well have been custom built for just such an explosion of a diverse mixture of culture – for even as the Old Town lives in harmony with the New, so do the activities of the Festival merge the artistry of great names with new, young, experimental talents. Visitors of all nationalities give the city a boost of adrenalin which can be felt in the spring of each step along Princes Street, suddenly frivolous with bunting and hanging baskets of flowers. Old hands feel superior watching the awe of newcomers as yet unaccustomed to the one o'clock gun.

It was not always thus. The first year of the Festival – 1947 – was a grey year. Britain was still in the grip of austerity. Rationing did not end until 1952. Dior's New Look was in fashion with its nipped waistline and flowing skirts succeeding years of utility clothing and coupons. Platform shoes clumped precariously over the cobbled streets of the city and trams still clanged their cheerful way along Princes Street.

Edinburgh was not renowned for her contributions to culture at this time, although there was talent in plenty to be found in the Rose Street pubs, with writers, painters, poets vying to capture the accolade of the wittiest, pithiest *bon mot* of the evening. From a theatrical point of view, there was little beyond the occasional visiting pre-London show, pantomime at Christmas and the semi-professional resident Gateway Company Theatre. Yet it was out of this post-war malaise that Rudolf Bing, then with the Glyndebourne Festival Opera, had the courage to persist in his vision of a British festival comparable in stature to those of Salzburg and Bayreuth.

Rudolf Bing became the Festival's first director. His worldwide connections proved invaluable in contracting Bruno Walter, reunited with his Vienna Philharmonic, Sir John Barbirolli and the Hallé, Arthur Schnabel, Pierre Fournier, Joseph Szigeti, William Primrose and the Louis Jouvet Company. A spirit of alliances recreated was behind the rebirth of artistic vitality in Europe urged to life by the uphill task of creating the very first Edinburgh Festival. It was with this concept in mind that the honour of playing the opening concert was given to the Orchestre des Concerts Colonne, Paris.

The sun actually shone – for three weeks. Visitors complained of the heat. The critics were impressed. The new Festival was a success. Later, of course, there were niggles about the predominance of music at the expense of drama. Criticism was made about the proportionately small Scottish contribution, despite the participation of the prominent Glasgow-born violist William Primrose,

the Scottish Orchestra and the Scottish Singers. Over the following years the situation was to be rectified, aided by a mercuric rise in the standards of Scottish performers. This gave rise to the eventual formation of a Scottish Opera and Ballet Company, a Scottish National Orchestra, Chamber Orchestra and the Scottish Baroque Ensemble – all developed to an internationally accepted level.

It is hard to remember today that in the late 1940s Scottish television was in its infancy, there was no stereo, and the Scots were isolated from first-hand knowledge of the standards of cultural activity in other countries until the Festival brought it all to their doorstep. It was particularly thrilling in those early years to listen to orchestras from Europe or the United States and to their interpretation of the works of great composers.

The Usher Hall, in Lothian Road, is Edinburgh's main concert hall. Within its Edwardian elegance, audiences have been privileged to hear the best soloists in the world, to listen to leading orchestras performing under the contrasting influences of various distinguished conductors.

Live theatre

The Mound snakes southwards up that great castle-bearing glacial rock, both floodlit each festive night to dominate Princes Street. It is a stiff climb to reach the Gothic-style dignity of the Assembly

Hall of the Kirk of Scotland. It seems as though the Mound has had to bend to go respectfully round it, yet this was to become the unlikely home for the Scots breakthrough into their own festival with a bawdy play in 'the auld tongue' which satirized and challenged the very authority of the Church. Much to the astonishment of all, the Church authorities gave consent to Tyrone Guthrie's production of *The Thrie Estaites*, although mildly suggesting that nails should not be knocked into the Moderator's throne. No restriction was made against singing or dancing or even against the provision of a bar.

In 1948 the play had its first performance since the original seven-hour version of 1540. Robert Kemp adapted it to a more acceptable length and under Guthrie's magic touch it became a recurring feature, giving Scottish actors their vehicle in many future Festivals. Few who saw the production will forget the exquisite gyrations of the late Duncan

A taste of the variety
the main Festival offers:
the Scottish National
Opera's *Hermiston;* Carlo
Maria Giulini and
Leonard Bernstein conducting;
Dietrich in
cabaret and Max Wall
as Buster Keaton.

Macrae as Flatterie, the droning of James Gibson's Deceipt, the resonant power of Tom Fleming and the vigour and pageantry of this ancient satire. The supporting music was by a Scottish composer, Cedric

In daytime rehearsals for a main Festival concert conductor Daniel Barenboim relishes the challenge of sorting out a difficult passage of music with his principal violinist and goes on to lead the field in a tea-break football match.

Thorpe Davie, who later set the music for another Scottish triumph, *The Jolly Beggars.*

During the three years of Rudolf Bing's directorship, he commissioned *The Cocktail Party* by T.S. Eliot. He brought to Edinburgh Trevor Howard, Bernard Miles and Patricia Burke in *The Taming of the Shrew*; Alec Guinness in a production by Ralph Richardson of *Richard II*; Margot Fonteyn, Beryl Grey and Frederick Ashton with the Royal Ballet, then known as Sadlers Wells; Leslie Caron and Jean Babilée with Les Ballets des Champs Elysées. Naturally the Glyndebourne Opera was well in evidence. Mozart's *Le Nozze di Figaro* and Verdi's *Macbeth* were presented. The late, incomparable Kathleen Ferrier sang with the Vienna Philarmonic one year and with the Hallé another. Her *Das Lied von der Erde* still haunts the Usher Hall and those fortunate enough to have been there. Even doubting Sir Thomas Beecham

was prevailed upon to conduct with his Royal Philharmonic Orchestra in 1949, Bing's final year as director.

Over the years the Festival has benefitted enormously from the widely varying influences imposed upon it by its six very different directors. Each built upon the work of his predecessors. Each had something new and individual to contribute.

Ian Hunter became the second director in 1950 for a period of seven years. He will be remembered particularly for his promotion of exhibitions – a new feature in the Festival programme. He initiated exhibitions which were acclaimed throughout the art world and which became an important aspect.

Art shows

These collections were shown at the National Gallery of Scotland and the Royal Scottish Academy, neighbouring buildings at the foot of the Mound.

Planning and organization of these major visiting exhibitions were in the hands of a committee representing both galleries and the Arts Council. Paintings from the principal art galleries of the world were gathered in Edinburgh in order to mount a unique collection of the featured artist – the Cézanne year, the 78 Gaugin paintings shown in 1955, 86 paintings by Braque in 1956, Corot in 1965, Derain in 1967 were memorable examples.

The first exhibition, the Rembrandt, had perhaps the greatest impact. Thirty-six of his paintings were on view in the Scottish capital, giving additional prestige to the Festival and exciting art lovers who had probably never had the opportunity to study the development of Rembrandt's genius over his lifespan.

Military Tattoo

Another stroke of genius, in 1950, was to add the tattoo to the ever-widening field of Festival

activities. Although independent of the main administration, the Tattoo has become an inseparable part of the festivities. The performance – a highly polished, well-rehearsed military event – takes place in that quiet hour before dusk on the esplanade of Edinburgh Castle which provides a dramatic backdrop to historic tableaux, gymnastics, highland dancing, pageantry, mock battles and other popular entertainment devised by the military. It has all the attractions of the Royal Tournament, from horses to the occasional elephant. Each year visiting military groups display colourful regimental costume and custom, some appearing to have come straight out of Ruritania. Perhaps most popular of all is the stirring sight and sound of the massed pipe bands.

As dusk falls, the floodlights dim and a spotlight picks out a solitary piper on the battlements. In the sudden silence of the summer evening, he pipes a farewell lament.

Music

In that same year of 1950, the Castle was the setting for an after dark, open-air performance of Handel's *Music for the Royal Fireworks*, complete with firework display and live cannon obligato from the Castle battery. The conductor was Beecham himself, a figure of rare distinction in tails and a steel helmet provided by the Quartermaster's Stores as a protection against sparks.

Sir Thomas's proximity to the Tattoo may have given rise to a story about his advice to a mother who wanted her son to learn a musical instrument which would not offend the parental ear in the early stages. Sir Thomas advocated the bagpipes, saying they sounded no worse at the beginning than they did when one had learned to play them.

The administration

In 1952, the Festival administrators faced up for the first time to the inherent problems of in-

viting an overseas opera company to perform at the King's Theatre. The exterior of the theatre, built in 1906, is undistinguished but the interior is a gem of plush and gilt baroque – like an opera house in miniature. Its smallness was the main problem for the first visitors, the Hamburg Opera Company, which was accustomed to its own vast stage. For one thing, the scenery would not fit. All in all, the size of German operas presented at the King's looked a trifle shabby that year. The problem persists, but years of experience have taught ways and means of making the best of it. Measurements are sent well ahead to visiting companies so that they may plan their compromises.

Robert Ponsonby, 6 feet 6 inches tall, took over from Ian Hunter in 1956. It was he who encouraged and developed the late night satirical aspect of the Festival which spread on to TV screens with such success. Anna Russell was allowed to make a little fun of the hallowed Festival itself. Then, in 1959, Michael Flanders and Donald Swan appeared in *At the Drop of a Hat. Beyond the Fringe* hit the boards in 1960.

Ponsonby's interest in ballet was clearly marked by 12 new works especially commissioned for 1958. Until then the major balletic contribution had come principally from the Sad-

from Madrid, the Royal Ballet and the new excitement of Jerome Robbins with his Ballet USA.

Robert Burns had his 200th anniversary at that time, an event which inspired Iain Hamilton to create his *Sinfonia for Two Orchestras.* There were intensive Burns readings and the premiere of *The Jolly Beggars* to boost Scottish

Russian performers was exciting and justifying. For other tastes there were thrilling appearances by Rex Harrison, Martha Graham and Marlene Dietrich; in the theatre there were new plays by Dylan Thomas, Lawrence Durrell and Nigel Dennis.

It was during this phase of the Festival's growth that conductor Alexander Gibson formed

The colourful costumes of singers in Don Giovanni at the King's Theatre and a group from the Scottish National Orchestra playing in the Library of the Signet.

ler's Wells Company, which had presented a varied classical and modern programme ranging from *Swan Lake* to early works by the talented young choreographers John Cranko and Scotland's Kenneth MacMillan. There had, of course, been other visiting companies – Ram Gopal with his Indian ballet, Les Ballets de Champs Elysées, the Yugoslav Ballet and the American Ballet Theater.

In 1959 and 1960 there were performances at the Royal Lyceum by The National Ballet of Finland, Les Ballets Babilée, the Little Ballet Troupe from Bombay, The Ballets Européens de Nervi, Susana y José

morale.

The Ponsonby period was also distinguished by his introduction of Maria Callas to Edinburgh. She took the Festival by storm as Amina in *La Sonnambula* with the La Scala Company from Milan.

Lord Harewood's reign – 1961 to 1965 – was both stimulating and controversial. He introduced the concept of featuring a particular composer each year, and Edinburgh was treated to 24 performances by Schoenberg in the first Harewood Festival. Subsequent years were saturated with Boulez, Tippett and Janácek. Some critics felt, however, that such a policy was departing somewhat from the original concept as expressed by Lord Provost Sir John Falconer in the inaugural year: '...the programme should be for the delight of the average listener'. But Shostakovitch played by

the Scottish Opera Chorus, later to become the Edinburgh Festival Chorus and the basis of the Scottish Opera company.

The first appearance of Scottish Opera at a Festival came in 1967 with productions of *The Rake's Progress* and *The Soldier's Tale.* By this time, Peter Diamand had been appointed as director and was continuing the policy of featuring composers each year. It was Schubert and Britten year in 1968, during which the new national opera company presented *Peter Grimes.* At that time a performance of Britten's *War Requiem* underlined the emotional intensity aroused by the Soviet-led invasion of Czechoslovakia which had reached its climax during the Festival. Drama was transferred to the streets in the form of pickets and demonstrations outside the Usher Hall where the State Orchestra of the USSR was playing.

During the 13 years of Peter Diamand's control the Festival had its 21st birthday. In its maturity the proportion of younger artists invited to take part was increased. The new policy demonstrated that the Festival was now sufficiently established to become a patron – perhaps too it was aimed at reducing the gap between the official events and the essentially young Fringe movement which had been developing alongside.

Among the highlights of this prolonged administration was an adaptation of Ariosto's *Orlando Furioso* by the Teatro Libero Rome, which took place in 1970 at the Haymarket Ice Rink using the open-stage technique to bring the audience into the performance as Guthrie had done with *The Thrie Estaites*. At the Assembly Hall the Prospect Company enlivened Shakespeare's *Much Ado About Nothing* with John Neville playing Benedict. The Royal Lyceum Company – Edinburgh's new Civic Theatre – presented *The Changeling* by Thomas Middleton, and thus established itself as a company able to hold its own.

The actors' cooperative

In 1972 came the birth of The Actor's Company, a co-operative venture in which there were no stars and '...all decisions were made through mutual discussion'. The cast included Moira Redmond, Ian McKellen and Frank Middlemas. The new company contributed lunch-time and evening performances and was highly praised. Londoners subsequently became familiar with *Joseph and the Amazing Technicolour Dreamcoat*, with music by Andrew Lloyd-Webber, which was playing at the Haymarket Ice Rink along with and in striking contrast to the Japanese Hosho Noh Theatre. These few examples reflect the care and skill with which an interesting mix of content was planned for each year's programme in the face of ever-increasing costs. It had taken £60,000 to launch the 1947 Festival. Towards the end of the Diamand administration, the figure had risen to £190,000.

John Drummond took over in 1978 for the 1979 Festival. Formerly head of the BBC Television Music and Arts Department, he may be remembered as the director who preserved the Edinburgh International Festival through the years of world recession. At one time visiting companies had subsidized part of the cost of coming to perform, but they can no longer afford to do it. Art galleries are increasingly reluctant to risk letting valuable paintings out of the country. The sale of tickets covers less than half the outlay and the balance of the burden falls on the Edinburgh City and the Scottish Arts Council. In addition the amount contributed by private sponsors and donors has increased substantially in recent years.

Performing for the Fringe Festival in a former municipal poorhouse overlooking Greyfriars churchyard a company of Polish actors provoke their audience.

In 1983 Frank Dunlop was appointed director, the first to come from the world of theatre, and under his leadership the Festival's scope was widened considerably. The celebration of the Auld Alliance between Scotland and France produced in 1985 one of the most successful festivals with a record number of ticket sales. In 1986 the numbers of performances taking place rose to over 300, in more venues throughout the city than ever before. A particular highlight was the World Theatre Season which brought to Edinburgh productions from France, West Germany, Spain, Sweden, Poland, South Africa, China, Japan and USA.

The Festival Club, now using the facilities of the Edinburgh University Staff Club, 9-15 Chambers Street, provides cafeteria, snack bar, lounges, bar and restaurant. It is a good place in which to collapse when one is weary! Open 9am to 1am daily during the festival. Membership is modestly priced and is available by the day, for a week or for all 21 days. Apply to the Festival Office, 21 Market Street, or during the Festival at the Festival Club, 9-15 Chambers Street.

The Film Festival

The Edinburgh Film Festival has been an event in the capital since the Festival as a whole started in 1947.

At first it was confined to one week of documentary films, but it has grown in size and prestige to compare with the festivals at Cannes and Berlin.

The Film Festival is now based at Filmhouse, 88 Lothian Road, occasionally using other cinemas for special gala screenings. Filmhouse houses two cinemas, and the smaller Film Guild cinema for workshop screenings, a bookshop, bar, restaurant and dubroom. The Festival spreads over the first two weeks of the main Festival, and presents over 100 films. It is independent of the Festival Society and therefore receives no financial assistance.

An august amateur body, the Edinburgh Film Guild, established the first festival with the aim of showing 'unusual films not normally seen in the ordinary cinema' such as the documentaries pioneered by Scottish-born John Grierson. By the second year, feature films had been introduced as well and the programme extended to three weeks to cover over 100 entries from 25 countries.

Film directors were soon appearing personally to explain their work to the public. Flaherty, Grierson, Michael Balcon, Vittorio de Sica, Charles Frend, Samuel Fuller, John Huston, Douglas Sirk, Joseph Losey and Peter Ustinov are a few who have appeared over the years to help clarify new trends and techniques seen for filmgoers.

In 1986 the first Edinburgh Film Prize was inaugurated by the Edinburgh District Council; an award of £1,000 to the person who has contributed most to film and video in Scotland.

The Film Festival has a reputation for giving the first British screenings of some of the most celebrated films – like *ET* in 1982, and *Paris, Texas* in 1984. The film to provoke the strongest reaction in 1985 was *My Beautiful Launderette*. 1984 also saw a big retrospective of Japanese cinema, and 1986 featured films, lectures and workshops on cinema in the third world.

Coming just before Venice in the International Film Festival diary, Edinburgh is not a competitive festival, but very much one for the public.

In such ways the Film Festival has added an extra dimension to the rich tapestry of the Festival as a whole, while making a major international contribution to increasing public knowledge of the art of film.

The Edinburgh Book Festival

The newest element in the world's largest arts festival is

Modern dancers in action at the Festival. Over the years ballet and dance has increased in importance at both festivals.

cabaret drawn from the rest of the Festival, Fringe and Jazz Festival.

Edinburgh International Jazz Festival

There is a healthy traditional jazz movement in Edinburgh all year round, and a Jazz festival evolved out of it, now sponsored by McEwan's, and counted as one of the best festivals in the country. Stars from the Festival take part in the magnificent jazz opening parade through the centre of the city, heralding the start of a week of performances in more than 20 venues throughout Edinburgh, beginning with the grand International Opening Ball.

The Fringe

Can 474,429 people be wrong? That was the astounding number of tickets sold for Fringe events in 1986 when 494 companies presented 959 shows, plays, concerts, reviews, dance, mime, recitals, exhibitions and even operas. The Oxford Dictionary defines 'fringe' as an ornamental bordering of threads left loose – a fairly fitting description of this colourful embellishment to the official Festival. It was born 'spontaneously' in the same year as its more staid parent, by virtue of eight theatre companies which simply set out to do their own thing. The university theatre companies of Oxford and Cambridge were early on the scene, using small halls in the Old Town. By the end of the fifties the bordering had grown to some 30 groups spread all over Edinburgh, a central box office had been organized, a programme published yearly and a Fringe Club opened.

the Book Festival, first held in 1983 and occurring biennially. This festival redresses the balance, and gives literature and the printed word a prominent place at the cultural feast. It is held in the central location of Charlotte Square Gardens which, for two weeks, is bedecked with tents full of books. All the books in the large exhibition for books can be browsed through and bought; most are from British publishers, but some are from abroad – the 1985 Book Festival boasted fine selections from China, France and Germany. In amidst the books are craftsmen demonstrating the traditional skills of paper-making or paper-marbling, but alongside is the most uptodate technology now used in book production.

Two theatres house a very full event programme with over 150 writers taking part. Star authors of the past include John Updike, James Baldwin, Anthony Burgess and André Brink. The Children's Fair within the Festival has a huge array of books, competitions, workshops and author visits. The cafe and bar is housed in the magnificent Dutch Spiegeltent, built in 1920, and here the Book Festival brings together

Today's printed programme has grown to an 88-page brochure. Each listing gives some idea of what the event is about. With such a wealth of choice, the bewildered visitor often turns for guidance to the review pages of *The Scotsman* – a review here can make or break a Fringe show. The paper also makes the prestigious "Scotsman Fringe First" awards for outstanding new drama.

As well as premieres, well-tried classics, revue and dance, the Fringe acts as the platform to some of the most unusual shows ever seen. *The Warp* at the 1979 Fringe made the Guinness Book of Records as the longest play in the world, taking over 24 hours to perform. And none of its tiny audience will forget *2001 – A Space Odyssey* performed in the front of a Hillman Avenger (the audience sat on the back seat) while parked outside the Fringe Office.

Visitors are often surprised at the world-wide success of the Fringe; its story is an interesting one. It was in 1960 that Jonathan Miller, Alan Bennett, Peter Cook and Dudley Moore first captured international attention with their show *Beyond the Fringe*. They were allocated four performances in the official venue of the Royal Lyceum theatre, put new life into British humour and are now part of an unorthodox establishment of their own making. They also set beyond challenge the Fringe's early reputation for the quality of its late night shows.

The Oxford Theatre Group's premiere of *Rosencrantz and Guildernstern Are Dead* brought Tom Stoppard the attention he deserved and the controversial Traverse Theatre Club, with stimulating interpretations of Shakespeare, was founded in Edinburgh in 1963 as a result of Fringe events.

Joan Littlewood, already well known for her theatre in east London, was quick to see the advantage of taking her Theatre Workshop to the Fringe. *Hinge and Bracket*, now nationally famous, first charmed Edinburgh in 1974, and a 1977 production of *Writer's Cramp* by John Byrne transferred successfully to London's West End.

A wealth of experience can be gleaned by all the young participants gathered together in one compact city whose normal population is under 500,000. The Fringe Club in the university union building, Bristo Square, provides a social meeting place for actors and audience. There are two restaurants and four bars open til late. Club membership is a modest sum for the three-week season, and is also available per day.

A recent development on the Fringe has been the increasing number of multi-venues, where visitors can find a number of theatres, bar and restaurant under one roof. This is undoubtedly due to the influence of Bill Burdett-Coutts and Assembly Theatre. In 1981 the main Festival vacated the magnificent Georgian Assembly Rooms on George Street, taking its Festival Club elsewhere, and the building was converted for the three weeks into 5 theatres for 37 different shows, plus exhibitions. It now houses some of the most popular names in light entertainment as well as international companies during the Fringe.

The Fringe supports as many as 40 exhibitions, many of them free. The scope is wide and varied. There might be British glass at the Scottish Crafts Centre in Canongate, or sculpture open-air in Inverleith Park. An annual exhibition shows 200 of the best entries in the Fringe Poster Competition, open to all Scottish schoolchildren, and sponsored by the Life Association of Scotland. The opening of the Richard Demarco Gallery in 1966 was an important event in Fringe history. In defiance perhaps of the established giants on show at the official exhibitions, this new gallery concentrated on twentieth-century art, and has ever since been a strong, often controversial force in the Scottish art world all the year round. The Demarco Gallery had its origins in the Traverse Theatre, now located in the Grassmarket.

The Traverse Theatre has become a permanent and important feature of Edinburgh's culture. The capital certainly needs entertainment between Festivals, although its citizens maintain a characteristic reserve over supporting anything new and experimental.

How then does the Scot in the street react to the Festival after all these years? As far as the expense of supporting it is concerned, it may take a few pence out of his sporran but it returns pounds to his wallet in terms of tourist spending and side benefits from publicity. He may still feel a little wary about all these foreigners swarming in each summer, but his deeply inbred sense of hospitality never wavers.

The
Stately Homes

Although Edinburgh has its fair share of fine houses and architecture commissioned by the rich and aristocratic inhabitants, some of the greatest displays of wealth and grandeur are outside the city.

Many of the stately homes were built as impressive edifices to money and power on massive estates within a few miles of the capital. They contain superb collections of every conceivable art form and, indeed, their architecture is some of the finest to be seen in Scotland.

There are those, the majority, built after the Union with England in 1707 when Scotland, at last, could trade freely and fill the coffers. But others are the ancient seats of families who led Scotland long before peace with the southerners. These stand, steeped in history and memories of Scotland's turbulence, without any pretentions to the mighty ostentation of the newer houses.

Of the mansions around Edinburgh there are four which represent the many styles, periods and riches of Scottish architecture.

Traquair, home of the royal Stuart family, has its roots in the previous millenium and has been constantly occupied ever since – at times by some of the most romantic figures in the realm's history, like Mary, Queen of Scots

In sharp contrast, there is Hopetoun House, founded on the huge new riches (of the Leadhills mines) acquired by the 1st Earl of Hopetoun. It was designed to display the family's new social status and almost aspires to the Sun King's Palace of Versailles, near Paris.

The original house was begun in 1699, drawn up by William Bruce and added to, 20 years later, by the illustrious Adam family, William and his sons Robert and John. It is possibly Scotland's most magnificent mansion.

Nearby is Dalmeny House, the home of the 7th Earl of Rosebery. It was the first Tudor Gothic revival house in Scotland, designed by William Wilkins in 1815 on the open country of the shores of the Firth of Forth.

Here are two of the nation's finest collections – the Mentmore Collection from Baron Meyer de Rothschild's Buckinghamshire estate; and the Rosebery Collection based on the historical, literary and artistic interests of the 3rd Earl.

Lastly there is Sir Walter Scott's Abbotsford, 40 miles southeast of the capital on the banks of the Tweed. Bought as a farmhouse and transformed into a grand Scottish Border Laird's residence by Scott on the profits of his writing, it stands as a tribute to all that is, and has been, Scotland.

Traquair

This head of Bonnie Prince Charlie is engraved on a glass that is part of a rare collection of Jacobite mementoes kept at Traquair. Legend says the Prince visited his loyal kinsmen while making preparations for the uprising in 1745.

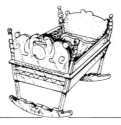

Left Among the many relics of Mary, Queen of Scots at Traquair is this bed in which she slept and the silk counterpane she and her 'four Maries' so carefully worked. In the cradle (**below**) she tended her infant son, the future King James VI and I, of Scotland and England.

Above This harpsicord is now restored to working order. It was made in Antwerp by Andreas Rucker in 1651 and is the only one in Britain with the original decoration.

Traquair is perhaps the most romantic house in Scotland. Only 28 miles (45 km) south of Edinburgh, it is also the oldest inhabited dwelling in the realm. Traquair has grown from the original foundation which legend dates back to AD 950, and is filled with the memorabilia of one family.

That family is the Stuarts, related to the Scottish Royal Family, who have lived here since 1491. In fact the three most tragic members of the House of Stuart – Mary, Queen of Scots, Charles I and Bonnie Prince Charlie – are inextricably connected with the story of the house.

The famous Bear Gates, the main entrance to the tree-lined drive, have remained closed (so the story goes) since Bonnie Prince Charlie passed through them on his way to defeat in England. Family tradition says that they will remain closed until a Stuart King sits on the Scottish throne.

From the castle forecourt, you can see the development of the house which began life in its current form in about 1100 as a royal hunting lodge. It grew into a fortified tower house in the

fifteenth century, and was extended into the present structure in the mid-seventeenth century. Its castle-like appearance, with corner turrets and tiny ground floor windows, reflects the times of border feuds and years of political and religious unrest in Scotland.

Pass through the nail-studded seventeenth-century door, make your way to the end of the ground floor corridor. The last room was part of the original hunting lodge, later becoming the basement of the tower house. The walls are immensely thick, the windows mere slits. During a border raid, the family would have brought their cattle in here.

The first-floor sitting room is part of the seventeenth-century addition. Partially exposed in the ceiling are seventeenth-century painted beams which, along with medieval-style wall paintings, formed the original decoration of the room.

The room was remodelled in the eighteenth century when the ceilings were plastered and the paintings covered with wood panelling. There is still a fine, unusual wall painting in the museum room directly above.

More sophisticated decorative painting was done by the Norries, an Edinburgh firm of decorators, and a seascape was inserted above the fireplace. The furniture is mostly eighteenth century, too. This room is still used, and has a lived-in, cluttered air about it.

The beautiful harpsicord is by Andreas Ruckers, Antwerp, 1651, and is the only known example from this workshop with its original paintings and decoration. It is also in perfect working order, and it is possible to hear a tape of music recorded from it.

The dressing room next door is arranged to show off Victorian clothes discovered in the attics, including two wedding dresses and a pair of the last Earl's stockings.

The King's Room, in the Old Tower, is the most atmospheric room in the house. This was the room Mary and her husband, Lord Darnley, occupied when they visited Traquair on a hunting trip in 1566. The cradle at the foot of the bed was the one she used to rock her infant son, the future James I. The beautifully embroidered white silk bedcovering is said to have

The chapel was built after the Catholic Emancipation Act of 1829. *Joseph Flying to Egypt* (**above**) is one of 12 sixteenth-century wood panels in the chapel. The figure of Mary and the dead Christ (**right**) is in front of the altar.

been worked by the Queen and her ladies-in-waiting, the 'four Maries' of the song.

The portrait between the windows is of Anne, second wife of the 2nd Earl of Traquair. She was descended from the same family as Mary Seton.

The Earldom of Traquair was created by Charles I and the 1st Earl supported him in the Civil War. Upon the defeat of the Royalists by Cromwell, he was imprisoned for four years. John, the 2nd Earl, also fought against Cromwell and his family suffered severe harassments from the Presbyterians. Catholicism was banned, and though the Earl was an Episcopalian, he was fined £5000 for marrying Henrietta Gordon, a Catholic.

Henrietta died young, and his second wife, Anne Seton, was also an ardent Catholic. Her husband died soon after their marriage, and she is portrayed here with a widow's peak. After her husband's death, she was continually persecuted by the local presbytery, who often searched the house for 'popish' objects. At this time she converted the topmost floor of the tower into a private chapel with a secret stair, hidden in the cup-

board, so that the priest could escape into the woods.

Her eldest son, William, was taken from her to be educated against Catholicism. He, however, died young, and his younger brother Charles succeeded as 4th Earl and continued to practise Catholicism which remains in the family to this day.

The Earls of Traquair were also ardent Jacobites. A portrait in the Library depicts the 5th Earl wearing the end of his neckerchief tucked through his buttonhole – a secret Jacobite sign; and the museum contains some fine examples of Jacobite glass including the 'amen' glass with the inscription:

God bless the Prince of
Wales,
The true-born Prince of
Wales,
Sent us by thee;
Send him soon over
And kick out Hanover,
And soon we'll recover
Our old libertie.

Though the 4th Earl was not imprisoned for his part in the 1715 uprising, his brother-in-law, the Earl of Nithsdale, was

incarcerated in the Tower of London under sentence of death. His escape from the Tower disguised as a woman – aided by his wife – was the only escape ever from the Tower and is yet another of the romantic stories connected with the family.

The 5th Earl was also imprisoned in the Tower for two years after the 1745 rebellion. His wife voluntarily joined him in his Tower apartments. It was he who made the dramatic gesture of closing the Bear Gates.

The family fortunes have been less adverse since then, and with the passage of the Catholic Emancipation Act of 1829, the family was able to practise their faith openly. Then they built the present Chapel, furnished with an Italian marble altar and 12 sixteenth-century Flemish-style woodcarvings bought by the 5th Earl.

The last of the direct line was Lady Louisa Stuart who lived to be almost 100. An acquaintance of Burns and friend of Sir Walter Scott, she founded the local Catholic Church of Peebles and Innerleithen which commemorate her centenary.

Hopetoun House,
a/mansion/built
on the wealth of lead
mining interests to
bolster the social status
of Charles, the 1st Earl.

Hopetoun House

Nathaniel Dance painted this portrait of the 3rd Earl and his brother Charles with their tutor William Rouet, in Rome where they stayed on their Grand Tour of Europe. It hangs in the Red Drawing Room designed by Adam.

Left The Yellow Drawing Room was created by the Adam family. The silk brocade on the walls was made around 1850.

Above Hopetoun's back door, the visitors' entrance, was part of the first phase of the mansion, started in 1699, designed by Sir William Bruce.

Hopetoun is the most magnificent house in Scotland, something of an equivalent to Blenheim Palace or, in a much smaller way, to Versailles. Built in the eighteenth century for the Hope family, approximately 10 miles (16 km) west of Edinburgh, it was consciously designed to proclaim their newfound wealth and social status.

The 1st Earl's grandfather had married well – the heiress to the Leadhills mines – So the family fortune was made. The Earldom was only created in 1703, most probably through the ambitions of Lady Margaret Hamilton, mother of Charles, the 1st Earl. It was she who commissioned William Bruce to begin work on the original mansion in 1699.

However, the Bruce House was not quite grand enough for Charles and his wife, Lady Henrietta Johnstone, the sister of the cultured and cosmopolitan Marquess of Annandale. She inherited his extensive collection of Italian art in 1721. Perhaps it was to house this collection that the most fashionable architect of the day, William Adam, was engaged to enlarge the house.

He designed the great façade with its colonnades and flanking pavilions. After William Adam's death in 1748, the remodelling and decoration were completed by his sons, Robert and John. Their main contribution was to the interiors and, in particular, to the magnificent suite of state rooms on the ground floor.

Perhaps the best way to see Hopetoun is to start in the oldest part of the house. Pass through the neo-classical entrance hall by Adam with its antique roundels from the Annandale Collection set high into the walls, and enter the original Bruce House. The restrained decoration and wooden panelling give these rooms a warm and intimate character. You can imagine a family actually living here, something a bit more difficult to do in the more imposing Adam rooms. The ground floor rooms are not exactly as envisaged by Bruce. The Library has been made by joining two bedchambers, and the Bruce bedchamber was painted in the eighteenth century to give a lighter, more decorative effect. The marvellously theatrical bed was designed for the Adam State Bedchamber.

If you mount the original staircase, encrusted with exquisite wood-carved friezes (the murals were painted in 1967 as a memorial to the present Marquess' first wife), you enter rooms which Lady Margaret Hamilton would still recognize and feel at home in. Her portrait by Karel de Moor hangs at the top of the stairs.

The tapestries depicting pastoral scenes were specially made by the John Vanderbank Soho Tapestry Company as were a series of decorative paintings extolling the Virtues by the Dutch painter Tideman.

It is quite a psychological and decorative jump from the cosy West Wainscot Bedchamber to the rather ostentatious Yellow Drawing Room. This is the first room of the Adam Suite, originally laid out as Dining Room, Drawing Room and State Bedchamber.

The Yellow Drawing Room was originally the dining room and much of the furniture is Adam-designed and made by James Cullen, the 'Scottish chippendale'. The elegant mirrors between the windows were meant to reflect candlelit

Right The Red Drawing Room, with a ceiling by Robert Adam and the 10-foot-long marble fireplace by J. Michael Rysbrack.
Below A London craftsman, Mathias Lock, supplied this bed of gilt

dinner guests, and the two beautiful plump commodes on either side of the Adam fireplace come from the State Bedchamber.

In the early nineteenth century, the 4th Earl, who was a professional soldier and knew little of the arts, delegated Andrew Wilson, an Edinburgh art dealer, to take care of the Hopetoun art collection. Though some of the most spectacular pictures were bought by Wilson, he also sold important works, taking a commission on all his transactions, much in the manner of a present-day stockbroker. Wilson's attributions were often inaccurate; for instance, the *Doge of Genoa* in the Red Drawing Room, purchased by him as a Tintoretto, is actually a *Doge of Venice* and most certainly not painted by Tintoretto. However, he must be given credit for the purchase of the *Adoration of the Shepherds* in the Yellow Drawing Room. Though not by Rubens himself, it is a very fine product of his school and may well have been done under the master's supervision. Note also the rather fine School of Rembrandt of an old woman and the

little Teniers *Temptation of St. Anthony* with its nasty Bosch-like demons.

The Red Drawing Room is the only room in the house which retains its original function. Its furniture was designed to be kept against the walls so guests could promenade and show off their finery. It is the grandest room in the house. The elaborate Robert Adam ceiling is wonderfully elegant and the grand fireplace by Rysbruck is particularly impressive.

Apart from the misattributed *Doge* above the fireplace there are some good Italian pictures from the Annandale Collection. Passerotti's *Brothers of the Manaldini Family* is a particularly fine example. But the two most interesting paintings in the room are the full-length portraits of James, the 3rd Earl, and his brother, Charles, by Nathaniel Dance. These were done in Italy while the brothers were doing the 'Grand Tour', and include details of Roman architecture in the background to prove their literary and artistic cosmopolitanism.

Also by Dance is the little conversation piece which

shows the two boys with their tutor in the Borghese Gardens with St. Peters Cathedral in the background. It is a particularly charming and intimate rendering, lacking the bombast of the full-length portraits.

The final room in the suite is the State Dining Room, originally the State Bedchamber. Apart from Versailles, State Bedchambers were never really very practicable, and the 4th Earl had the room converted into a dining room in 1820. It was here in 1822 that George IV dined on turtle soup and three glasses of wine before knighting the painter Henry Raeburn. There is, in fact, a Raeburn portrait of the 4th Earl hanging here, as well as fine portraits by Ramsay and Gainsborough. The most interesting, if not the best, picture is David Allan's posthumous portrait of the 1st Earl shown at his desk with the plans for the house, while the actual building of it goes on in the background. Painted 40 years after the Earl's death in 1792, this portrait underlines most succinctly the importance which the family attached to their own little Palace of Versailles.

A late portrait of Sir Walter that shows clearly his high-domed skull which was possibly the result of the poliomyelitis attack he suffered as a child.

Abbotsford

The baronial mansion of Sir Walter Scott, overlooking the Tweed, is a dream come true. Writing brought Scott, one of 13 born to an Edinburgh solicitor, a baronetcy, fame and a fortune which he used to build his Gothic fantasy.

Left The view from the dining room turned bedroom where the dying Scott could enjoy his favourite sight of the lawns by the Tweed.

Above Scott found sitting for artists tedious but admirers constantly demanded his likeness and dozens were made: this one by Raeburn.

To visit Abbotsford, about 40 miles (64 km) southeast of Edinburgh, is to step directly into the life of Sir Walter Scott. Scott, who began his career as an Edinburgh lawyer, became, during his own lifetime, one of Europe's most successful novelists. With his sudden rise to fame he became obsessed with the idea of becoming a Border laird and in 1811 he bought the little farm of Carthyhole with the intention of creating himself a country seat. At first he only made additions to the existing building but in 1822 he had the old farmhouse entirely pulled down to build the main block of Abbotsford. Sir Walter had paid just 4000 guineas for the 110-acre (44.5 ha) property standing on the right bank of the River Tweed. The land had at one time belonged to the monks of Melrose. This, plus the fact that there was a ford across a nearby stream, prompted Scott to change the name from Carthyhole to Abbotsford.

The tour of Abbotsford begins in Scott's book-lined Study. One would not be at all surprised to see the white-haired old man walk through the little

door in the gallery which leads from his bedroom. It was in the comfy leather armchair at this desk that Scott wrote the famous Waverley Novels. Despite their phenomenal success Scott's life story became a romantic tragedy worthy of one of his own novels. At the height of his fame, in 1826, his publisher, Constable, went bankrupt leaving debts of over £120,000. Scott, with his immense sense of pride, took on these debts and worked himself almost to death to honour them. It is a tribute to his tenacity that he virtually paid the debt in full.

Among the masterworks produced at Abbotsford were such classics as *The Heart of Midlothian* and *Rob Roy*. In response to public demand, Scott turned to English history as well, notably with *Ivanhoe*, though with *Redgauntlet*, the last of his novels, he returned to the Scottish theme with which he was always more at home.

The desk at which he wrote was made from pieces of wood from the wrecked ships of the Spanish Armada. And wooden panels line the Study which

contains part of Sir Walter's collection of 9000 books. Here too is a portrait of the hero Rob Roy.

Move through to the Library which is surveyed by the idealized bust of Sir Walter by Chantrey. As in the Raeburn portrait in the Sitting Room he appears every inch the Border laird he tried so hard to become.

He was a magpie of a collector with a passion for anything to do with Scottish history, particularly objects with romantic connotations or associations with his own novels. The heavy moulded plaster Gothic ceiling is copied from Roslin chapel which features in several of his novels. If you look in the glass case in the window you will find Bonnie Prince Charlie's quaich, Rob Roy's purse and a tumbler with a few lines of poetry scratched on it by Robert Burns. As well as Scottish romantic novels Scott wrote a scholarly life of Napoleon and also on display is Napoleon's cloakclasp, in the form of two golden bees, found in his carriage after Waterloo.

Many of the objects in the house were presents from admirers. The two elaborately carved Italian chairs, said to

The dirk of Rob Roy whose real name was Robert McGregor. He was a highland outlaw with Jacobite loyalties who was romanticized by Scott.

Right Scott's carefully kept writing materials and notes are still at Abbotsford where he worked himself to death trying to pay off his publishers' debts. Apart from his many novels Scott wrote poems, ballads, reviews and histories.

The original keys to the Old Tolbooth in Edinburgh hang on a wall in the entrance hall, one item in Scott's massive collection.

have come from the Borghese Palace in Rome, were donated by his publisher. The beautiful handpainted Chinese wallpaper in the sitting room came from Sir Walter's brother-in-law, while the ebony roll-top desk was a present from King George IV and the silver urn in the niche beside it was a gift from Byron.

The walls of the Armoury are encrusted with weapons of great beauty as well as those of historical interest – note the superbly inlaid ivory butt of an Austrian rifle. Rob Roy's broadsword, dirk and gun also hang here.

In the Anteroom to the Armoury hangs a painting of Ginger, one of Sir Walter's dogs, by Sir Edward Landseer.

A glass case in the Dining Room contains an important relic of Scottish history – the sword of James IV, later given by Charles I to the Marquess of Montrose. It was here in the Dining Room that Sir Walter lay on his deathbed propped up by the window so that he could see his beloved River Tweed.

The Entrance Hall is panelled with oak from the Auld Kirk of Dunfermline. The two semi-circular cupboards were constructed out of the pulpit and, rather irreverently, Sir Walter kept wine in them. The walls are adorned, baronial style, with antique weapons and suits of armour – echoes of *Ivanhoe*.

On the exterior wall just above the entrance porch is set the condemned criminals' door of the Old Tolbooth of Edinburgh and in the centre of the Courtyard is a fountain which once formed part of Edinburgh's Mercat Cross, which in 1660 ran wine for the citizens at the Restoration of Charles II.

Sculptured medallions from the same cross are set into the south wall of the court alongside antique Roman reliefs from Hadrian's Wall. Maida, Sir Walter's favourite dog, is buried near the front porch beneath a stone effigy (Maida's likeness also appears on the Scott Monument in Princes Street Gardens). An inscription in Latin runs around the marker. Scott translated it as:

Beneath the sculptured form
    which late you wore
Sleep soundly, Maida,
    At your master's door.

The garden archway leads to the family's private apartments through the Chapel, with its fifteenth-century Flemish altarfront and painting of *Madonna and Child* by Ghirlandaio. This is also open to the public. Cardinal Newman was a friend of Scott's descendants and frequently celebrated Mass here.

This wing was added in the mid-nineteenth century and Scott's two great-great-granddaughters still live here. They see the house very much as a shrine to Sir Walter who they would like to think would still feel perfectly at home here since hardly a thing has been changed since his death in 1832.

Indeed electricity was installed scarcely 20 years ago; Sir Walter was an amateur scientist and until then the family made do with a gas lighting system of his own design. (Abbotsford was one of the first gas-lit houses in Britain.)

The whole house testifies to the personality of the man whose romantic view of Scotland caused the whole world to take note of Scotland's unique contribution to European culture.

The splendid home of the
Earls of Rosebery on the
Firth of Forth has some of
the world's greatest
treasures in two collections.

Dalmeny House

John Millais's sensitive portrait of the 5th Earl was painted in 1886. The Earl was a great scholar, writer and politician who became a Liberal Prime Minister and was an avid collector of works of art, books and objects that are now on view.

Left Treasures of the Mentmore collection - stately French furniture, tapestries, clocks and other 18th century works of art.

Above Mementoes of Napoleon, including his shaving stand and harpoon gun, are arranged in the room devoted to the Emperor.

*J*ust seven miles (11 km) outside Edinburgh stands one of the area's most celebrated historic houses – Dalmeny House, the home of the Earls of Rosebery. Dalmeny is important for two reasons; first, because of the role played by the 5th Earl as Prime Minister and leader of the Liberal Party in the 1890s and second because it houses some of the principal items from the fabulous Mentmore collection. These came into the family through the marriage of the 5th Earl to Hannah Rothschild, heir to Mentmore, the Rothschild's rambling Buckinghamshire mansion.

But the links between the Roseberys and Dalmeny go much further back than this – in fact, to 1662, when the estate of Dalmeny and Barnbougle was bought by Sir Archibald Primrose – Primrose is the Rosebery family name – when he was Lord Clerk Register of Scotland. He and his family lived in the thirteenth-century castle of Barnbougle, right on the shores of the Forth, which had belonged to the English Moubrays, Knights Templars in the Crusades. It was to Barnbougle

that the smuggling Moubray descendants brought contraband to be stored in the castle cellars.

Sir Archibald's son, who followed in his father's legal footsteps, became the 1st Earl of Rosebery in 1703 in Queen Anne's Coronation honours. He, too, continued to live in the cold and primitive castle.

It was the 3rd Earl's family who began to complain bitterly about the old castle but the Earl would have none of it. 'What was good enough for my grandfather, is good enough for my grandchildren,' came the reply. It took a huge wave, crashing through the dining room window, knocking him off his feet, to overcome his obstinacy and convince him that the castle did need rebuilding.

He commissioned Robert Adam to redesign the ancient castle but the results were not acted on, since the thrifty Earl considered them too extravagant.

When the 3rd Earl died, at the age of 88, in 1814, however, the 4th Earl acted quickly. He commissioned William Wilkins, whom he had known at Cambridge, to set about plan-

ning Scotland's first Tudor Gothic Revival house, a little way up the hill from Barnbougle Castle. The new house became, after its completion in 1817, a model for many nineteenth-century Scottish country houses, being noted for its comfort and modernity.

Though the Roseberys had always been important Scottish figures, it was the 5th Earl who was the first to take the national stage. He had three overwhelming ambitions: one was to marry the richest woman in England, another to become Prime Minister and the third to win the Derby. He achieved them all – he married Hannah Rothschild, heir to Mentmore, in 1878; followed Gladstone as Liberal Premier in 1894; and eventually won the Derby three times, with horses bred at Mentmore.

This Rosebery was a complex character. As well as being a politician, he was also a scholar, with a fascination for Napoleon, on whom he wrote one of the classic books. He also collected objects and portraits with Napoleonic connections and these, with the eighteenth-century portraits that also in-

Left Dalmeny House contains an unsurpassed collection of furniture. **Above** Wilkins, architect of the House, designed this table. **Middle** A Scottish bible box. **Below** An eighteenth century chair.

Right The joys of childhood is the theme of Goya tapestries adorning the hall stairway. A rare art form for the Spanish master, the works demonstrate an uncommonly lighthearted style.

terested him, formed the basis of his great collection.

His marriage to Hannah, the only child of Baron Meyer de Rothschild, brought him the exceptional collection at Mentmore in Buckinghamshire. The Baron had bought largely French eighteenth-century works of art between 1830 and 1850 – at the same time that the Wallace collections were put together – classic examples of which are now at Dalmeny. He also amassed a vast amount of Victorian works which were not brought to Dalmeny but were auctioned at Mentmore.

The 5th Earl thus set the pattern of Rosebery life over the years. Six months of the year was spent at Dalmeny and the rest of the time in the south. The treasures were similarly divided. The classic collections – notably the French furniture – remained at Mentmore, while Dalmeny was filled with pieces in the Scottish baronial style.

The decision to sell Mentmore and its collection completely changed this. The family decided what to keep according to a deliberate philosophy. This was that Dalmeny should remain a home and not

become a museum. The fine pieces from Mentmore, therefore, were chosen just as much for personal reasons as for their financial or artistic value, though the last factor also played an important part. The care that has gone into selecting what the visitor sees at Dalmeny today thus reflects the love the Roseberys have for their home and their possessions.

Inside the Gothic entrance hall, beneath the hammer beams and a fan-vaulted ceiling, is a large and impressive portrait of the assiduous 5th Earl by Millais. It is one of Millais' best portraits, with the figure dramatically set off against a dark background. The Earl's face is painted in sensitive detail.

On the stairway hang some of the rarest treasures of the house: the very unusual Goya designed tapestries. They were made by the Royal Tapestry Factory to fit into decorative schemes for Spanish royal palaces. They are four lighthearted, merry scenes of lovers and children and, apart from being a rare art form for Goya, they are also distinguished by

their jollity compared to Goya's more common gloominess.

On the top landing is Hogarth's *The Painter's Wife*. Like the Goya works it is untypical of the painter who was largely concerned with social comment. This is a personal and honest portrait, direct and concerned with the person beneath the image.

The Library, rebuilt in the 1950s following a wartime fire, is still used by the Rosebery family as a sitting room. It houses the book collection the 5th Earl, who collected books all his life.

Among the portraits in the room is one of the 6th Earl who inherited both Mentmore and Dalmeny and, justly, divided his time between the two. He was an all-round sportsman and a very keen racehorse enthusiast. He had a distinguished career with Allenby in World War I and as military governor in Egypt, and in World War II became Regional Commissioner for Civil Defence in Scotland. Racing mementoes are also on display.

The 6th Earl's wife, a pianist, was very involved with the arts and much of the planning for the

Edinburgh Festival was discussed in the Library. Indeed, Lady Rosebery was on the Programme Committee of the Festival for 25 years.

In the neo-classical Drawing Room are the greatest treasures from the Mentmore Collection. They are the pieces selected lovingly and carefully from the Buckinghamshire house by the present Earl of Rosebery and his wife before the sale in 1977, forced on by heavy death duties when the 6th Earl died.

They are largely French works made between 1680 and 1780 during the reign of the Sun King Louis XIV, Louis XV and Louis XVI. On the floor are the earliest Savonnerie carpets, from a series of 900 made for Louis XIV's palaces, which have taken the Roseberys more than two years to restore – with the help of the Rosebery children soaping them with sponges on their feet.

The Beauvais tapestries, designed by Boucher, were also under the caring eye and hand of the restorers for two years. They now clearly show the original design of François Boucher from about 1740, showing the European fascination with life in China at the time.

In the Drawing Room are some stately examples of French furniture, like the desk with the dolphins at the corners designed for the Dauphin in rococo style in about 1756; or the beautiful Louis XVI Secretaire designed by Oeben and finished by his son-in-law Riesener, the best and most expensive French cabinetmaker of his time.

The safe in the room weighs a ton and takes six men to move it. Baron Rothschild bought it as one belonging to Louis XV. The story is that Louis XVI, when Dauphin, helped to make the safe and helped the locksmith forge and fit the locks. When, as king, he was imprisoned during the Revolution, he had locks and clocks sent in to work on.

There are many priceless pieces in the Drawing Room and the Roseberys plan to open a further room for French furniture and so demonstrate stately and more homely furniture and the changes in style over a hundred years. With it will be displayed a large collection of Sevres and Vincennes porcelain that is not yet on show.

On the way to the Napoleon Room, along the Scottish Corridor, is a portrait of a 76-year-old man attributed to Rembrandt. The man, dressed in a sweeping, dark cloak and black cap, is Joannes Uytenbogaert and it is similar to a portrait that hangs in the Hermitage in Russia.

When the corridor was restored with the splendid Gothic tracery overhead and the fan-vaulting, it was furnished with a few pieces of Scottish country-house furniture. The Roseberys discovered more of the 5th Earl's collection of Scottish furniture from the fifteenth and sixteenth centuries in Barnbougle Castle and brought it into the Corridor, where it now stands as an authentic reminder of its period in a neo-Gothic setting.

The 5th Earl, who was a renowned expert on the life of Napoleon and wrote a definitive work about the Emperor, also collected pictures, objects and furniture associated with him. The works have been arranged by the present Earl and his wife in one room – the Napoleon Room.

This room also contains David's sketch of Napoleon's coronation ceremony with the new Emperor snatching the crown from the Pope, so that he could crown himself. A bust of Napoleon stands in a corner and the shaving stand he used when in exile on St. Helena is here. There are also portraits of his wives, Josephine and Marie-Therese, and his brothers, Joseph, Louis and Lucien, whom he made rulers of lands he conquered.

Among other memorabilia is a model of *The Northumberland*, which took Napoleon to exile; watercolours of St. Helena; furniture used by him in exile; and a portrait of him as a sad old man with his sun hat on.

When the Roseberys organized the Dining Room, which the family still use during the holidays, their idea was to hang portraits of people who lived at much the same time and who might well have dined together.

There are several Reynolds works – of Dr. Johnson, compiler of the famous dictionary; the politician George Selwyn; the opera singer La Contessa della Rena; and of Edward Gibbon, the historian.

Thomas Gainsborough's Lord Rodney, who beat the French at the Battle of the Saints in the West Indies; his painting of Lady Mary Fordyce; and a portrait of the powerful Henry Dundas, 1st Viscount Melville, by Sir Thomas Lawrence hang nearby.

Neil, 3rd Earl of Rosebery, painted by Henry Raeburn, shows the old Earl at the age of 84 with thick, curling hair – in fact he went bald very young in life and had three wigs, a short, a medium and a long one so that he could go to Edinburgh in the long wig and pretend to have a hair cut, next appearing in the shorter wig.

Dalmeny House has four principal rooms on show to the public at present but there are plans to open more to display additional parts of the magnificent collections. These will include Rothschild family portraits and more relics of the 5th Earl.

Dalmeny, with its surrounding estate, is one of the greatest pleasures in its area and contains some of Scotland's unique treasures.

Scottish Products

A wealth of goods results from the blend of tradition and innovation

Scotland, and especially its capital, offers a treasure trove to the shopper. Everyone will be familiar with the country's well-known products such as smoked salmon, oatcakes, haggis and kilts. But Edinburgh's shops and workshops offer an infinite variety of handmade and manufactured goods which should not be overlooked. Bagpipes and Edinburgh rock are just two of the products still made in Edinburgh itself, while there is a thriving coterie of craftsmen producing local wares.

Arts and crafts shops are generally located in areas around the Grassmarket and the High

A wealth of goods results from tradition and innovation

Street. Look in the "Yellow Pages" telephone directory under "Arts and Crafts" for a list of shops and producers. Appointments should be made to visit most workshops, which often work on a commission basis rather than holding a large amount of stock.

The Scottish Craft Centre exhibits and displays selected Scottish craft work, and the Scottish Tourist Board produces a booklet entitled *See Scotland at Work* which lists craft workshops and industrial concerns in Edinburgh, the rest of mainland Scotland and the Islands. All of these can be visited, some require an appointment to be made in advance and others not.

Edinburgh's crafts include candles, ceramics, dolls, embroidery, furniture and woodwork, glass, pottery, jewellery and silversmithing, knitwear and crochet, leatherwork, musical instruments, textiles, weaving.

Products which are still made in Edinburgh or for which a significant number of retail outlets and stockists exist in Edinburgh include kilts and all the elements of highland dress, tweeds, woollens such as cashmere and Shetland, bagpipes, whisky, Drambuie, Glayva, smoked salmon, oatcakes, kippers, haggis and cheeses. The articles on the following pages describe their origins and processes of production.

Away from shops and craft workshops, browsing around Edinburgh's two main markets will prove entertaining if not rewarding. The largest is at Ingliston behind the Royal Highland Showground on each Sunday of the year. Take the road to the airport, the A8 towards Glasgow, and turn off at the sign 'Ingliston, Airport'. The site has 1400 stalls where you can buy anything from a jacket to a catamaran; and you can visit a chiropodist, the mosque, the funfair or give the children a pony ride. The traders offer excellent bargains.

Edinburgh's own market, the Lane Sales, has existed for over 100 years and is especially useful for household goods. Old books and photographs are sold too, among a welter of interesting items. The market is situated between Hanover Street and Frederick Street on Thistle Street Lane Southwest Tuesdays and Fridays at 11.00. Since parking space is restricted, it is better to walk.

Antiques

The Scots have always been great travellers – sometimes for pleasure, more often through necessity – and they have always sent or brought back to Scotland a most remarkable variety of antiques from all over the world. From Chinese porcelain to Peruvian pottery and American Indian and Eskimo artefacts, antiques continually make their way onto the market. But apart from such international treasures the visitor to Edinburgh is more often looking for items which are distinctively Scottish.

When antique-hunting, the conventional bagpipe and tartan image, so often fostered by the Scots themselves, must be discarded. This aspect of Scotland's past was largely confined to the Gaelic, clan-based society of the northwest, although it is true that the highland drover, with his pistols and broadsword and dressed in short kilt, was once a familiar sight in the Old Town.

The famous highland pistols with their all-steel construction and ball-shaped triggers are now largely to be seen only in museums, but good eighteenth-century broadswords can still be found.

Another nationally distinctive antique is high-quality Scottish pewter. The famous 'Tappit Hen', a tankard with a distinctive nobbed lid, derivative in shape from the French 'Pichet' used in Normandy for cider, is perhaps the best known and most sought after of all Scottish pewter objects. The Scots pint was equal to three Imperial pints and the 'Hen' was made both in this size and in intermediate sizes of 'Chopin' (about two pints), 'Mutchkin' (just under a pint) and 'Half Mutchkin'. It also appeared in Imperial capacity, with and

A rare Bohemian liquer glass from about 1720 and a traditional pewter 'tappit' hen.

without a crest, and even in a lidless form, so its permutations are many.

As a poor country Scotland had little church plate or silver but it had a great many churches, each with its pewter flagons and chalices and alms plates. All of these are distinctively Scottish in shape and many bear attractive makers' marks or 'touches'.

Despite comparative poverty the Scots loved fine silver and it was worked in most of the royal burghs. Early Scottish silver, even the humblest of articles, is distinguished by a respect for the metal, a severity of line which is very much reflective of the national character. While fine examples from the seventeenth and early eighteenth centuries fetch very high prices, most Scottish silver from the later period is priced

about the same as its London equivalent. Edinburgh silver bears the attractive hallmarks of the city, the Thistle denoting the sterling quality of the metal and the Castle derived from the city's coat of arms. Most Scottish silver was made and assayed in Edinburgh and there is no better buy for the discerning visi-

The present Edinburgh assayer's mark stamped on silver.

tor today than Edinburgh silver of the late Georgian period, even if only a modest set of spoons.

Edinburgh during the eighteenth century was a centre for the production of fine quality goods of all kinds. Apart from silver, glass and pottery, much fine furniture was made, marked by a particular robustness in design which set it off from London-made furniture, particularly during the neo-classical period. Earlier Scottish furniture – chests, coffers and chairs and tables from the seventeenth century – exists in surprising quantity. It is usually made of oak.

The eighteenth century was also a halcyon time for the Scottish clockmaker who, at least in the larger towns, often doubled up as a maker of barometers as well. Almost every village or town boasted its clockmaker and these country clocks, often with attractive painted faces and usually of the longcase or 'grandfather' variety, are much preferred to English-made clocks of the same period. Scottish clocks always have a movement of eight days' duration while the country-made English clock had a simpler movement without a second hand and had to be wound daily.

Country-made French furni-

tend to be centred in two areas within easy reach of each other.

Start in the Grassmarket, in the Old Town below the Castle. The Grassmarket was the original centre of the antiques trade in Edinburgh, for the area was in decline and property was cheap. Today it is still the place where the 'knockers' and the 'runners', those casuals of the business, unload their goods, and from time to time a real discovery can turn up here.

The second area is scattered through the New Town. Queensferry Street off the west end of Princes Street contains a group of quality shops and the street runs down to Dean Village where there is a large cabinetmaking and antique furniture warehouse.

Situated on George Street

for the buyer much less predictable, but by the same token the fun and the chance of making a real discovery are even greater.

Furniture

Over the years cabinet-making in Edinburgh grew from a rough trade to a fine art, the brilliance of which was not to be submerged until the onset of the Victorian Age. Its early history features criminal episodes quite uncharacteristic of the staid image of this craft.

Edinburgh was a centre for furniture-making by the mid-fifteenth century when the Incorporation of Wrights was formed, admitting only those who made their living working in wood. However, for almost three centuries their products were crude copies of English and French designs. The business ethics of these early craftsmen seem to have been equally crude for in the 1670s they seized and closed down the workshop of a colleague whose only crime was making superior furniture.

The renaissance of design and craftsmanship in England which followed the Restoration of Charles II in 1606 was not mirrored in Scotland. The first step towards such a boom north of the border was taken by Alexander Peter, considered by some experts to be Scotland's finest cabinetmaker. There are records showing he supplied furniture to George Dundas of Dundas Castle in 1734 and a flood of orders from other aristocratic clients followed. Among these was an order for some 150 pieces for Lord Dumfries.

He also commissioned Edinburgh's second outstanding cabinetmaker, Peter's ex-apprentice William Mathie, to

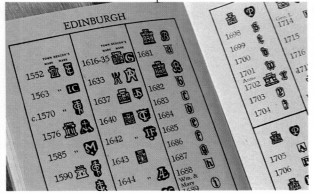

The Scottish capital's hallmarks, used between 1544 and 1792.

ture from the eighteenth century can also be found easily in Edinburgh, and this is undoubtedly an additional attraction for the many continental dealers who travel here regularly.

Other collectors' items of Scottish type which are easily found include snuff boxes, or 'Mulls', made in great variety from sheeps' horns and traditional Scottish brooches and other jewellery.

Edinburgh is a compact city and most of its antique shops

are some of the oldest auction rooms in Edinburgh and there are many antique shops at the junction of George Street and Hanover Street, some overflowing to Thistle Street. Dundas Street, the northern continuation of Hanover Street, runs down to St. Stephen Street where several intriguing shops may be found.

The opportunites which exist in Edinburgh for the antiques' enthusiast are indeed rich and varied. The lack of specialized outlets make the opportunities

make a series of carved mirrors for his castle. As Lord Dumfries had been made a Knight of the Thistle in 1752, Mathie varied his usual rococo and Chinese style of decoration to include a naturalistic thistle and the entire insignia of the Order on certain mirrors.

was probably financed by Rannie, Chippendale's partner, who came from Leith. His brother was a prosperous wine and spirits merchant there and Chippendale and Rannie received many orders through this connection.

The Director's illustrations of

cess, and from Hamilton's cabinetmaking skills. Within a few decades it had changed from a small upholstery and soft-furnishings importing business into a major furniture supplier for the burgeoning New Town and statelier homes in the area.

Antique dealers' shop front with neo-classical sculptures.

However, fine as the work of these craftsmen was, they did not create an Edinburgh style. Indeed, among the Dumfries furniture is a side table which so meticulously copies a Chippendale design that only Peter's account for it convinces experts it is local work. The source of this design was Chippendale's book, *The Gentleman and Cabinet-Maker's Director*, first published in 1753 and subscribed to by many Edinburgh cabinetmakers including Peter. The book had tremendous impact on furniture design throughout Europe but there was a special reason for its popularity in Edinburgh. It

Chinese-style furniture undoubtedly contributed to the thought behind the popular Cockpen Chair, so-called because several early examples stood in the Dalhousie pew at Cockpen Church. But the actual creation of this charming chair, with its lattice-work back resembling a Chinese puzzle, is now attributed to James Hamilton. He was employed by a firm called Young and Trotter founded in 1751. The first records of his activities there date from 1774 but he became a partner very soon after, probably as a result of the enormous success of the Cockpen Chair. The firm also benefited from its suc-

The rapid rise of Young, Hamilton and Trotter can partly be attributed to the even more abrupt downfall of the Brodie family's business. Francis and his son William were both Deacon of Wrights and sat on the Town Council, thereby cornering the market for civic furniture and fittings. While in the mid-eighteenth century the Brodies continuously supplied furniture to the Town College, as the university was then known, tradesmen's accounts show that Young and Trotter only picked up minor work such as stripping wallpaper and replacing it with rat-proof material in the paste.

But in 1788 a bungled raid on the Excise Office revealed that William (Dean) Brodie, libertine and gambler but a very competent cabinetmaker, was less capable in his secondstring occupation of burglar. His execution brought disgrace to the firm.

The other factor promoting the success of Young, Hamilton and Trotter was William Trotter, a descendant of John Knox who became sole proprietor of the firm in 1809. Despite active involvement in public life, in-

in Paxton House where he furnished the library and picture gallery in 1815. He also supplied furniture to the university, the Assembly Rooms and the Parliament.

There are survivors from the 100 cabinetmaking businesses in Edinburgh in 1812. The firm of Whytcock and Reid founded in that year still flourishes in Belford Mews, Dean Village, and it supplies and restores furniture for Holyrood House. But the death of William Trotter in 1833 brought the golden era

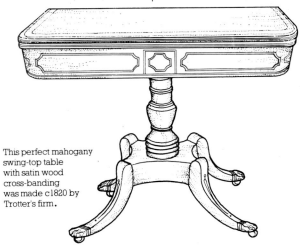

This perfect mahogany swing-top table with satin wood cross-banding was made c1820 by Trotter's firm.

cluding being Master of the Merchant Company and Lord Provost of Edinburgh, he created the version of Regency furniture known as the 'Trotter' style. From his premises in Princes Street with its workshop in Waverley Market he did a roaring trade by supplying the local customers with value for money and a distinctively Scottish style.

This furniture can be recognized by its air of masculine solidity, the use of high quality materials including wood and brass inlays and most notably by the carved lion's paws which frequently replaced the Engish Regency brass feet. One of the largest collections of his work is

of Edinburgh cabinetmaking to a sudden close. The pleasing and distinctive designs of the eighteenth century disappeared as cabinetmakers turned to producing much heavier pieces. These conformed with Victorian standards of taste but have certainly not found such favour with twentieth-century furniture connoisseurs. It is the older pieces which are sought after.

Clocks

Though clockmaking in Scotland started in Aberdeen in the 1400s, a hundred

years were to pass before Edinburgh entered the stage. And it was not until the sixteenth century that a native school of craftsmen emerged in the capital. By 1600, however the art had reached a fairly advanced stage, as is evident from the work of David Ramsay, watchmaker to James VI. Originally from Dundee, he possibly worked for a while in France before coming to Edinburgh and then finally travelled to London in the wake of his royal patron as 'Clockmaker Extraordinary' to the King. Ramsay's skill was rewarded by James, who made him Page of the Bedchamber in 1627, while in 1631 he became one of the founder members of the Clockmakers' Company of London.

Throughout the seventeenth century the development of the craft accelerated. By the middle of the 1600s there were sufficient clockmakers for them to be recognized as a distinct branch of the locksmiths' trade and thus form part of the Edinburgh Incorporation of Hammermen. The first qualified 'knokmaker' to be admitted to this august body was a George Smith, on September 6, 1649.

One of the earliest members of the Incorporation, an example of whose work has survived, was Humphrey Milne or Mills who became a freeman in 1660. He has left a very fine example of a brass lantern clock. This type of clock, so called because of its lantern-like shape, was introduced in England around 1620 and continued in popularity until the first half of the eighteenth century. Such clocks usually stood on wall brackets and normally had one hand. They were probably among the first clocks produced in Scotland to meet the demand for individual time pieces.

During the second half of the seventeenth century there began the development of what was to become the most popu-

Above Brass lantern
clock by Humphrey
Milne, 1660-1692.
Right Engraved silver
and brass pocket
watch by David Ramsay,
1600-1650. **Far right**
Marquetry longcase
clock by Paul Roumieu
Jnr, 1682-1712.

lar type of clock in Scotland – the longcase or grandfather clock. Humphrey Milne is thought to have produced some early longcase clocks and one of his apprentices, Andrew Brown, made several very beautiful clocks of this type. By far the most famous clockmaker of the late seventeenth century was Paul Roumieu. His father, Paul senior, arrived in Scotland from France sometime before 1677 and, after David Ramsay, is the earliest watchmaker recorded in Scotland. He passed on his skill to his son, who became a freeman of the Incorporation of Hammermen in 1682. The Roumieus' French

connection is a good example of the close economic links which existed between the two countries, and no doubt both father and son introduced technical advances which originated in France. The Roumieus' shop and house is thought to have been in the clockmakers' land at the top of the West Bow. Dr. Chambers in his *Traditions of Edinburgh* records that on the fourth floor of this house, which was demolished in 1835, were the remains of a curious piece of mechanism, namely a gilt ball representing the moon which was made to revolve by means of a clock.

By the middle of the eight-

eenth century Edinburgh clockmakers' skills could be compared favourably with those of clockmakers in any other part of Britain as the clockmakers responded to the demands accompanying economic prosperity.

By this time the craftsmen had perfected the movements of ordinary clocks and were becoming more adventurous. This manifested itself in a profusion of 'performing' clocks which could play complicated series of tunes or had ingenious automata. This development reached its climax in the production of extremely complicated astronomical clocks. One such was made by John Scott, who worked in Princes Street and East Register Street between 1779 and 1798. He was described as clockmaker to the Prince of Wales, and certainly he must have been a craftsman of the highest order.

The final phase in the development of the longcase clock began during the period of the painted or white dial clocks, which were popular from about 1790 to 1870. They were made in their thousands by clockmakers in virtually every town and large village in Scotland to satisfy the increased demand for a good quality 'knok' at a reasonable price. This was the era when the possibility of owning a clock came within the reach of the ordinary man. The earlier dials were decorated rather sparsely with much of the white enamelled underpainting showing, while the later dials tended to show much more flamboyant and picturesque painting. One of the reasons for the comparative cheapness of these clocks was that the faces came from clock face factories – firms specializing in making the painted dial plate and supplying them to the local clockmakers who fitted them to their own movements. Edinburgh was in the forefront of this trade, with several firms producing these dials, including Bell and Meundell, Russell and Clark and Dallaway and Son. Because of the numbers produced, this type of longcase clock is the one that has survived best and has become synonymous with the term grandfather clock.

Books

*E*dinburgh has a long tradition of books and bookselling. The city has even erected statues to the memory of some Allan Ramsay, bookseller, wigmaker and poet, stands in Princes Street Gardens, and Provost Chambers, bookseller and publisher, looks down from a pedestal in the street named for him.

The early history of the business is obscure but when James IV was encouraging the spread of the European Renaissance into Scotland, two printer–booksellers called Chepman and Myllar were setting up a little shop in the Cowgate. Their books, which appeared around 1508, are the earliest dated works known to be printed in Scotland – only a few decades after Gutenberg's invention of moveable type.

Bookselling and publishing tended to be in the same premises right up to the beginning of the twentieth century and even now a few of Edinburgh's secondhand booksellers have their own presses.

In the eighteenth century when Adam Smith and David Hume were revolutionizing economics and philosophy, the literati met in Edinburgh bookshops in the way they now do in pubs. Allan Ramsay had a shop, first at Netherbow, then by the Luckenbooths, where he combined bookselling and poetry with hairdressing and wigmaking. He was, he said, attending to both the inside and outside of his customers' heads.

In 1777 there were 98 hairdressers and 20 bookshops in the city but by 1867 the balance had changed to 43 hairdressers and 128 booksellers. One of the

Edinburgh has some fine bookshops. Scotland's largest bookshop is James Thin, 53-62 South Bridge, Edinburgh, founded in 1848 and still a family business.

best of these was run by William Creech, the first Edinburgh publisher of Burns. Creech was Lord Provost from 1811 to 1813; it was remarkable how many of those involved in bookselling won high office in the city in the nineteenth century. Bookselling was very big business indeed.

In fact, one of the world's largest publishing houses started in a small Edinburgh close at the end of the eighteenth century – the *Encylopaedia Britannica*. Its publisher, Archibald Constable, who also produced the *Edinburgh Review*, was also the publisher of Walter Scott's first novel, *The Lay of The Last Minstrel*, which sold 44,000 copies between 1805 and 1830.

Ballantyne, Adam Black, John Blackie, William Blackwood, William Collins, William and Robert Chambers, Archibald Constable and Thomas Nelson are just some of the big names of nineteenth-century Scottish publishing and bookselling. Some, like Bartholomew the mapmakers, specialized; others leant more heavily towards bookselling, like Thins or the now ubiquitous John Menzies which began in Princes Street in 1833.

If you are a book collector, Edinburgh can still surprise with its great treasure trove of old books. The city has dozens of bookshops, spread through both the Old and New Towns, selling second-hand books by the thousand, from cramped quarters that can take hours to scour for titles.

It is still possible to spot a good bargain – perhaps a first edition Scott or Stevenson at the very best – in among the many more common volumes that line the shelves and those that are displayed with pride within the shops.

Books are very much loved in Scotland and there is a busy trade in them, so the turnover,

even in some of the smaller bookshops, can be faster than you think. If you find nothing the first time around, visit again, talk with the bookseller, make your wants known, and you may well walk out with the very volume the next time you visit.

Prices vary greatly, of course, with the condition and scarcity of the book in question, but it is usually possible to strike a good bargain with a bookseller. And it is certainly worthwhile having a chat with the bookseller and showing your fascination for the subject. He will certainly be interested and knowledgeable about his books and it is possible that he will open up for you an intriguing world of literary back-alleys.

Bagpipes

Bagpipes consist essentially of a bag of skin which is inflated under pressure from the arm to produce a stream of air to the pipes. The invention of the bag did not represent a new musical instrument but merely an addition to pipes blown by the mouth. Reed pipes were known well before the time of Christ, particularly in hill countries where shepherds and cowherds played the pipes during their long hours of solitude.

The earliest surviving examples of the reed-sounded pipe or pipes have been found in Babylonia and ancient Egypt, but it is likely that the principle was discovered independently in innumerable countries all over the world, and certainly they were known in ancient Greece and Rome. Reeds or pieces of straw when pinched flat and blown with compressed lips yield a crude musical sound, and this principle was

This shop has dealt in kilts and bagpipes for nearly 150 years.

*I*t is said that there is no inhabited continent where the Scottish highland bagpipe is not played, and certainly most people are familiar with its distinctive sound. Bagpipes are an essential part of Scotland's national heritage and their long history is indefinably embodied in the awe-inspiring sight of the pipers in full highland dress in the streets of Edinburgh.

named the double reed after the two surfaces created by compression. The single reed is constructed by a cut a short way along the straw, which when played produces a musical sound.

Today's bagpipes comprise a bass drone (the longest pipe), which is essentially the single reed type; two tenor drones (identical in appearance) both of single reed type; a blow pipe (the short pipe which narrows at the end for use as the mouthpiece); and the chanter, which with its finger holes enables a tune to be played according to the double-reed principle. The bag acts as a reservoir and pump to supply air to the pipes. The modern version is basically the result of adding a bag to the hornpipe, the generic name

Bridgeness in East Lothian which has carvings of the double pipe.

The pipes of ancient Britain however are thought to have developed from the Egyptian model, the parallel pipes, as a result of the earliest Mediterranean migrations between 2000 and 3000 BC. This theory is supported by the fact that the

1437) played the pipes, and bagpipes were the national music of England during the reign of Henry V (1413-1422). James II of Scotland (1437-1460) passed an act for the suppression of the pipes in 1449, but they were restored by James III, (1460-1488) and James IV (1488-1513) had English pipers playing at the gates of Edinburgh Castle until 1507. Up until this time pipers had traditionally been associated with the English Court from the reign of Edward III (1327-1377) but by the end of the fifteenth century there were town or burgh pipers as well. The bagpipes acquired battle status in the mid-sixteenth century in Scotland, being associated with Scottish armies, and the clans employed their own pipers. The English Court dispensed with the pipers in the 1660s, from which time bagpipes in England were relegated to folk music. It was about this time that the third pipe, the base drone, also known as the great drone, was added.

After the Jacobite Rebellion of 1745, the second (and far more vicious) Disarming Act was passed. It was judged in the High Court that bagpipes were an instrument of war, being associated with armies, and, together with weapons and symbols of nationalism such as tartan, were banned.

The result for the piper was disastrous – and furthermore there was far less employment by the clans owing to their own impoverishment because of the forfeiture of their estates. In 1757, however, the new highland regiments were formed in response to troubles abroad, and they were allowed once more to play the pipes. The Disarming Act was repealed in 1782 from which time Scotland enjoyed its piping tradition without interruption to the present day.

There is now a College of

An array of drones, chanters and reeds used in sets of pipes.

for double, single and parallel pipes.

Although the double pipes existed in ancient Britain, it is known that the Romans introduced them after their invasion of Britain in the first century AD. The National Museum of Antiquities, Edinburgh, possesses the Roman stone found at

highlanders did not adopt the Romans' double pipes.

Up until the twelfth century the pipes comprised the hornpipe, a type of chanter fitted with a bag or skin and the blowpipe. It was not until the fourteenth century that a drone was added.

James I of Scotland (1424-

Piping in Glasgow, and Edinburgh, like other towns in Scotland, has its own bagpipe makers. The water reed gave way first to cane and then to hard woods such as laburnum, cocus, rosewood and, in this century, African blackwood or Canadian maple. The hardness of the wood is essential, since the harder the wood, the better the tone. If Canadian maple is used, it has to be specially treated, it 'works' better than the other woods and can be bored without the need for mounts. Square sections of about ten inches (25.4 cm) in length and two inches (5.1 cm) in width are turned on a lathe into pipes. Plastic, ivory or silver are used for the embellishments and so is the traditional horn. A set of pipes will cost not less than £300 and a full-mounted silver set with hand engraved family crest or runic devices may be £2000. The pipes will last for ever, except for the bag which is made of sheepskin or cowhide and needs replacing every year or two. If the pipes are not played regularly, the skin will harden within two months.

William Sinclair has been making bagpipes in Edinburgh since the 1920s and started his own business in 1963. You have to wait several months after placing an order for the authentic article. Sinclair & Son produce about 100 sets a year mostly for professional pipers in Edinburgh. They have also exported to South Africa, Canada, the United States, Australia, France, Norway, Sweden and Finland. The United States is one of the biggest importers but the continental countries are apparently increasing their orders.

Allistair Sinclair's advice to the hopeful piper is to start learning by the age of ten and he emphasizes the importance of a good ear since you have to tune the instrument yourself.

The pipes are pitched at B flat to play with brass bands and possess just eight notes – which do not represent a true scale. The notes relate to the white notes of the piano which means there is no minor key. The instrument is tuned by rotating the two ends of the pipe, decreasing or increasing the space from end to end according to the desired sound.

The sound of the bagpipes is a uniquely haunting one which compels the ear and, with its evocation of Scotland and its history and traditions, perceptibly moves every foot.

Tartan

Of everything that is exclusively associated with Scotland, tartan is the most vivid and the most instantly recognizable particularly in the form of the kilt. But the tartan has an uncertain history and the misconceptions are many.

Many writers claim that the word tartan is English, the Gaelic being breacan but, it now seems accepted that tartan derives from tiretaine, French for a coloured woollen material.

Scotland has produced lengths of cloth since medieval times. The basic garment for both nobleman and peasant until the end of the sixteenth century was the leine croich, a linen tunic. Over this was worn a woollen mantle, which developed into a large tartan blanket, the breacan filleadh, or folded plaid.

The wearer would lay it flat on the ground, pleat it to reduce the width, leaving a short length at either edge unpleated. He would then lie on it, with the lower edge in line with his knees. The two unpleated ends were folded across the body, overlapping, and the whole garment held in place with a belt at the waist.

The excess of fabric above the belt was either raised and draped over the head and shoulders or draped around the torso where it was fastened on the shoulder with a brooch, button or pin.

The garment was obviously an encumbrance, and towards the end of the sixteenth century the forerunner of today's kilt emerged: the lower section of the plaid had pleats stitched in place and the upper half was cut away. This became the length of plaid that today is worn over the left shoulder and fastened with a decorative brooch.

Claims that the clansmen adhered rigidly to one particular tartan so that they would not kill their own clansmen in disputes and retaliations are clearly insupportable: you would be unlikely to cross someone else's territory wearing an outfit that marked you as a target for assassination.

Some experts on the subject say that it was an Englishman, Thomas Rawlinson, manager of a Glengarry ironworks, who invented the little kilt, as it was then known. He felt his workers were too restricted in the belted plaid and so, in about 1727 he dispensed with the plaid, had pleats sewn in the lower part of the garment and hence the kilt was born.

But there are references and engravings well before 1727 which show the little kilt, and so the story of Rawlinson's invention must have been embroidered.

The tartan chosen for the kilt depended largely upon where the wearer hailed from and was not necessarily related to his clan. Since chemical dyes did not exist, vegetable dyes were used in the making of the cloth: so it was a matter of personal preference combined with the plants available that would determine the colours of the kilt. And if a great many Macdonalds, for example, existed in one area, then no doubt many of them wore kilts of the same or similar colours.

Although there was no rigid organization concerning a clan's tartan, there were personal preferences and tartan had become a symbol of the highlander.

requiring six square feet in which to read it) was a response to the revival in popularity of Scotland in general and tartan in particular due to George IV's visit to Scotland in 1822 and his fascination for it – rivalled only by Queen Victoria's interest and affection.

By the 1850s and 1860s, the

advise you on the selection of a tartan. If you know which area either you or your ancestors are associated with, Kinloch Anderson will be able to arrange the design of a new tartan according to the predominant colours of the plant life in that area.

Men normally wear the kilt,

The tartan marks the clan of each child here but not until the 1840s, when the Sobieski Stuart brothers published their disputed works on the classification of tartans, did each clan adhere to one pattern.

After the Jacobite Rebellion of 1745, all such symbols were banned under the Disarming Act of 1747. Tartan was not worn, legally at least, until 1782 when the Act was repealed.

Fragments of the old tartans that exist today, and these include those in Edinburgh's Museum of Antiquities, show that the later tartans conceived in the nineteenth century bear little or no relation to those worn before 1745 and must have been the product either of misguided historians or imaginative entrepreneurs.

Two such entrepreneurs, the Brothers Allan, also known as the Sobieski Stuart brothers, produced The Costumes of the Clans in 1842. The brothers claimed to be grandsons of Bonnie Prince Charlie and thus party to information known to no one else.

Their astonishing publication (weighing 22 pounds and

tartan industry was thoroughly established and the vogue for Scotland and its symbols was at its peak.

There are now over 500 clan tartans and it is accepted that if you have links with a particular clan, then you may assume its tartan – and, if not, you should not really wear any tartan.

If you wish to establish your crest or any other heraldic device, the Lord Lyon office in Edinburgh can advise. If you wish to establish whether you are descended from a particular clan, you should contact the Scots Ancestry Research Society in Edinburgh. The terms in 1987 are a £10 (plus VAT) non-returnable registration fee and an authorization for research to be carried out up to a maximum of £100.

Shops such as Kinloch Anderson operating from its historic site in Edinburgh's Royal Mile will then be able to

while women wear kilted skirts. The women's version usually takes about six to seven yards (5.4-6.4 m) of cloth, while the kilt proper requires eight to nine yards (7.3-8.2 m). The kilted skirt is complemented by a coordinating blouse and a tam.

There is nothing to rival the kilt as a symbol of Scotland. Parades and ceremonies with Scotsmen in full highland dress are an awe-inspiring sight – a reminder of Scotland's chequered history.

Tweed

*E*dinburgh is one of the best market places you can find for tweed and Harris tweed.

Tweed comes in an infinite variety of colours, weights and in herringbone or check.

The weight is selected according to the garment the tweed is destined for and the use it will receive. Men's suits, women's suits, coats, jackets, skirts and trousers can all be made up in Edinburgh once you have selected the preferred colour from the roll, or you can buy ready-mades.

Tweed was made in southern Scotland from about the 1840s and the main centres of production, in a textile industry that was otherwise depressed, included Galashiels, Jedburgh and Hawick in the Tweed river basin. The Border towns found a ready market for the tweeds in the south. Demand increased with Queen Victoria's affection for Scotland and all things Scottish.

It was the English that unwittingly gave tweed its name, rather than the river of the same name. *Tweel,* the Scottish version of the French word for cloth, *toile,* was misread – and so tweed was born.

The best quality tweed is Harris tweed, a 100 percent wool cloth, which is handwoven on the islands of the Outer Hebrides, notably the isles of Harris and Lewis. It is usually a heavyweight cloth, and it is legally protected from imitation.

The traditional cloths come in subtle shades of browns and greens. Its internationally recognized standard of durability makes tweed an attractive investment.

Cashmere

Cashmere is sheer magic. With its uniquely soft and velvety touch, it has become a supreme symbol of luxury and opulence. And the hard-wearing quality, colours and design of cashmere clothing produced in Scotland have given it undisputed leadership

in the world's knitwear markets. Some designers, such as Bonnie Cashin, will work only with cashmere made in Scotland.

Expensive – of course. Just 2.2 pounds (1 kg) of cashmere is worth £90 today, even before any garment is produced. The reason for its high cost lies partly in the difficulty of obtaining the raw material.

The word cashmere is an anglicization of Kashmir, the province of India where the goats that supply the wool were found. Nowadays, however, the necessary undercoat of the fleece is provided by goats from China, Iran and the Soviet Union. Great expense is involved, not only because the animals roam high up in the mountains, but also because much time and skill are required in the manufacturing process.

The development and availability of cashmere can be traced most recently to the conglomerate known as Dawson International. Joseph Dawson in 1901 invented a machine which could separate the hair of the goat, a process that had previously been done entirely by hand, in preparation for yarn-spinning. As a result, Dawson's were one of the largest cashmere processors anywhere. It was not until the 1950s, however, that cashmere became the status symbol it is today.

Towards the end of the 1940s, a mixed textile company named Tood & Duncan started making lambswool yarn and, subsequently, single ply cashmere as well. By 1960, Todd & Duncan were using 70 percent of Joseph Dawson's production. Dawson, by then a public company, bought Todd & Duncan which meant that the world's largest cashmere buyer and dehairer had joined the largest cashmere spinner. One year later, the spinning strength of the company was increased by the

acquisition of Laidlaw & Fairgrieve, the firm which had pioneered in Shetland yarns in the 1950s.

Dawson's then acquired a variety of good quality Scottish knitwear manufacturers between 1966 and 1970: Barrie, Pringle, McGeorge, Glenmac, Ballantyne Sportswear and Braemar – the oldest name in Scottish knitwear. Dawson's injected the companies with capital, the principal aim being to update the machinery which, in some cases, was hopelessly antiquated.

Dawson's chairman, Alan Smith, recognized that irregular supply of the raw material was a continual problem and so, in the early 1960s, he began visiting mainland China. Between 1961 and 1971, he established a unique relationship with his suppliers, on the understanding that Dawson would buy all the cashmere they could offer, even in excess of need, in return for price stability.

The Dawson group, based at Kinross on the shores of Loch Leven, now occupy a market – the top 5 to 10 percent in price and quality – which is quite unaffected by low-cost imports that have hit the manufacturers of less luxurious knitwear.

Direct exports exceeded £40 million in 1980, with Italy being the largest individual market, followed by Switzerland. Export represents about 75 percent of their total production, but much of the remainder is exported as well: large quantities are sent to London and sold on, and this is classed as invisible export.

The six different companies comprise a huge range of colours and styles in women's suits, skirts, jerseys, cardigans, twin-sets, scarves and men's ties. A plain Ballantyne jersey retails in 1987 for about £70 to £90, while an intricate intarsia design may well cost over £200. Top designers, such as Karl

Lagerfeld, are commissioned to produce designs, and certainly the tailoring is enviable.

Inlaid design, or intarsia, is one of the features of the group. The word has been borrowed from the woodworking craft of marquetry. Of the many intarsia designs, the original Argyll remains popular, while flowers, birds, butterflies, diamonds and geometrics are much in demand.

Ballantyne's intarsia knitters are based just outside Edinburgh in a large, modern factory. Their training takes two years, after which time they can produce a diamond pattern jersey front on a single bed machine in about three and a half hours – the more complex designs may take as much as eight hours.

Assembly of the fronts with the backs and sleeves produced in Innerleithen is carried out here as well. The stitch length selected on the different machines ensures that the hand-knitted intarsia front matches exactly the machine-knitted sleeves and back.

The matching and seaming carried out during assembly is a skilled process, subject to several quality checks at each stage. Assembly training takes about one to one and half years. Batch numbers will have been attached to the collars and other trims so that each whole garment is produced from the same batch of wool. When the garment has been assembled, it goes to the milling house with its corresponding trims.

The garments and trims are thoroughly scoured in special detergent to remove the oil, and the fibre is broken down in a milling process to produce the characteristic softness. The millman estimates just how long each batch requires in the machine: the time factor is crucial as the machine may contain £1000 worth of garments at any one time.

The garments are then spun and dried, boarded (pulled over steel frames and set to size by steaming and vacuuming), and then sent out for hand-finishing. Necks are cut out for V-necks, and collars, buttons, pockets, trimming, binding, braiding constitute the next stages. A series of examinations determines whether the garment can be passed for pressing, when it is again checked for quality.

The quality, colours and designs of cashmere garments produced in Scotland ensure that they retain a supreme position in the world's knitwear markets. Although much of the total production goes for export and invisible export, Edinburgh nevertheless offers, in its concentrated shopping area, many shops specializing in Scottish woollens and tweeds. As well as cashmere, you will find lambswool, botany wool, Shetlands from the Shetland Isles, and Fair isles which originated from the sparsely populated Fair Isle off northern Scotland. Fair isles are knitted in colours and designs which are said to be Moorish and are traceable to survivors of the Spanish Armada in 1588.

Whisky

D o not ask for whisky, do not request a Scotch—you are in a land where brands and blends can be as individual as the wines of France. If you apply yourself diligently to the task, you can soon become a true Scot and pick out the particular glass of golden liquor to suit your mood. It will probably be one of the scores of 'single malts', the pure and crowning glory of Scottish distilling. But it might be one of hundreds of blends, which are made from a mixture of malt and grain whiskies and account for 98 percent of all whisky sold.

Whether the choice is a light and delicate blend or the dark, smokey tang of an island malt, what you are sampling is the Gaelic 'water of life'. That is the meaning of the word *uisge-beagh,* from which whisky got its name.

The malts are a pure product made from malted barley in a series of processes known as malting, mashing, fermentation and distillation in pot stills. The barley is steeped in water so that the germination process is triggered and rootlets start to sprout. A grain of barley is in fact a small store of starch which is insoluble. After about seven days, the conversion of the starch will have taken place and the maltster then dries it, in a kiln fired by peat.

The distiller grinds the soluble starch and adds water during the process known as mashing. A sugary liquid, maltose, is extracted and fermented with yeast. During the course of about 40 hours, the sugar is converted into a crude alcohol of about 12 percent strength, known as wash.

The final product requires two distillations in large copper pot stills. The first distillation separates the alcohol from the fermented liquid and the resulting distillate, known as low wines, is then passed to another still where it is distilled a second time. The first runnings from the second distillation, the foreshots, are very strong and are set aside. Towards the end of the distillation, the strength and quality of the spirit is reduced and these runnings, known as feints, are drawn off and, together with the fore-shots, are redistilled in the next distillation of low wines.

It is the mixture of the three elements, the low wines, the foreshots and the feints, that is largely responsible for the character of the whisky. The middle cut, the runnings that

The Magic of Malt Whisky

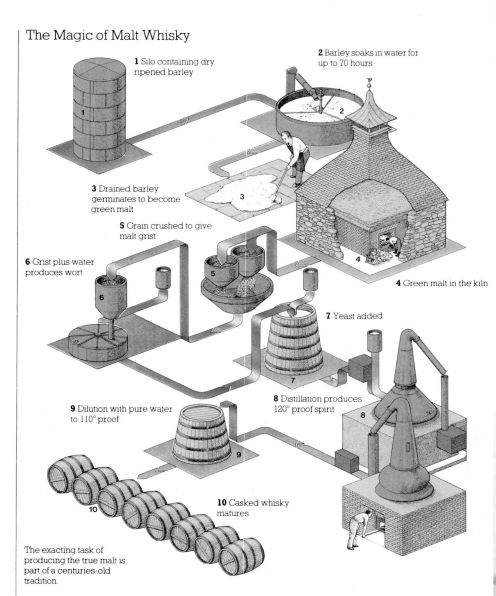

1 Silo containing dry ripened barley

2 Barley soaks in water for up to 70 hours

3 Drained barley germinates to become green malt

5 Grain crushed to give malt grist

6 Grist plus water produces wort

4 Green malt in the kiln

7 Yeast added

9 Dilution with pure water to 110° proof

8 Distillation produces 120° proof spirit

10 Casked whisky matures

The exacting task of producing the true malt is part of a centuries-old tradition.

are taken off between the foreshots and the feints, are pumped into casks and left to mature for a minimum of three years. It is often left for considerably longer – The Glenlivet, for example, is not bottled until 12 years later. About 1½ percent a year is lost in evaporation, but the process of maturation is an important one since it results in a smoother and more mature whisky. After about 15 years or so, the whisky becomes progressively smoother and less recognizable for what it is. One might guess that it is a cognac which is being offered. After maturation, the whisky is coloured with an infinitesimal quantity of caramelized sugar, if the casks have not already imparted sufficient colour. Once bottled, the whisky does not then change in state or flavour – so you can drink it straightaway.

Malt whisky comes from four distinct regions, the Highlands, the Lowlands, Islay and Campbeltown on the Mull of Kintyre, which together represent Scotland's total 130 distilleries, of which 116 are malt distilleries. Although generalizations can be made about the malt whiskies to come from these geographical areas, it is worth remembering that each still produces a whisky that to someone in the trade is as individual as a fingerprint. Glenfiddich and Balvenie, for example, which are literally across the road from each other and use the same water and the same barley, make noticeably different products.

Longmorn, Linkwood, Glen Rothes and Glengoyne; around Dufftown and Keith, the group including Glenfiddich, very much responsible for promoting the single malt in recent years, Strathisla, the oldest distillery, founded in 1786, Bal-

whiskies. The Islay distilleries make a characteristic heavy, peaty, pungent, almost medicinal style of malt for which an acquired taste is needed. The single malts from Islay include Bowmore, Laphroaig, Lagavulin and Bruichladdich.

A whisky company has occupied this New Town building since 1799.

The Highlanders, the largest group, can be subdivided into three areas: those around the Livet valley, which include The Glenlivet, Glen Grant, Glenfarclas, Tormore, Cardhu,

venie, Dufftown-Glenlivet and Mortlach; and, thirdly, north of the Spey from Inverness almost to John O'Groats, a group including Glenmorangie, Old Pulteney, Dalmore and Clynelish.

The Highland malts have traditionally been regarded as the best, with the Speyside products, from around the River Spey, being regarded in the trade as excellent malts. The Lowlanders are much lighter and are most often used in the production of blended

A blender or broker can appreciate the difference between the malts sufficiently to enable him to identify its age and area of origin and to pinpoint it to one of three or four. An Edinburgh broker, with many years in the trade, said in 1981 that of all the malts, those that commanded high prices included Aultmore, Glen Grant, Longmorn, The Glenlivet, and Mortlach, all of them Highland Malts. He added that Glenmorangie, one of the best sellers, is a very fine malt – but, natu-

There is nothing like owning <u>the</u> original

<u>The</u> Glenlivet.
The original, unblended malt wh
from the oldest licensed distillery in
the highlands of Scotland is widely
acknowledged to be the finest in the
world.
The supreme malt with a unique
character and exceptional smoothne
<u>The</u> Glenlivet is unchanged since 18
There is nothing like <u>The</u> Glenliv

The Glenlivet

<u>The</u> malt.
12 years old and the finest in the world.

rally, no one in the trade will commit themselves to naming the best.

Your own tasting is probably best carried out with a selection of miniatures, a good range of which are carried by Lambert Bros., 9 Frederick Street, and William Cadenhead Ltd., 172 The Canongate. Lambert's stock a huge range of whiskies, both malts and blends, carry books about whisky and have their own export service. Cadenhead's specialize in old and rare malts, and also have their own export service as well as mail order.

Whereas the malt whiskies are made purely from barley, the grains are made from a mixture of malted barley with unmalted cereals such as maize. The process, which is far less costly, is a continuous one, with the distillation carried out in a Patent or Coffey still, rather than a pot still, and the spirit is collected at a much higher strength. Since the whisky can be run at a much higher strength, and continuously, the Coffey stills can produce as much as 14,000 gallons per hour. Grain whisky is not influenced by geographical factors and it has a less pronounced aroma and flavour than the malts.

The well-known brands of blended whisky, exported all over the world, make up 98 percent of Scotland's total whisky, and so it is to the manufacture of the blends that much of the malt and grain production goes. A blend may contain between 15 and 50 different whiskies, the process of blending being known as vatting. Blending is an art, in which the malts and grains are selected to complement their respective flavours, so that the best qualities of each are brought out. Once mixed in a blending vat, after a battery of testing, they are returned to the cask to 'marry' for several months before bottling. Some

are vatted separately and only combined during bottling.

Blending was pioneered by Andrew Usher in Edinburgh in the early 1860s. It was only when this practice became common that a taste for Scotch whisky spread first to England and then throughout the world. Pot still malt whisky, although its popularity has increased greatly in the last 20 years, is inclined to be rather strongly flavoured, particularly for those in warmer climates and sedentary occupations.

To the Scotsman of the cold, rugged hills in centuries past, however, the pure malt must have been more than welcome. It is thought that distilling started in the East many centuries ago; the fact that eastern civilizations had bamboo tubes which would have been good for conducting vapour when the West had only crude implements seems to support this assumption. From the Far East the practice seems to have spread through India and the Middle East with the Crusaders to the monastic houses of Europe in the Middle Ages. The centres of learning were keeping the practice alive by distilling medicinal preparations of herbs and perhaps by

making something akin to whisky for their own consumption, a practice which spread to Ireland and then to the west of Scotland. A fifth-century Welsh song refers to 'strong liquor', while the first recorded reference in Scotland is an entry in the Exchequer Rolls of 1494: 'eight bolls of malt to Friar John Cor wherewith to make aquavitae' – eight bolls is well over 2645 pounds (1200 kg), so it is clear that Friar John Cor was involved in the distillation of

Window-shopping — a parade of Scotland's matchless whiskies

rather more than would be required for one monastery.

It seems that the monasteries constituted a cottage industry, and the crofters in the highlands, too, would have been producing their own fire-water. After centuries of illegal distillation, 1823 saw the imposing of a £10 tax on stills of over 40 gallons' capacity. Although illicit distillation continued, the industry was eventually brought under control.

Scotch whisky can only be made in Scotland. It is not, by law, Scotch whisky otherwise. The words whiskey and whisky used to be confused, but whiskey is now confined to Irish whiskey, which is subjected to three distillations and uses a wider range of cereals. Before

The art of one family
reflected through five generations.

Three distinctive whiskies, each individual in character.
The result of distilling and blending skills perfected by the
generations of the Mackinlay family. An experience of
quality which continues unbroken today.

Charles Mackinlay & Co Ltd.

Distillers, Leith, Scotland.

the product can claim to be called whisky, it has to mature in wooden casks for a minimum of three years.

The casks used were traditionally, and until recently, the sherry casks that are imported from Spain. These would impart a certain flavour and colour to the whisky depending on which type of sherry the cask had been used for. Other factors are involved, however, in the production of a drink that has not been repeated successfully anywhere in the world. (Much whisky is now matured in bourbon casks from the United States.)

The natural elements of water, peat (which is introduced in the malting process) and the climate, affecting the crop as well as the final product during maturation, all influence flavour of the malt whiskies. The distilling process is crucial, too. The amount of secondary constituents retained in the spirit depends upon the shape of the still, the way in which it is operated and on the strength at which the spirit is drawn off.

Whatever its origins and whatever the secrets of distillation, whisky in 1980 represented £746 million in export earnings, accounting for 83 per cent of total production. Of the remaining 16 percent, it is estimated that about one-quarter is consumed in Scotland. When you are in Edinburgh, you should not miss the chance of sampling the range of one of Scotland's oldest and most revered products.

Drambuie

Drambuie owes its origins to a royal debt. Disguised as a serving maid, Bonnie Prince Charlie, head of the Stuarts, fled to Skye towards the end of the 1745 rebellion after suffering a crushing defeat at the hands of the English. Mackinnon of Straithard, ancestor of today's chairman and managing director of the Drambuie Liqueur Company, sheltered the exhausted Prince and, at the end of the Jacobite Rebellion, engineered his escape from the English.

Charles Edward Louis John Sylvester Maria Casimir Stuart, before leading his faithful followers into battle, had travelled the courts of Europe, where he had achieved fluency in four languages and a considerable knowledge of food and wines.

It is said that Drambuie was the Prince's favourite drink and in grateful recognition that he owed his life to Mackinnon of Straithard presented him with the recipe.

Drambuie uses the very best quality Scotch malt whiskies which may vary in age from 8 to 21 years. For over 150 years the recipe was handed from father to eldest son, small quantities being made for members of the Mackinnon clan. It was not until the beginning of this century that Malcolm Mackinnon decided to experiment with the treasured recipe on a commercial basis. In the first year of production, 1906, only 12 cases were sold in Edinburgh. Edwardian conservatism gradually weakened, however, and in 1916 the cellarman of the House of Lords gave it the seal of his personal approbation. By the end of World War I every British officers' mess and wardroom had its stock of Drambuie, and in the United States, sales soared once the era of Prohibition ended.

The Drambuie Liqueur Company now exports 90 percent of its production to 157 countries, the United States being the largest consumer. The company employs about 200 people, but the recipe remains a secret known only to Norman Mackinnon and his wife. The only written copy is lodged with an Edinburgh bank. On his death in 1945 Malcolm Mackinnon passed on the secrets of the Drambuie essence to his son, Norman, the present chairman, who in accordance with tradition will eventually pass it on to his eldest son.

Different ways of drinking Drambuie and recipes for its use in cooking abound, but the purists recommend that it is drunk on its own after dinner. It can be drunk at any time, as an aperitif for example, and like whisky can be drunk over ice. A Rusty Nail is said to be excellent: a good measure of Drambuie is mixed in equal proportions with a good Scotch whisky, stirred gently and served in a chilled glass.

Recipes include the addition of Drambuie to meat or fish as a substitute for vinegar in hors d'oeuvres such as avocados, in strawberry sponge cakes, and in pancakes, trifle, flans and soufflés.

Cheese

Scotland has a long tradition of cheesemaking, and although farm cheesemaking has virtually died out, there are still a number of creameries in the north. Edinburgh sells the full variety of Scottish cheeses and you should not miss the opportunity of sampling them. The quality is assured by the richness and fertility of the soil which provides lush pastures for the cattle.

Caboc has been made in the highlands since the fifteenth century and is made purely from cream, shaped like a thick sausage and rolled in coarse oatmeal. As it is comparatively bland, it is best accompanied by oatcakes or cheese biscuits and sprinkled with freshly milled black pepper.

Crowdie is a soft cottage cheese which is best when

Worth the little extra for the extra we put in.

BAXTERS OF SPEYSIDE, FOCHABERS, SCOTLAND.

made with fresh milk. It is regarded as the traditional cheese of the highlands.

Dunlop is one of Scotland's traditional cheeses, having been made first towards the end of the seventeenth century. Not unlike Cheddar, it is somewhat softer and more mellow.

Hramsa cheese is a soft cheese made with cream and flavoured with garlic. It is specially recommended for spreads, dips and canapés.

Orkney cheese is fairly similar to Dunlop and it can be white or red and is sometimes available smoked. Orkney was originally a farmhouse cheese produced in the Orkney Islands.

Stewart cheeses are made in two varieties: the white Stewart is something of an acquired taste owing to its saltiness, but the blue is mild and certainly worth trying.

Other cheeses to look out for include *Gaelic*, a full fat soft cheese with chopped leaves of fresh garlic coated in flaked oats, almonds and hazelnuts, *Campbeltown*, *Galloway*, *Gigha*, *Lockerbie* and, not least, *Scottish Cheddar*.

The Choosa Cheese chain which has several branches in Edinburgh affords the best opportunity of buying a wide selection of cheeses.

Glayva

*G*layva means 'very good' and this was the name Ronald Morrison and his partner, George Petrie, a chemist, thought the most apt christening for the liqueur they first produced in Leith, the port town of Edinburgh, in the 1940s.

Glayva is made from malts and grain whiskies which are blended by Ronald Morrison and Co. Ltd. Herbal oils, heather honey, sugar and, finally, colouring are added to the blend.

Only three people know the exact recipe for the herbal oils, and these are Ronald Morrison's· two sons, Michael and Gordon, and the blender. In accordance with the mystique of the drink trade, they are not prepared to divulge the formula.

Ronald Morrison's family were in the whisky business and he subsequently spent several years in Spain, learning the sherry trade. Before his death, Ronald Morrison passed on the secrets of the recipe to his two sons.

Michael Morrison mixes the essence and it is then passed to the blender, who has performed the task since the 1950s. From dissolving vats, the ingredients are pumped into compounding vats and are then filtered and bottled.

The company says that it is, of course, a matter of personal taste which of the Scottish liqueurs one elects to drink. They believe that Glayva is less sweet than Drambuie, for example, and thicker.

Ronald Morrison's company produces 100,000 cases each year, with about 75 to 80 percent being exported. Of the 70 countries importing, the largest consumers are those where Scots have settled – Canada, Australia and New Zealand.

Glayva is said to mix well in cocktails, particularly with soft drinks such as orange, lemon and lime, and is frequently used in cooking.

Haggis

*H*aggis is probably the most traditional and certainly the best known of all Scottish dishes. It is sometimes maligned by the foreigner, but its undistinguished ingredients amount to a flavoursome, nutritious and satisfying delicacy.

The word haggis derives

from the French *hachis,*to chop. Haggis in different forms has been known since the early Greek and Roman civilizations. Its origins in Scotland are referred to by the French who knew it as *le pain bénit d'Ecosse* in the days of the Auld Alliance, the first formal treaty of which was made in 1295 and which was renewed a number of times until the end of the fifteenth century.

Haggis has ever since been consumed in large and regular quantities both by local Scotsmen and Scots abroad. It is significant that Charles Macsween's, established in 1953, sell haggis for consumption abroad. Such is the fame of haggis that it has been immortalized many times in literature, approved of by Queen Victoria and paid tribute to by Robert Burns, Scotland's revered poet, in his eight-verse ode *To a Haggis:*

... O what a glorious sight,
warm-reekin, rich!

Haggis comprises essentially the sheep's 'pluck', the windpipe, lung, heart and liver. The windpipe is removed and the rest is boiled for three hours with beef fat. The fat is then skimmed off and the liver, heart and lungs minced. Oatmeal, onion, seasoning (usually pepper, salt and spices) and gravy from the boiling are then mixed into the mince.

The basic recipe has never changed, although the casing has. A number of different cases are used today and these even include plastic. Since the casing is not eaten some people maintain it is of no significance but most Scotsmen prefer their national dish properly prepared in the traditional way.

The correct casing, if only a matter of aesthetics, is the sheep's paunch, or stomach which is filled with the mixture and then blanket-stitched with

Traditional fare — haggis with battered neeps and tatties.

cotton thread. A sheep's stomach will take anything from 10 to 20 pounds (4.9 kg) of the prepared mixture and, when it is boiled, shrinks to fit. Smaller haggises are encased in a length of caecum, known as a bung, from the ox or sheep. The caecum, part of the large intestine, is about three to four feet (1-1.3 m) long in an ox and it is therefore cut to size and fastened with string or clips.

When the sheep's stomach or bung has been filled it is replaced in the boiler for a short time. It is then simmered wrapped in foil, at home, for one to one-and-a-half hours and served steaming hot with mashed potatoes and turnips, or swedes as they are called in England. 'Bashed neeps and champit tatties' are the only acceptable accompaniment to be served with haggis, according to the traditionalists.

The haggis is served as hot as possible, slit lengthways and the mixture scooped out. Care has to be taken when splitting open the haggis or it may well rain its contents over you!

There is virtually no limit to the variations in size of the haggis. Three to four people will require about one to one-and-a-half pounds (0.4-0.6 kg) but miniatures are available.

Natural Scottish thriftiness and perhaps an element of barbarism is well demonstrated by the success and long history of the haggis. Use of ingredients which alone would not be particularly desirable ensures that very little of the animal is wasted. Plenty of Scotsmen eat haggis once a week, it is served for school lunches and, more prestigiously, features on Taste of Scotland menus. These menus are organized by the Scottish Tourist Board and include other Scottish specialities such as smoked salmon, venison and whisky mousse. Some hotels serve miniature haggis or just a slice of it as an hors d'oeuvre.

John Macsween, son of the founder, supplies not only the people of Edinburgh but the English, who he says are large consumers of haggis, and the Americans. (You should check with Customs beforehand if you wish to take haggis out of Britain for regulations relating to meat import into other countries.)

Macsween's sell haggis all the year round up to the three or four pound (1.3 or 1.8 kg) size and, on receipt of an order the day before, will supply any of the larger sizes. They produce about ten tons (18,000 kg) of haggis each year. The com-

pany also sell haggis boxed in tartan presentation packs, which show Edinburgh Castle, Burns' poem *To a Haggis* and serving instructions.

Demand fluctuates according to the time of year, since haggis is traditionally a winter dish, but it is January when consumption is at its highest. Burns Night, Robert Burns' anniversary, is on January 25 and this is marked by banquets and dinners where it is customary to serve haggis and to drink a glass of neat whisky with it. The haggis is piped in by a highlander in full regalia, and the haggis is slit with a dirk (the dagger worn with highland dress). Apart from Burns Night, other festivals and occasions where haggis is *de rigueur* include Hogmanay on December 31, St. Andrew's Day on November 30 and every meeting of Masonic lodges.

Kippers

*K*ippers were once regarded as food just for the masses, but the tasty smoked herring have long graced the tables of rich and poor alike. Few foods can beat that special breakfast flavour, a fact recognized by the perceptive French who have made a habit of importing kippers from Scotland to add to their own distinctive cuisine. One important tip – don't boil them in water as so many English people do. Let them cook gently in the oil that emerges when they are heated.

Until 1977 the kipper bought in Edinburgh would be the result of smoking home-caught herring, which has always been considered superior both in size and texture. Since then, only very limited quantities of fresh herring have been available from the Clyde fishery and Edinburgh's remaining two kipper producers have had to rely upon importing frozen herrings from Ireland, Iceland and Canada for fear of decimating Britain's stock.

It has been recorded that herring was smoked in England in 1349, but it was not until the 1890s that Eyemouth on the east coast became a principal centre of Scotland's herring industry. Other important centres included the Clyde in the South Minch, Mallaig and Ullapool in the Minch, Peterhead, Fraserburgh, Aberdeen and North Shields.

were available, the fish had to be passed on racks by one man to another perched high up in the kiln who would hang each one up on hooks. The smoking process took eight hours and kilns varied in capability from 140 pounds (63.5 kg) of herrings to 14,000 pounds (6350 kg). Today's Torry kiln, developed by the Torry Research Station at Aberdeen, takes 1680 pounds (76.2 kg) (420 pounds on each rack) and can perform three cycles a day.

Croans sell all their produce within the United Kingdom, half

salmon has been netted or rod-caught, rather than farmed, the fins will be properly formed and the flesh will be firm to the touch. The flesh will also be coarser grained than the farmed fish with a richer colour and flavour.

Salmon are netted from the sea around the northwest of Scotland, the Moray Firth areas of the northeast or from the east coast rivers, the Tay and the Tweed. The sale of netted fish is permitted from the last week in January until September 15 or until late October for rod-

Kippers and shellfish are a speciality of Brown's in Elm Row.

Campbell's shop smoke your own salmon.

Robert Croan & Sons Ltd, one of the last two companies producing kippers in Edinburgh, started business in 1882 in the Holyrood district and still smoke herrings in the traditional way.

The fish are split and rubbed with salt. When they have been brined, they are placed on racks in a kiln and smoked over a mixture of oak chips and sawdust at 85°F (29.4°C) for about four to five hours. The temperature has to be strictly maintained because if it is too high the fish will be cooked and if too low the 'kippers' will be wet and soggy. After removal from the kiln, the kippers are left to cool and then boxed.

Before modern electric kilns

going to England and the remainder being sold in Scotland. The company believe that Loch Fyne kippers are the very best, since the fish come from inland lochs where there is a mixture of fresh water and salt which seems to produce a particularly succulent, tasty herring.

Salmon

Scotland's smoked salmon is world famous. Although the process of smoking has been sophisticated by chefs from London and Paris, the taste of the product remains unique and distinctive.

Either fresh or smoked, if the

caught fish. The quality of the fish deteriorates at about the end of August, with the body becoming thinner and the head larger.

Farmed fish is heavy bellied with unformed fins, and the flesh will be fine-grained with an oily texture and bland flavour.

Salmon is still smoked by the traditional cold-kiln method, whereby the fish are placed in the kiln at a low temperature for three consecutive six-hour periods. First, however, the head and tail are removed, the fish is gutted and the backbone removed. The body is split into two and placed in pickle for 12 to 24 hours, depending on its size. The average size for salmon is 8 pounds (3.6 kg) but they may be as large as 35 pounds (16.3 kg).

The pickle varies according to local taste but the traditional Scottish recipe requires demerera sugar and salt and pepper. The mixture is smoothed over the two sides of the fish and within one hour they are quite wet, the sugar and salt drawing the liquid. The salmon is left in the mixture overnight and the surplus is then washed off. The fish is removed to the smokehouse to drain and dry so that no surplus moisture remains before it is placed in the kiln. The fire is lit and another lit once it has gone out. The fish is smoked over three consecutive fires, each for a period of six hours at a very low temperature.

The salmon is left to 'set' after removal from the kiln and, once cool, is sliced by hand. After an initial period of about two months, a fishmonger can slice a 12 pound (5.4 kg) salmon into fine slices in ten minutes; a 12-pounder (5.4 kg) will yield about 5¾ pounds (2.6 kg) of smoked salmon.

Of the many fishmongers in Edinburgh where smoked salmon is available, Campbell's of Stafford Street and Dickson of West Harbour Road, Port Seton, will smoke your own fresh salmon for you.

Porridge & Oatcakes

*O*atmeal, from which both porridge and oatcakes are made, has been a food staple for many hundreds of years. The grain was processed in local mills and dried out in a kiln. The old-fashioned mills provided a variation in the flavour of the meal, which is still appreciated by Scots today. It seems to be a matter of personal taste, however, whether fine, medium or coarse oatmeal is used. Today's processes of mass milling and mechanical drying are said to detract from the flavour of the meal and to reduce the nutritional qualities.

Oatmeal should be closely packed and kept airtight. It was traditionally stored in an oak chest in a dry place. If it is well packed, it may keep for over a year, and it is said to improve in sweetness and digestibility.

Of the many Scottish dishes requiring oatmeal, the best known is probably a fresh herring dusted in coarse oatmeal and served with a piquant mustard sauce and, of course, porridge and oatcakes. The list includes an endless variety of crowdies and sowans, which are somewhat similar to porridge, white (or mealie) puddings and black puddings.

Porridge
Sir Walter Scott (1771-1832) wrote to his son-in-law J. G. Lockhart: 'What meal does Johnnie want for his porridge? I will send it up from Abbotsford. I think it will agree with him better than the southern food of horses.' Scott evidently believed passionately not only in the orgin of the oatmeal but in the importance of local mills.

The sole ingredients of porridge are oatmeal, salt and water. The traditional bowl was made of a local hardwood such as birch. Horn spoons were used, and it was the custom to eat the preparation standing up. General Sir Ian Hamilton in *When I Was a Boy* wrote that 'the small nursery critics formed their most private opinions of guests a great deal on the porridge ceremonial. The worst and most deplorable giveaway was when the lady or gentleman took sugar.'

Each person should be allowed one cup of water, a handful (about 1¼ ounces/35 g) of oatmeal and a good pinch of salt. The oatmeal is added to boiling water in a steady rain from one hand, stirring briskly with the other. When the mixture is boiling, it should be taken off the heat, the lid put on and then allowed to simmer for 20 to 30 minutes. The salt is added after about ten minutes. The porridge is served very hot with cream, milk or buttermilk.

Oatcakes
In the days when oatcakes were served with every meal, each community traditionally had its own mill, grinding oats from the surrounding crofts to supply oatmeal.

Jean Froissart (1337-1404), French chronicler and poet, wrote that the Scottish soldier's equipment included a flat plate at his saddle and a wallet of meal at his back. When he had tired of meat, Froissart reported, the soldier would moisten some meal in water and lay it on the heated plate, and 'hence it is no marvel that the Scots should be able to make longer marches'.

Oatcakes are now eaten as an accompaniment to herrings, sardines, cheeses or with marmalade, honey or jams. The original oatcake was made of oatmeal and water, but it is now customary to add fat or dripping, baking soda and salt as well. Time and patience are required to make the authentic oatcake, but there are a good variety of manufactured oatcakes to choose from.

Shortbread

*S*hortbread owes its origins to Yule-bread, a thin bannock (circle) of oatmeal baked during Christmas and Hogmanay, and divided into farls (quarters). The ancient Yule-bannock, from the early days of sun worship, was notched, by pinching with finger and thumb around the edge, to symbolize the sun's rays just as shortbread is today.

The increasing popularity of white flour eventually ousted the ancient Yule-bannock and led to the development of the familiar rich, crisp shortbread of today.

Shortbread is eaten throughout the year now but it is still

Sun symbols in a range of shortbread.

associated particularly with Christmas and Hogmanay. It is traditionally offered to the 'first-footers' – those who call upon house after house in the early hours of New Year's Day.

You can choose from the several makes of shortbread on the market when you are in Edinburgh or make your own, since it is a quick and easy recipe. Cream four ounces (113 g) of butter and two ounces (57 g) of caster sugar together and then add a mixture of four ounces (113 g) of plain flour and two ounces (57 g) of rice flour, sieved. The resulting dough is pressed out by hand and laid on two ungreased sandwich tins. The rounds are cut into quarters or eighths with a knife, notched around the edges, pricked lightly all over and then baked at gas mark 4 (350°F/175°C) for 30 minutes.

Edinburgh Rock

dinburgh rock, one of the cheapest sweets on the market, is said to owe its origins to Alex Ferguson who travelled from Doune in Perthshire to Stirling in 1822 where he tossed a coin to decide whether to set up in Edinburgh or Glasgow. Ferguson started his business in the Bow, a steep twisting street between the Grassmarket and the Lawnmarket beneath Edinburgh Castle.

Sugar, water and colouring is boiled in pans at a temperature of over 300°F (131°C), flavour is added in some cases, and the mixture is then poured onto a metal slab and partially cooled with a fan. It is then folded over, moved to a stone slab (ideally Caithness flagstone, according to Ferguson's in 1981), cooled, folded and pulled out.

The pulling-out process is basically one of extrusion whereby the huge, unmanageable, sticky mass is spun on a device of moving arms to inject it with air. The unwieldly skeins are then laid over six horizontal rotating rollers where the mass cools further and changes shape from plump oblong to tubular. The 'tube' is then passed through a half-inch (12.7 mm) space on to a slab where it is rolled by hand. A wooden measure marks off where each cut should be made, the cuts being made by tapping gently with the open blades of a pair of scissors. If it were actually cut through, it would splinter.

Ferguson's export about 5 per cent of their Original Edinburgh Rock, particularly to the United States, Canada and Australia. Flavours included in each of their presentation packs are the traditional ginger, vanilla, lemon, raspberry and orange.

While Ferguson's have the monopoly on the name 'Original Edinburgh Rock', another long-established company, Ross, have claim to 'Edinburgh Castle Rock'. Ross's was established towards the end of the nineteenth century and now produce the standard flavours of cherry, strawberry, orange, vanilla, ginger and lemon in their boxed packs.

Ross's explain that the difference between Edinburgh rock and letter rock (associated with Blackpool and Brighton) rests with the fact that Edinburgh rock is practically 100 percent sugar whereas letter rock is a mixture of sugar and glucose. In both appearance and taste it is completely different from the conventional variety.

Edinburgh rock is normally marketed in packs of five or six

A traditional Scottish sweet that is tasty and inexpensive.

different flavours in a presentation pack and in 1981 each stick was retailing at about sixpence, a comparatively low price for any sweet.

Useful Information

Baby-sitter

Bruntsfield Helping Hands Agency

*45 Barclay Place
Bruntsfield Place
Phone: (031) 228 1382*

Open: Monday to Friday, 09.00-17.30
Baby-sitters, nurses, help with the old, there is a 24-hour answering service for emergency nursing help

Head Post Office

2 Waterloo Place

Bureau de Change open:
Monday to Friday 08.30-18.00,
Saturday 08.30-12.30

Tourist Information Office and Accommodations Service

*Waverley Market
Bureau de Change*

Hours: October to April:
Monday to Friday, 09.00-18.00;
Saturday, 09.00-13.00; closed on Sunday
May/June/September: Monday to Saturday, 08.30-20.00; Sunday, 11.00-20.00
July/August open until 21.00 hours daily
Bureau de Change closes ½ hour earlier and at 3p.m. on Sundays

Tourist Accommodation Service
Phone: (031) 557 1700

Tourist Information Service
Phone: (031) 557 2727

GUIDES

A list of approved guides can be obtained from:

The Tourist Information Office

*Phone: (031) 557 2727
or*

The Scottish Tourist Guides Association

*9 Jordan Lane
Phone: (031) 4477190,
overseas and general enquiries
(031) 661 6038 UK enquiries and bookings*

Health

Medical Emergencies
In an emergency – find the nearest telephone, dial 999 (no money is required) and ask for an ambulance
In the event of an accident or acute illness go directly to the nearest hospital with a Casualty Department. The following hospitals have 24-hour casualty services.

The Royal Infirmary of Edinburgh

*Lauriston Place
Phone: (031) 229 2477*

Casualty – first gate East Drive

Western General Hospital

*Crewe Road South
Phone: (031) 332 2525*

In the middle of Crewe Road – for casualty follow the arrows

The following has a casualty service Monday to Friday 09.00-17.30

Leith Hospital

*Mill Lane
Leith
Phone: (031) 554 4433*

Casualty – in main door, turn right

All patients receive emergency treatment free of charge

Visiting a Doctor
For less serious problems make an appointment to see a doctor at his surgery. Local police stations have lists of doctors and Health Centres, information can also be obtained from:
The Health Board
'Primary Care Section'
Phone: (031) 225 1341
In addition, most hotels will have addresses of doctors.

Lost Property

If you lose a personal possession while in Edinburgh, try ringing one of the city's Lost Property Offices – who may well be able to help.

Police Lost Property Office

*Fettes Avenue
Phone: (031) 311 3131*

Open: Monday to Friday, 09.00-17.00

Railway Lost Property

*Waverley Station
Phone: (031) 556 2477*

Open: Monday to Sunday, 08.30-13.00, 14.00-17.00

Lothian Regional Transport Lost Property (Buses)

*14 Queen Street
Phone: (031) 554 4494*

Open: Monday to Friday, 09.00-17.00

Scottish Omnibuses Lost Property (Eastern Scottish Buses)

*Bus Station
St. Andrew Square
Phone: (031) 556 8126*

Open: Monday to Friday, 08.30-12.30, 13.30-17.30

Police

In an emergency – find the nearest telephone, dial 999 (no money is required) and ask for the police

In Scotland, policemen wear black uniforms and flat black caps with a black and white chequered-band around the brim. They are based at the following principal Police Stations

Lothian & Borders Police Headquarters

(opposite Inverleith Park)
Fettes Avenue
Phone: (031) 311 3131

South Edinburgh

South Side Police Station
98 Causewayside
Phone: (031) 667 3361

North Edinburgh

Gayfield Square Police Station
near top of Leith Walk
Gayfield Square
Phone: (031) 556 9270

West Edinburgh

West End Police Station
near Haymarket
Torphichen Place
Phone: (031) 229 2323

East Edinburgh

31 Queen Charlotte Street
Phone: (031) 554 9350

The police have the power to tow away a car if a serious parking offence has been committed. It can be retrieved after payment of a maximum fine of £22.00, phone: (031) 311 3131 and ask for 'Traffic Link'.

Post Offices

Head Post Office

2 Waterloo Place
Phone: (031) 550 8232

Edinburgh's main post office with Bureau de Change, Passport Service, Philatelic Sales Service for stamp collectors, and a 24-hour service area – telephones, British telephone directories stamp machines and lists of postal collection times.

Open: Monday to Friday, 09.00-17.30;
Saturday, 09.00-12.30.

Branch Offices
Branch Post Offices can be found throughout the city. Most have passport and foreign currency services. Normal opening times are 09.00-17.30, although some close for lunch between 12.30 and 13.30

Useful Addresses

Edinburgh Book Festival

First two weeks of International Festival

Opening House 10.00-18.30 every day

For information: 25A South West Thistle Street Lane, Edinburgh EH2 1EW
Phone: (031) 225 1915

Edinburgh Film Festival

The Filmhouse
88 Lothian Road
Phone: (031) 228 6382

Edinburgh Festival Society

21 Market Street
Phone: (031) 226 4001

Most of Year Open Monday to Friday, 08.45-17.00
From 1 August same plus:
Saturday, 10.00-12.00
During festival open Monday to Saturday, 8.45-18.00; Sunday, 10.00-17.00

Information and booking

Edinburgh Fringe Festival Society

170 High Street
Phone: (031) 226 5257/5259

Most of year open Monday to Friday, 10.00-18.00
From July same plus Saturday, 10.00-18.00
During Festival Monday to Sunday, 10.00-19.00

Programme available from late June each year. To obtain by post, send 2 first class stamps (programme quite bulky)

Edinburgh Military Tattoo Office

1 Cockburn Street
Phone: (031) 225 1188

Open: Monday to Friday 10.00-16.30 in summer. Monday to Thursday, 10.00-21.00; Friday and Saturday, 10.00-22.30 during the Tattoo

Parliament Hall and Buildings

High Street

Overlooking West Parliament Square are Lothian Regional Chambers, which are adjoined by the Signet Library built slightly earlier in 1810-12. Near the statue of the 5th Duke of Buccleuch are some heart shaped cobbles which mark the site of the Old Tolbooth, featured in Scott's novel – "The Heart of Midlothian". Parliament Hall, Sheriff Court and City Chambers all stand close by.

Opening Times: Tuesdays to Fridays, 10.00-16.00
Closed on Public Holidays

Royal Highland Show

Royal Highland Show Ground
Ingliston (7 miles/11 km from city centre on main road to Glasgow)

Phone: (031) 333 2444
Agricultural Show takes place in June each year

Scottish Experience

2 Rutland Place
Phone (031) 228 2828

Open Monday to Saturday,
10.00-19.00, Sunday, 14.00-18.00
Visitors centre – including Craft
Shop, information service, 15
minute audio-visual show,
40-foot (12m) illuminated relief
map of Scotland.

Speaking Clock

Dial 123

St. Giles Cathedral

High Street

Present church is the third on
the site. First church of the 9th
century was replaced in 1126
but this was burnt down by the
English in 1385, after which the
present Cathedral was built.
The building has been changed
much over the centuries,
particularly at the time of the
Reformation.
John Knox became its minister
in 1560. As St. Giles became
Edinburgh's main church it
became a meeting place for
Parliament and the General
Assembly.
The original cruciform shape
was lost due to many alterations.
Many aisles and chapels added,
for instance the Thistle Chapel,
designed in 1911 by Robert
Lorimer in Gothic Style for the
most Noble Order of the Thistle
founded in 1687 by James VII.
Opening Times: April–
September: Monday to Saturday,
09.00-19.00; Sunday, 07.30-21.00
October–March: Monday to
Saturday, 09.00-17.00; Sunday,
07.30-21.00
Phone: (031) 225 4363

Section II –
Art galleries,
Museums, Stately
Homes and Town
Houses

**This section of the
directory gives details of
various places of interest
in Edinburgh and the
surrounding area. The
lists are not intended to be
complete, but to point out
the major sights.**

Art Galleries

City Art Centre

1–4 Market Street
Phone: (031) 225 2424

The City Art Centre presents
changing displays of works
from the city collection. This
includes Scottish paintings
dating from the mid-19th
century, as well as prints,
drawings and sculpture. It also
provides facilities for films and
lectures and holds a limited
number of selling exhibitions.

Open: June to September:
Monday to Saturday, 10.00-18.00;
October to May, Monday to
Saturday, 10.00-17.00
During the Festival: Sunday,
14.00-17.00

The Fine Art Society

12 Great King Street
Phone: (031) 556 0305

The Edinburgh branch of the
Fine Art Society (established in
London in 1876) was opened
here in 1973. The original
character of this New Town
house, built around 1815, is
preserved by the well-
appointed furniture and
decoration. There is a regular
exhibition programme of works
by both international and
Scottish artists, though the main
emphasis is on the latter.

Open: Monday to Friday, 10.00-
18.00, Saturday, 10.00-13.00

The Fruit Market Gallery

29 Market Street
Phone: (031) 225 2383

A large gallery with a varied
exhibition programme,
including both Scottish and
international artists. The gallery
also stages exhibitions which
have been proposed to the
Scottish Arts Council by
members of the public.

Open: Monday to Saturday,
10.00-17.30

The Malcolm Innes Gallery

67 George Street
Phone: (031) 226 4151

This gallery specializes in 19th-
and 20th-century Scottish
sporting and natural history
paintings. It also represents the
interest of 13 living Scottish
artists, including Elisabeth
Cameron, Brian Rawling and
Louise Wood.

Open: Monday to Friday, 09.30-
18.00
During exhibitions open
Saturdays

National Gallery of Modern Art

Belford Road
Phone: (031) 556 8921

The national collection of 20th-
century art has been housed
here since 1984. Most of the
major modern artists like
Picasso, Hepworth, Matisse and
Moore are represented in this
exhibition of painting, sculpture
and graphic art. There is a
programme of changing
exhibitions and a very good
collection of modern Scottish
artists. There are also some
sculptures in the garden. (For
further details see the Art
Galleries article in the main
body of this book.)

Open: Monday to Saturday
10.00-17.00; Sunday, 14.00-17.00

The National Gallery of Scotland

2 The Mound
Phone: (031) 556 8921

This is one of the best of the
smaller galleries in Europe.
Opened in 1859, it houses a fine
collection of works by
Continental and English
masters from the 14th century to
Cezanne. The National Gallery
also features a section devoted
to Scottish artists. (For further
details, see the Art Galleries
article in the main body of this
book.)

Open: Monday to Saturday,
10.00-17.00; Sunday, 14.00-17.00

National Portrait Gallery

2 Queen Street
Phone: (031) 556 8921

In the same building as the
National Museum of Antiquities,
the gallery was opened in 1882
to 'illustrate Scottish history by

likenesses of the chief actors in it'. The Scottish characters portrayed date from the mid-16th century to the present day in all media including 29 calotypes by the pioneering photographers David Octavius Hill and Robert Adamson. There is an annual exhibition which illustrates a different aspect of Scottish social or art history.

Open: Monday to Saturday, 10.00-17.00; Sunday, 14.00-17.00

During the Festival: open until 18.00, and from 11.00 on Sundays

Netherbow Arts Centre

High Street
Phone: (031) 556 9579

The Netherbow is the Arts and Communication Centre for the Church of Scotland. There are 12 exhibitions a year in each gallery – a small number of paintings on display in the restaurant, and craftwork, paintings, sculpture, weaving, macrame and photography in the Solstice. Centre policy tends towards exhibiting works by lesser-known living Scottish artists.

Open: Monday to Saturday, 10.00-16.00, plus evening theatre performances
During the Festival: late opening 18.30-22.30

The Printmakers Workshop

23 Union Street
Phone: (031) 557 2479

The only gallery with continuous exhibitions of contemporary original prints. The work of modern Scottish printmakers is shown alongside those of printmakers from around the world. Prints from the workshop are also on sale.

Open: Gallery, Monday to Saturday, 10.00-17.30; Studio, Monday to Thursday, 10.00-21.00; Friday and Saturday, 10.00-18.00; Sunday, 14.00-17.00

The Royal Scottish Academy

The Mound
Phone: (031) 225 6671

From March to July the galleries of the Academy house the Academy's own Annual Exhibition for which 500 works are selected from those submitted by members and non-members of the Academy. During the Festival exhibitions of well-known foreign artists are held. The Academy also presents its Diploma collection once a year, which includes the diploma works of aspirant members of the Academy. During the rest of the year they show the work of three societies of practising Scottish artists the Royal Society of Scottish painters and watercolourists in January and February, the Society of Scottish Artists in October and November, and the Society of Women Artists in November and December. An annual student's competition is organized during February and March and the work of the successful students can be seen on display.

Open: Monday to Saturday, 10.00-21.00 during Annual Exhibitions; Sunday, 14.00-17.00. For other exhibitions check local press.

Stills

The Scottish Photography Group Gallery
105 High Street
Phone: (031) 557 1140

This gallery holds between eight and ten exhibitions by national and international photographers every year. Their exhibitions in the past have ranged from the work of Bill Brandt to examples of the photographer as printmaker.

Open: Tuesday to Saturday, 12.30-18.00
During the Festival: Tuesday to Sunday, 10.00-18.00

Talbot Rice Art Centre

Old College
South Bridge
Phone: (031) 667 1011 ext. 4308

The Centre has two main exhibition spaces; one houses the university's permanent collection, the other being given over to temporary exhibitions of which there are approximately ten a year. The permanent collection includes examples of 17th-century Dutch painting

(Meindert Hobbema, Jan Both and Hercules Seghers), and a number of 16th- and 17th-century bronzes. The major exhibitions are based on an interesting three-point policy of promoting Scottish artists in one-man shows, housing major touring exhibitions from abroad, and presenting historical exhibitions (again with a Scottish emphasis).

Open: Monday to Saturday, 10.00-17.00

Museums

The ancient City of Edinburgh is rich in historical and especially literary associations. The following is a selection of museums which should cater for most tastes, from the fire-engine fanatic to the bibliophile. Opening times tend to change according to the season, so telephone before making your visit.

Agricultural Museum

Showroom Ground
Ingliston
Phone: (031) 333 2674

A branch of the National Museum of Antiquities of Scotland which holds an annual exhibition on an agrarian theme.

Open: 10.00-17.00 during Royal Highland Show in June
Other times by appointment for special parties

Braidwood and Rushbrook Fire Museum

McDonald Road Fire Station
Phone: (031) 229 7222 ext. 53

This museum contains fire-fighting equipment and fire engines ancient and modern, from hand pump to high speed apparatus. There is also a collection of curious artefacts such as a German fireman's helmet which glows in the dark.

Open: Appointments only

Canongate Tolbooth

Phone: (031) 225 1131

The Canongate Tolbooth, built in 1591, was a burgh court house and prison for 300 years. Today it serves as a museum with a collection of Highland dress and tartan. Downstairs is a brass-rubbing centre containing a brass commemorating Robert the Bruce.

Open: June to September: Monday to Saturday, 10.00-18.00; October to May: Monday to Saturday, 10.00-17.00 During the Festival: Sunday, 14.00-17.00

Museum of Childhood

38 High Street
Phone: (031) 225 6961

A storehouse of memories of childhood – games, dolls, Hornby trains, clockwork mice, costumes and books. A treat for children and a nostalgic experience for their parents. The most spectacular exhibit is the doll's house *circa* 1897, with its running water, electric lighting, full complement of tiny furniture and even a minute orange tree in the guest room. There is also a range of educational toys on display.

Open: June to September: Monday to Saturday, 10.00-18.00; October to May: Monday to Saturday, 10.00-16.00 During the Festival: Sunday, 14.00-17.00

Museum of Flight

East Fortune Airfield
North Berwick
Phone: (062) 088 308

Twenty miles (32 km) east of the city, the Royal Scottish Museum's collection of aircraft includes aero-engines and rockets.

For details of special excursions and open days, phone: (031) 225 7534

Open: July and August: Monday to Sunday, 10.00-16.00

Museum of Lighting

59 St Stephen Street
Phone: (031) 556 4503

Part of a lighting emporium is dedicated to the exhibition of the proprietor's collection of early domestic, transport and marine lamps from the past.

Open: Saturday, 10.00-18.00

National Library of Scotland

George IV Bridge
Phone: (031) 226 4531

This was formerly the Advocates Library, founded in the late 17th century. It obtained the right of copyright deposit in 1710, and as a consequence obtained the best works of continental scholarship. In 1925 the Faculty of Advocate's presented their library to the nation. The library has about 4½ million printed items, and its collection of Scottish books and manuscripts is unrivalled. There is a map collection, a music collection dating from the early 19th century, the Haxton collection of Bibles, and material relating to the Celtic language, ships and shipping and labour history as well.

Reading rooms: Monday to Friday, 09.30-20.30; Open: Saturday, 09.30-13.00 Exhibition room: Monday to Friday, 09.30-17.00; Sunday, 14.00-17.00

National Museum of Antiquities of Scotland

Queen Street
Phone: (031) 556 8921

This museum has collections which show the history of Scotland from earliest times to the present day. There are relics from the Stone Age, Roman times and the Viking invasions. There is also a fine collection of Scottish weapons and tartans. (For further details see the Museum's article in the main body of this book.)

Open Monday to Saturday, 10.00-17.00; Sunday, 14.00-17.00

New Town Conservation Centre

13a Dundas Street
Phone: (031) 556 7054

The centre holds a permanent display of the conservation work in progress on the Georgian New Town. There is a conservation reference library and usually an exhibition on some aspect of architecture. Walks and guided tours are also organized from here.

Open: Monday to Friday, 09.00-13.00, 14.00-17.00

Reid Hall

Teviot Row, off Teviot Place
Faculty of Music
Edinburgh University
Phone: (031) 667 1011 ext. 2573

The Edinburgh University Collection of historic musical instruments is housed in glass cases in an ante-room off the Reid concert hall. Instruments include serpents, crumhorns, sackbuts, early recorders and tambours.

Open: Only during the Festival: 14 00-17.00 and in intervals of concerts on Thursday evenings during term

Museum of the Royal College of Surgeons of Edinburgh

18 Nicholson Street
Phone: (031) 556 6206

A specialist museum with exhibits of surgical, dental, pathological and historical material. Open: Appointments only

The Royal Scottish Museum

Chambers Street
Phone: (031) 225 7534

Scotland's national museum is housed in an imposing mid-Victorian building and displays range from primitive art to space material. There are also mammal and bird collections but the main emphasis is on science and technology. There is a programme of talks, lectures and films throughout the year. (For further details see the Museums article in the main body of this book.)

Open: Monday to Saturday, 10.00-17.00; Sunday, 14.00-17.00

St. Cecilia's Hall

Cowgate
Phone: (031) 667 1011 ext. 4415

The University's Russell collection of harpsichords and clavichords is on display in this elegant Georgian hall built by Robert Milne in 1762 as the concert hall for the Edinburgh Music Society. There are 36 keyboard instruments including virginals, regals and spinets. The room also contains period tapestries and textiles, and paintings by Giovanni Pannini and Jacob van Ruysdael.

Open: Saturday, 14.00-17.00
During the Festival. Monday to Saturday, 10.00-12.30

St. Cuthbert's Co-operative Association Ltd Transport Collection

Grove Street
Phone: (031) 229 2424 ext. 363

One of the last commercial firms to use horse-drawn transport for milk deliveries. At their stables they have a wonderful collection of coaches of every description, hearses, gigs, carts as well as harness and livery. They are responsible for the refurbishment of the state carriages which are used in royal cavalcades.

Open: Appointments only

The Scottish Experience

St. Thomas Church
Shandwick Place
Phone: (031) 228 2828

This comprises two multi-media presentations. 'Spectacular Scotland' is a relief map which helps to locate places of interest at the press of a button; 'The Edinburgh Show' uses back-projection techniques, music and commentary to outline the city's history.

Open: Monday to Saturday, 10.00-19.00; Sunday, 14.00-19.00

Scottish United Services Museum

Crown Square
Edinburgh Castle
Phone: (031) 226 6907

A military museum illustrating the history of the armed forces of Scotland. There are displays of uniforms, arms and equipment, decorations, portraits and a library. There is also a comprehensive collection of prints depicting the uniforms on display.

Open: April to October: Monday to Saturday, 09.30-17.00; Sunday, 11.00-17.00
November to March: Monday to Saturday, 09.30-16.00; Sunday, 12.00-16.00

Edinburgh Wax Museum

142 High Street
Phone: (031) 226 4445

The wax museum is housed in a Georgian building which was originally the New Assemblies Hall. The wax figures depict royalty, historical and media personalities, and fictional characters such as Peter Pan, Alice in Wonderland and Pooh Bear. Tableaux illustrate historical events and the waxworks are surrounded by period furnishing and realistic sound effects.

Open: April to September: Monday to Sunday, 10.00-19.00; October to March: Monday to Sunday, 10.00-17.00

Stately Homes and Town Houses

Edinburgh's status as the capital city of Scotland and seat of the Scottish monarch and court accounts for the numerous grand mansions and stately homes in the surrounding area. This section lists those which are well worth a visit, along with a selection of town houses which are of architectural or historical interest. Map references are included for houses which can be found within the area mapped at the end of this book. It is wise to telephone before setting out as opening times are variable.

Abbotsford

Melrose
Phone: (0896) 2043

Once a small farmhouse on the banks of the Tweed, Sir Walter Scott's home is now a museum to one of Scotland's favourite writers. The interior has been kept much as it was, and features as well as

paintings by Raeburn and Landseer, Scott's writing materials, his books and relics of Scottish history. (For further details see the Stately Homes article in the main body of this book.)

Open: Third Sunday in March to the end of October: Monday to Saturday, 10.00-17.00; Sunday, 14.00-17.00

Bowhill

Selkirk
Phone: (0750) 20732

Bowhill is the border home of the Duke of Buccleuch and Queensberry. The house contains the Duke's famous art collection, which includes some Elizabethan miniature paintings. There are also Nature trails, pony trekking, a gift shop and tea room.

Open: Weekdays, 12.30-17.00 Sunday, 14.00-18.00

Open Easter weekend: May, June, September open only Mondays, Wednesday, Saturdays, Sundays

July, August open daily except Friday

Dalmeny House

South Queensferry
Phone: (031) 331 1888

Only seven miles (11km) from Edinburgh, Dalmeny House is situated on the shores of the Firth of Forth, with walks through parks and woodland. It contains two fine collections; the Rosebery art collection gathered by the 3rd, 4th and 5th Earls, and the Mentmore collection of fabulous 18th-century furniture, tapestries, porcelain and paintings. (For further details see the Stately Homes article in the main body of this book.)

Open: mid April to end of September, Wednesdays and Sundays, 14.30-17.30

Also open Easter Monday and local Monday holidays

Edinburgh Castle

Castle Hill
Phone: (031) 225 9846

There has been a fortress on this site since about the 7th century. The oldest part of the present castle is the chapel built by David I and dedicated to Malcolm's queen, Margaret, in the 12th century. The Scottish crown, sceptre and sword are also kept here. (For further details see the Edinburgh Castle article in the main body of this book.)

Open: April to October: Monday to Saturday, 09.30-17.00; Sunday, 11.00-17.00

November to March: Monday to Saturday, 09.30-16.00; Sunday, 12.00-16.00

Floors Castle

Kelso
Phone: (05732) 3333

Home of the Duke of Roxburghe, and the site of the murder of James II of Scotland in 1460. William Adam helped to build this fine example of 18th-century architecture. The castle contains some porcelain, superb French and English furniture, and paintings, tapestries, and even some Gobelin. The collection of Battersea enamelled boxes is particularly worth seeing. There is also a walled garden, garden centre, gift shop and tea room.

Open: Easter weekend, then May to September. Monday to Friday, 11.00-17.30

Garden centre: Daily throughout the year, 09.30-17.00

The Georgian House

7 Charlotte Square
Phone: (031) 225 2160

The National Trust of Scotland has restored this magnificent piece of Georgian architecture in amazingly authentic detail. There are furnishings in the style of Chippendale, Sheraton and Hepplewhite, porcelain by Derby and Wedgwood, and paintings and engravings by Morland, Ramsay and Nasmyth. (For further details see the New Town article in the main body of this book.)

Open: April to October; Monday to Saturday, 10.00-17.00; Sunday, 14.00-17.00
November to December: Saturday, 10.00-16.00 Sunday, 14.00-16.30
Closed mid-December to April
Last admissions 30 minutes before closing time

Gladstone's Land

Lawnmarket
Phone: (031) 226 5856

Situated on the Royal Mile, this 17th-century house provides a contrast with the Georgian House, 7 Charlotte Square, in the New Town. Built by Thomas Gledstanes in 1620, the house was originally intended as a tenement with a separate flat on each floor. As it is now, it gives a valuable glimpse of living conditions in a medieval city.

Open: Monday to Saturday, 10.00-17.00; Sunday, 14.00-17.00

Palace of Holyroodhouse

Royal Mile
Phone: (031) 556 7371

Once a guest house, Holyroodhouse was turned into a royal palace by James IV in 1488. It is now the official residence of the Queen in the city. (For further details see the Palace of Holyroodhouse article in the main body of this book.)

Open: March to October: Monday to Saturday, 09.30-17.15; Sunday, 11.00-16.30
November to February: Monday to Saturday, 09.30-15.45

Hopetoun House

South Queensferry
Phone: (031) 331 2451

The magnificent home of the Marquis of Linlithgow, originally designed by Sir William Bruce, but completed by William Adam and his sons, Robert and John, the latter two being principally responsible for the interior decoration. The surrounding 100 acres (40.4 ha) contain deer, peacocks, St. Kilda sheep, a nature trail and picnic areas. (For further details see the Stately Homes article in the main body of this book.)

Open: From Easter to third Monday in September; Sunday, 11.00-17.30

Huntly House

142 Canongate
Phone: (031) 225 1131

Huntly House is a good example of a restored 16th-century town house. A number of the rooms have been decorated to show the changing life-style at various periods in the history of the house. The 17th-century room, for example, shows the elegance of a fairly well-off merchant, and the late 19th-century is recreated with a 'working class kitchen'. There is a collection of Edinburgh silver and glass dating from the 17th century onwards, Scottish pottery excavated from the Roman fort at Cramond and two rooms displaying relics of the World War I Field Marshal Earl Haig.

Open: June to September: Monday to Saturday, 10.00-18.00
Rest of the Year: Monday to Saturday, 10.00-17.00

John Knox's House

45 High Street
Phone: (031) 556 6961

John Knox, the leader of the Protestant Reformation in Scotland, lived here in one of the most ancient dwelling houses in the city. On display are a number of pictures and lithographs of Knox, usually in the act of pulpit-thumping. There are also letters, documents and early editions of his tracts and sermons, including the famous pamphlet *The First Blast of the Trumpet against the Monstrous Regiment of Women.*

Open: April to October: Monday to Saturday, 10.00-17.00
November to March: Weekdays, 10.00-16.00

Lady Stair's House

Lady Stair's Close
Lawnmarket
Phone: (031) 225 1131

This solid 17th-century town house contains relics of Robert Burns, Sir Walter Scott and Robert Louis Stevenson. These include the original manuscript of Burns's *Scots Wha ha'e,* locks of hair, knives, quill pens, snuff boxes and umbrellas. The most interesting exhibits are the portraits, including one of Stevenson by Girolamo Nerli.

Open: June to September: Monday to Saturday, 10.00-18.00
Rest of the Year 10.00-17.00

Lauriston Castle

Cramond Road South
Phone: (031) 336 2060

A fine mansion with beautiful grounds overlooking the Firth of Forth, this was once the home of William Robert Reid, a cabinet-maker and collector of objets d'art. A late 16th-century tower house has been incorporated in a Jacobean-style house built in the early 19th-century. Decorated by Reid in the early years of this century, it presents a prosperous Edwardian interior with mostly 18th-century English and European furniture, including a set of Chippendale dining chairs. Among the objets d'art are Reid's collection of ornaments in Derbyshire fluorspar, wool mosaic pictures, and tapestries.
Open: Monday to Sunday, 11.00-13.00, 14.00-17.00
April to October: closed Fridays
November to March: Saturday and Sunday, 14.00-16.00

Manderston

Duns
Berwickshire
Phone: (03612) 3450

A fine Edwardian country house surrounded by formal gardens and woodland park. As well as period furnishings in luxurious surroundings there is a marble dairy, stables and a lake. Gift shop and cream teas available.
Open: Any day by appointment for parties of 20 or more
Mid-May to mid-September: Thursday and Sunday, 14.00-17.30

Mellerstain House

Gordon
Berwickshire
Phone: (057381) 225

One of the most beautiful Georgian houses in Scotland, designed and built by William and Robert Adam. The interior is decorated with their fine plasterwork and pastel colours. There are paintings by the Old Masters (Gainsborough, van Dyck, Ramsay and Raeburn), an outstanding collection of 18th-century furniture, and a library still with its original decoration. Other attractions include the terraced gardens, lake, gift shop and tea rooms
Open: Monday to Sunday, 13.30-17.30
Closed Saturday, May to October

Stirling Castle

Stirling
Phone: (0786) 62421

A thousand-year-old castle where great battles of the Wars of Independence were fought by such Scottish heroes as William Wallace and Robert the Bruce. A multi-vision show with narration gives historic facts and details of the people associated with the castle – among them Mary, Queen of Scots and her son James VI and I, who was crowned here. The walled old town also has many historic buildings.
Open: May to September: Monday to Friday, 09.30-18.00; Saturday and Sunday, 11.00-18.00
October to April: Monday to Friday, 09.30-17.05; Saturday and Sunday, 12.30-16.20

Traquair House

Innerleithen
Peeblesshire
Phone: (0896) 830323

Twenty-eight miles (45 km) south of the city, Traquair is the oldest inhabited house in Scotland, dating back to *circa* AD950. The Stuart family has lived there since 1491 and entertained many tragic figures including Mary, Queen of Scots and Bonnie Prince Charlie. There is a working brewery, craft workshops, a nature trail and a chapel. (For further details see the Stately Homes article in the main body of this book.)

Open: Easter to mid-October: Monday to Sunday, 13.30-17.30
July to end of August: Monday to Sunday, 10.30-17.30

Other Places of Interest

The Camera Obscura and Outlook Tower

Castle Hill
Phone: (031) 226 3709

Installed in the 1850s in the Outlook Tower on Castle Hill, the camera obscura throws a clear image of Edinburgh onto a white, concave table top.
Remaining floors have exhibition of holography, pin-hole photography and space photography.

Open: April to September: Monday to Saturday, 09.30-17.30; Sunday, 10.00-18.00
October to March: Monday to Saturday, 09.30-16.00; Sunday, 10.00-16.00

Edinburgh Zoological Park

134 Corstorphine Road
Phone: (031) 334 9171

Dogs are not admitted. You will need at least half a day to see around the 80 acres (32 ha) of woodland and parkland at the Scottish National Zoological Park, Edinburgh. The animals are displayed sympathetically and the zoo's policy is to emphasize the educational aspects of a zoological garden but not at the expense of entertainment value. Don't miss the splendid collection of penguins. Facilities for the elderly, invalids, and the handicapped are available. (For further details see the Edinburgh Zoological Park article in the main body of this book.)

Open: April to October: Monday to Saturday, 09.00-18.00; Sunday, 09.30-18.00
November to March: Monday to Saturday, 09.00-16.30; Sunday, 09.30-16.30

Royal Botanic Garden

Inverleith Row
Phone: (031) 552 7171

Established as a Physic Garden in 1670, this is the second largest botanic garden in Britain. A scientific establishment, it is also famous for its collection of rhododendrons. The gardens and plant houses cover 70 acres (28 ha) and are only ten minutes from the city centre.
Invalid chairs are available. Dogs not admitted. (For further details see the Royal Botanic Garden article in the main body of this book.)

Open: Garden: Monday to Saturday, 09.00-sunset; Sunday, 10.00-sunset
During the Festival, 10.00-sunset
Closing time 1 hour before sunset during British Summer Time
March 22 to October 25
Closed 1 January
Plant houses and Exhibition hall: Monday to Saturday, 10.00-17.00; Sunday, 11.00-17.00

The Herbarium and Library are not open to the public. Researchers should apply in writing to the Regius Keeper

Section III – Culture and Entertainment

**The Edinburgh Festival
The Festival is always held for three weeks in August. Details are available from April onwards and throughout the Festival from:
The Festival Society
21 Market Street
Phone: (031) 226 4001**

Concert Halls and Theatres

The visitor to Edinburgh can normally rely on finding an opera, concert, ballet or play that is to his taste. During the hectic August and September weeks of the Edinburgh Festival the range of choices is overwhelming, but throughout the year there is an ever-changing cultural programme on offer at the concert halls and theatres listed below. Ring the Edinburgh Bookshop (031) 225 4296, which acts as booking agency for many halls; contact individual box offices at the venues; check the advertisements in The Scotsman and Evening News or ask at your hotel for details of the current programme.

The box office at the Usher Hall (10 1C) Lothian Road, phone: (031) 228 1155, will provide details of the special lunchtime and evening concerts that groups such as the Edinburgh Quartet and the Scottish Baroque Ensemble put on at country houses and churches in and around Edinburgh.

Standards of performance obviously vary with each company and are outside the scope of these reviews. However, visitors can use these reviews to identify the best seats, and get an impression of the acoustics and ambience of each hall.

Churchill Theatre

33a Morningside Road

A municipally owned theatre that presents amateur productions for most of the year, but is used by professional companies during the Festival.
Events: Amateur production of plays and operas by companies of variable ability.
Tickets: Box office at the theatre, phone (031) 447 7597
Edinburgh Bookshop, 57 George Street, phone: (031) 225 4296
During the Festival, 21 Market Street, phone: (031) 226 4001.
J. & A. Cruikshank, 62 Morningside Road, (opposite theatre).

Freemasons Hall

96 George Street

At one time Edinburgh's main recital hall, with 600 seats, the Freemasons Hall has become less popular in recent years.
Events: Recitals and chamber concerts, mainly during the Festival
Tickets: Box office only at the Edinburgh Bookshop, 57 George Street, phone: (031) 225 4296.
During the Festival, 21 Market Street, phone: (031) 226 4001

French Institute

13 Randolph Crescent

France's cultural headquarters in Scotland with seating for around 100 people and breathtaking views across the Dean Valley.
Events: Concerts, plays, film shows and exhibitions are presented in the first-floor salon; teaching facilities and a library are also available
Tickets: Box office at the Institute, phone: (031) 225 5366

George Square Theatre

south side of George Square

A modern auditorium with 334 seats, owned by Edinburgh University.
Events: Plays, university opera productions and occasional concerts
Tickets: Box office at the door before the performance Edinburgh Bookshop, 57 George Street, phone: (031) 225 4296

King's Theatre

*Tollcross
Leven Street*

Edinburgh's 'Festspielhaus' was formerly owned by Howard & Wyndham, but is now the property of the city. A handsome, decorative Victorian theatre, which formerly had 1650 seats—the number has been reduced by the brutal insertion of an ugly lighting switchboard at the back of the stalls and a crudely-extended orchestra pit. King's Theatre is used for international opera during the Festival, but is otherwise over-dependent on second rate repertory companies.
Events: Ballet, drama, light opera, opera, pantomime, touring productions, variety
Tickets: Box office in the theatre, phone: (031) 229 1201
During the Festival, 21 Market Street, phone: (031) 226 4001

Leith Theatre

28 Ferry Road

Once Leith Town Hall, this cavernous 1442-seat theatre presents amateur opera.
Events: Amateur opera, the odd pantomime
Tickets: Box office at the door before the performance, phone: (031) 554 1408
Edinburgh Bookshop, 57 George Street, phone: (031) 225 4296

McEwan Hall

Teviot Row, off Teviot Place

A familiar circular landmark in Bristol Street, McEwan Hall is the ceremonial hall of Edinburgh University.
Events: Apart from university ceremonies the hall is used for choral concerts, carol concerts, and organ recitals
Tickets: Box office at the door before the performance, phone: (031) 667 1011 ext. 4343
Edinburgh Bookshop, 57 George Street, phone: (031) 225 4296

Music Hall

54 George Street

Linked to the Assembly Rooms in George Street, the Music Hall has 1178 seats and is municipally owned

Events: Occasional recitals and chamber concerts. The hall is also used by amateur symphony orchestras, such as the Scottish Sinfonia, and by drama groups during the Edinburgh Festival

Tickets: Box office at the door before the performance, phone: (031) 225 3614
Edinburgh Bookshop, 57 George Street, phone: (031) 225 4296

Nelson Hall

2–8 McDonald Road

An annexe of the McDonald Road Public Library, that holds between one and two hundred people.

Events: Concerts at the Nelson Hall are, by a long established Edinburgh tradition, free. Joan and Hester Dickson, the cellist and pianist, organize monthly chamber concerts and recitals by various performers during the winter season.

Tickets: Box office at the door before the performance, phone: (031) 556 5630
From any public library

Playhouse Theatre

20 Greenside Place

A multi-purpose auditorium with 3500 seats that was famed in its day as the city's largest cinema—a stage and dressing rooms prove that it once has theatrical aspirations. In 1980 the building was renovated by the Playhouse Society for the Scottish Opera, the Scottish Ballet and anyone else who cares to use it, including rock groups. Between live shows the auditorium is still used as a cinema, and upstairs a small night-club provides a platform for jazz groups and other more specialized performers.

Events: The Scottish Opera hold short seasons several times a year, and concerts are presented by groups as large as the Scottish National Orchestra (SNO) and as small as the Scottish Baroque Ensemble

Tickets: Box office, 20 Greenside Place (4 3D), adjoining the theatre, phone: (031) 557 2590

Queen's Hall

89 Clerk Street

Edinburgh's best, most active and inviting concert hall, with a maximum of 800 seats (if restricted-view seats are used). Set in a renovated Georgian church, it is the home of the Scottish Chamber Orchestra (SCO) and Scottish Baroque Ensemble (SBE)

Events: Regular concerts are given by the SCO and SBE throughout the winter season. The SCO play mid-week and Saturday evening programmes, with conductors including Roderick Brydon (artistic director) and Raymond Leppard (principal guest conductor), with star soloists in concertos, and a repertoire ranging from Bach to modern music. The SBE, directed by the violinist Leonard Friedman, perform a wide repertoire of music for strings, usually mid-week. There are regular Wednesday lunchtime recitals with guest soloists, organised by the SBE. Lunch can be eaten in the auditorium itself, or in the adjoining bar. The hall is also hired to other groups such as the Edinburgh Bach Choir, the Meadows Chamber Orchestra and the New Music Group of Scotland, who appear there from time to time. Jazz concerts, lectures and workshop sessions are also given. The Hall has already become a major asset to the Festival, and the long bar is sometimes used for specialised small-scale concerts.

Tickets: Box office in the Hall, phone (031) 668 2019
Edinburgh Bookshop, 57 George Street, phone (031) 225 4296
During the Festival, 21 Market Street, phone (031) 226 4001

Reid Concert Hall

McEwan Hall,
Teviot Row, off Teviot Place

A lofty university hall with 310 seats, that was formerly known as the Reid School of Music.

Events: Much used for chamber music, recitals, programmes of choral music, student concerts and fringe events during the Festival. Though some performers have moved away to the Queen's Hall, the Reid remains a thriving, busy

place, with university concerts on most Thursday evenings between autumn and early summer; the hall is also let out to independent concert promoters

Tickets: Box office at the door, phone: (031) 667 1011 ext. 4577
The Edinburgh Bookshop, 57 George Street, phone: (031) 225 4296 for some events

Royal Lyceum Theatre

middle of Lothian Road
next to Usher Hall
Grindley Street

Edinburgh's main playhouse the 1200-seat Royal Lyceum is the home of the Lyceum Theatre Company. Apart from plays, there are occasional opera performances – Thea Musgrave's 'Voice of Ariadne' can be heard in a production by the Cologne Opera Studio at the 1981 Edinburgh Festival

Events: Drama performed by the resident repertory company; varied performances during the Festival

Tickets: Box office in the theatre, phone: (031) 229 9697. During the Festival, 21 Market Street, phone: (031) 226 4001

St. Cecilia's Hall

Cowgate

Edinburgh's original Georgian concert hall is now owned by the university, and has been renovated both as a concert hall and a home for the world-famous Russell Collection of harpsichords. But it is more than a museum; it is a 250-seat concert hall where these instruments are put to practical use, forming an ideal setting for the university's annual summer festival, 'Bach at St. Cecilia's Hall'.

Events: Chamber concerts and recitals, including a winter season by the Georgian Concert Society

Tickets: Seats bookable at the door before the performance, phone: (031) 667 1011 ext. 4415
Edinburgh Bookshop, 57 George Street, phone: (031) 225 4296
During the Festival, 21 Market Street, phone: (031) 226 4001

St. Mary's Episcopal Church

Palmerston Place

This lofty Anglican church was completed in 1917; it towers over Palmerston Place

Events: The cathedral choir gives concerts throughout the year, as do visiting choirs. In addition, there are organ recitals and occasional operatic performances e.g. Britten's three church parables, and Peter Maxwell Davies' 'Jongleur de Nôtre Dame', all staged during the Festival

Tickets: Box office at the door before the performance, phone: (031) 225 6293
Edinburgh Bookshop, 57 George Street, phone: (031) 225 4296

Usher Hall

Lothian Road

Edinburgh's principal large-scale concert hall, with 2780 seats, is owned by the city and hired out to those who wish to use it – mainly the Scottish National Orchestra during the winter season and a variety of artistes during the Festival

Events: Weekly concerts by the Scottish National Orchestra on Friday evenings between October and April – principal conductor Sir Alexander Gibson; principal guest conductor Paavo Berglund

Tickets: Box office inside the hall, phone: (031) 228 1155
Edinburgh Bookshop, 57 George Street, phone: (031) 225 4296
During the Festival, 21 Market Street, phone: (031) 226 4001

Scottish Evenings

These entertainments, which usually include dinner and a 'Scots Cabaret', are designed for those visitors to Edinburgh who do not have friends or relations in the city to show them a more authentic Scottish night out. They represent the popular image of a Scottish evening rather than the actuality – nevertheless, many find them thoroughly enjoyable, and the emphasis on the ghosts of Harry Lauder and Robert Burns and the steaming haggis make it necessary to book well ahead. Several of the venues at which a 'Scottish Evening' can be experienced are listed below.

Jamie's Scottish Night Out

King James Hotel
St. James Centre
Phone: (031) 556 0111

A slick, well-run show hosted by Larry Marshall, a veteran of the live audience. Dinner takes up the first hour, with a versatile Scottish dance-band in attendance, and the cabaret, with audience-participation, follows. Halfway through the evening there is a compulsory taste of haggis, and Burns's famous toast.

Scottish cabaret; five-course banquet; haggis supper.

May to October: Monday to Friday, and Sunday. 6.45pm-10.00pm. Price £23.00 per head.

Dalhousie Jacobean Banquet

Dalhousie Courte
Bonnyrigg (8 miles/13 km southwest of Edinburgh)
Phone: (031) 663 5155

The Jacobean Banquet at Dalhousie is markedly different from the other Scottish evenings. The setting is the year 1623 – guests sit at long trestle tables and the entire five-course meal is eaten with the fingers and small knife. Wine and mead flow freely and is served by 'court ladies', splendidly attired in the dress of the period. During and after the meal, these ladies sing from a well-chosen repertoire of contemporary music.

Jacobean banquet, with entertainment.

Monday to Saturday, 19.30-23.30. Price £20.00 per head, free transport available from and to city centre (bus leaves Edinburgh 18.45) – details on booking.

Region and City Maps

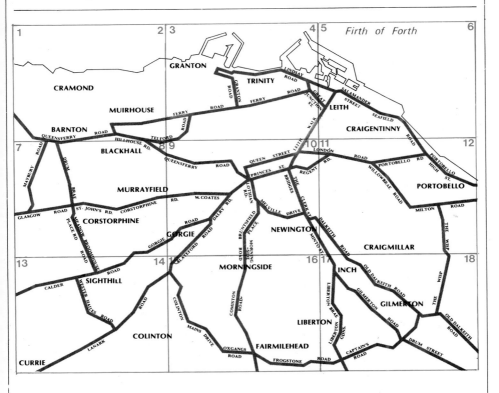

The New Edinburgh Bypass road is presently under construction. The section from Fairmilehead to Corstorphine (not shown in these maps) has just been opened. A new road from Milton Road to the A1, bypassing Musselburgh, has also just been opened (1987).

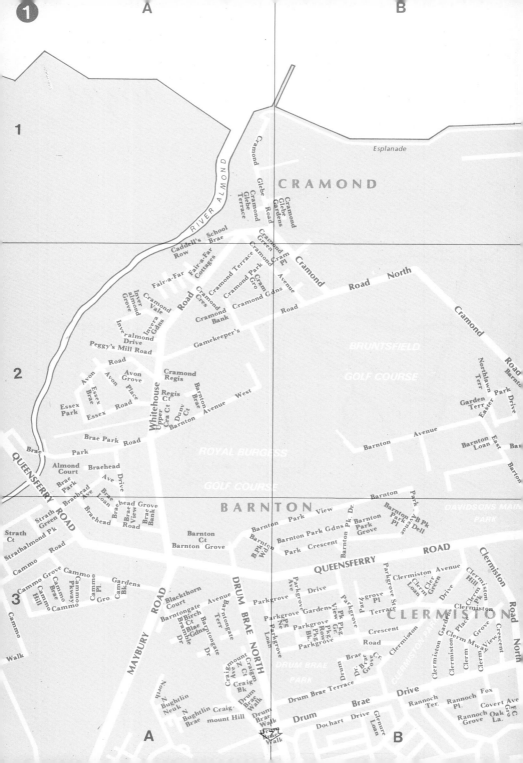

1

A   B

1

RIVER ALMOND

Esplanade

CRAMOND

Cramond Glebe Road
Cramond Glebe Gardens
Cramond Glebe Terrace
Cramond Green

Cram Pl
Cramond Green

Cram Gro
Cram Cres

Caddell's Row
School Brae

Fair-a-Far
Fair-a-Far Cottages

Cramond Terrace
Cramond Park

Cramond Avenue

Cramond Road North

Cramond Road

Fair-a-Far

Inveralmond Grove
Cramond Vale
Invera Gdns

Cramond Gdns
Cramond Cres
Cramond Bank

Cramond Gdns

Cramond Road

Inveralmond Drive

Peggy's Mill Road

Gamekeeper's

2

Road

Avon Road
Avon Grove

Cramond Regis

BRUNTSFIELD GOLF COURSE

Norhlawn Terr
Garden Terrace
Easter Park Drive

Avon Road
Avon Brae
Essex Brae
Essex Park
Essex

Cramond Regis
Regis Ct

Cra Ct
Duny Ct
Barnton Brae
Barnton Avenue West

Barnton Loan East

Barnton

Whitehouse Road
Upper

Barnton

Brae Park Road

Brae Park

Barnton Avenue

Barnton Loan

Brae Park

Almond Court
Braehead
Brae Park
Ave
Brae Roan
Drive

ROYAL BURGESS GOLF COURSE

Queensferry Road

Braehead Ave
Braehead
Braehead Grove
Brae Bank
Braehead Road

Barnton

Barnton Park View

B A R N T O N

DAVIDSONS MAINS PARK

Strath Green
Strath Ct
Strathalmond Pk

QUEENSFERRY ROAD

Road

Cammo

Barnton Park View
Barnton Park Gdns Dr.
Barnton Ct
Barnton Grove

Barnton Pk Dr.
Barnton Park Crescent

Barnton Pk.
Barnton Park Grove

Barnton YB Pk Pl
Park Dell

3

Cammo Grove
Cammo Brae
Cammo Hill
Cammo

Cammo Pl.
Cammo Gro

Gardens Bk

Blackthorn Court
Barntongate Terr
Barntongate Dr.

Birch Brae
Bramble Gdns
Barntongate Dr

Avenue

Parkgrove Ave
Parkgrove Gardens
Parkgrove

Parkgrove Drive

Parkgrove Pl
Parkgrove Terrace

QUEENSFERRY ROAD

Clermiston Avenue
Clerm
Clr Green

Clermiston Hill
Clermiston Loan Drive

Clermiston Rd
Clermiston Grove

CLERMISTON

Cammo Walk

MAYBURY ROAD

DRUM BRAE NORTH

Craigmount Ave
Craigmount Ave Z
Craig Ct
Drum Bk
Brae Walk
Craigmount Hill
Drum Brae Walk

Parkgrove Cr
Pkg Pl
Pkg Nk
Pkg Gdn
Pkg Rd
Parkgrove Bk

Parkgrove Road

Crescent

Road

Brae Cr
Brae Gro
Dr

Clermiston Place
Clermiston Gardens
Clermiston Medway
Clerm Grove
Rannoch

Clermiston Road North

DRUM BRAE PARK

Bughtlin Neuk
Bughtlin Craig
N Brae
mount Hill

Drum Brae Terrace

Drum Brae

Dochart Drive

Drive

Glenure Loan

Rannoch Ter.
Rannoch Pl.
Rannoch Grove
Oak La.

Covert Ave
Fox Gro

Walk

A   B

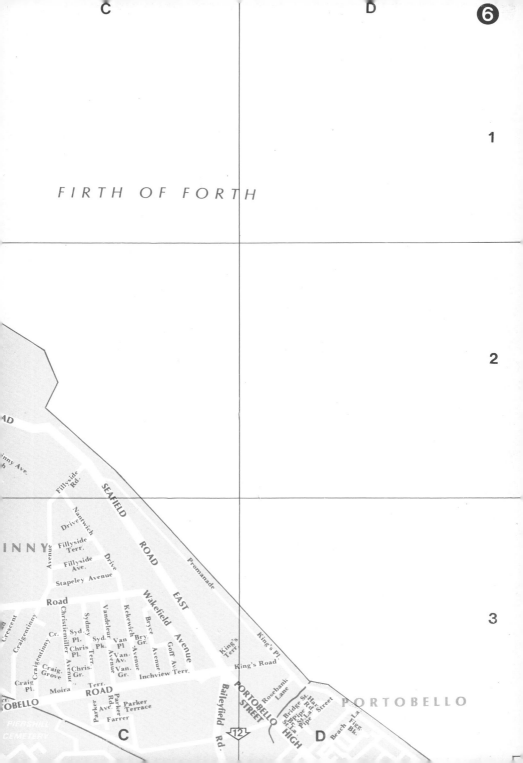

C   D   ⓺

1

FIRTH OF FORTH

2

AD

nny Ave.

Fillyside Rd.

SEAFIELD

Nantwich Drive

INNY Fillyside Terr.

Avenue

Fillyside Ave.

Drive

ROAD

EAST

Promanade

Stapeley Avenue

Road

Wakefield Avenue

Crescent

Craigentinny

Christiemiller Avenue

Christiemiller Cr.

Craigentinny Grove

Syd. Pl.

Chris. Pl.

Sydney Terr.

Syd. Pk.

Vandeleur Avenue

Kekewich Avenue

Bryce Avenue

Van Pl

Van. Av.

Van. Gr.

Bry. Gr.

Golf Av.

3

Inchview Terr.

King's Terr.

King's Pl.

King's Terr.

Craig. Grove

Chris. Gr.

Craig Pl.

Moira Terr.

ROAD

Parker Rd.

Parker Ave.

Parker Terrace

King's Road

Rosebank Lane

Bridge St

Harl St

Pipe La.

Pipe St.

Pipe La.

Pipe Street

PORTOBELLO

Farrer

OBELLO

PIERSHILL CEMETERY

C

Baileyfield Rd.

⟨12⟩

PORTOBELLO STREET

HIGH

D

Beach La.

Figg Blk.

13

A   7   B

SIGHTHILL PARK

Bro

Brhouse Path

BROOMHOUSE RD

Brho

1

Bankhead Broadway

Bankhead Broadway

Bankhead Crossway North

Bankhead Broadway

Bankhead Medway Terrace

Bankhead Crossway South

Bankhead Place

Bankhead Avenue

Loan

Cultins Road

Bankhead Drive

Bankhead Way

Bankhead Street

Sighthill Bank

S. Wynd

Sighthill Ct.

Sighthill Green

Sighthill

SIGHTHILL

Bankhead Drive

CALDER ROAD

Calder View Gardens

Calder

Calder Place

Calder Cres.

Calder Park

Court Gardens

Calder Gardens

Calder Drive

Neuk

Sighthill Place

Sighthill Road

WESTER Sighthill Street

Sighthill View

Sighthill Rise

Sighthill Terrace

Sighthill Gardens

Cres.

Dr

Murray

Murrayburn

Calder Grove

Murrayburn

HAILES

Mburn App.

Mburn Drive

Murrayburn

Hailesla

Murrayburn Gate

Pl. Place

Union Canal

Westburn Gdns.

Westburn Ave.

ROAD

Park

West

2

Riccarton Mains

Road

Grove

WESTER

Wester Hailes Dr.

WESTER

Brae Rise Lea

Baberton Mains Way

Dell Hill

B.M. Gardens

Baberton

B.M. Terrace

Mains

B.M.

Way

B.M. Wood

Grove

B.M. Park

Drive

Place

B.M.

BABERTON

Baberton Cres.

Row

BABERTON

Mains

Drive

B

GOLF COURSE

Bank Wynd Green

Ct.

Baberton Cres.

Foulis

3

JUNIPER GREEN

Juniper Pk Road

Juniper Gro

Belmont Rd

Juniper Terr.

Juniper Av.

Woodhall Terr.

Baberton Gro

Woodhall Rd

Baberton Av.

Woodhall Drive

Woodhall Ave.

Pk.

Baberton

LANARK

Baberton Loan

Nether Currie Crescent

Road

Muirwood Pl.

Muirwood Road

Knowe Crescent

Muirwood Pl.

Nether M'wood Gro

Crescent Drive

Corslet Rd.

Pl.

Thomson Pl.

Nether Currie Rd.

Thomson Drive

CURRIE

Riccarton Dr.

Riccarton Avenue

Bryce Pl.

Corslet Cres.

Thomson Crescent

Thomson Road

Water of Leith

F View Cres

Palmer Road

Curriehill Road

Riccarton Mains

Grove

Bryce Cres.

E. Currie Cres.

E. Currie Terr.

LANARK ROAD WEST

Blinkbonny Road

Forth View Cres

Palmer Pl.

Pentl Pl

A   B

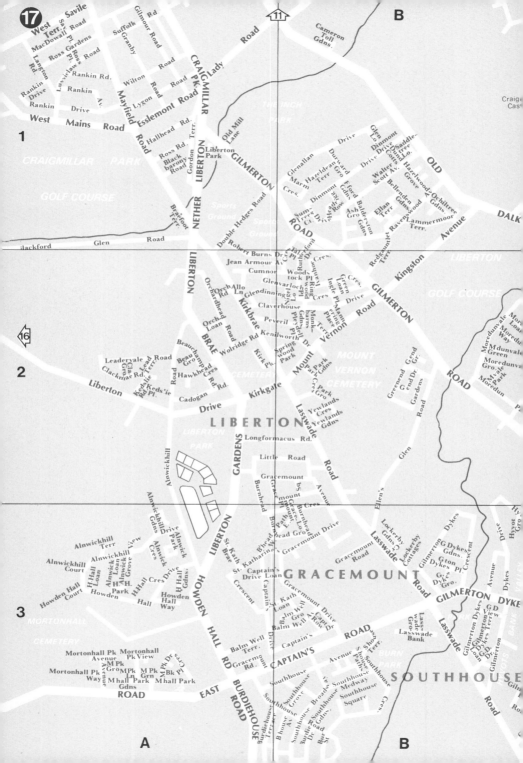

C

D

NIDDRIE
POLICIES

12

Greendykes Terr.
Niddrie
Ave.
Niddrie
House
Gardens
Wauchope House
Greendykes
House
Greendykes
Loan
Greendykes
Gdns
Greendykes
Road
Ho.
Road

Craigmillar
Castle
Road

Niddrie Burn

The Wisp

Cauldcoats Road

Millerhill
Road

Shawfair
Road

1

ROAD

The Wisp

DANDERHALL

Edmonstone
A. View
Cres.
Woolmet Cres
Arthur
View
Woolmet
The Cir
Arthur View
Cres.
Arthur View
Ave.
Forth View
Terr.
Drum View
Cres.
Edmonstone Terr.
Smithy Green Av.
Newton Church
Cres.
Danderhall
Cres.
Edmonstone
Road
Church Rd
Edmonstone
Dr.
Newton Church
Road
Campview
Campview
Cres
Cviewpl
Campview
Terr.
Wadsford Av.
Campview
Gdns
Cview
Grove
Campview Terr.

2

Craigour
Pl.
Craigour
Green
Avenue
Craigour
Drive
Craigour Terrace
Cgour.
Loan
Cgour
Cres
Terr.
Cgour.
Cres
Cgour.
Cgour. Gdns
Fernieside Drive
Fernieside Ave.
Fernieside
Park
Fernieside
Gardens
Fernieside
Road
Crescent
Fernieside
Grove

MOREDUN

Moredunvale
Moredunvale
Mdun.
Pk.Loan
Moredun
Pk Way
Moredun
Park Ave
GILMERTON PARK
Moredun
Pk Green
Mdun
Pk Green
Park St
Park Street

OLD

DALKEITH

FERNIEHILL

DRIVE

Moredun
Gardens
Mdun
Way
Mdun
Pk View
Mdun
Pk
Gro
Fhill View
Street
Fhill Terr
Fhill Sq
Ferniehill
Ave
Fhill
Pl.
Fhill
Ferniehill
Grove
Ferniehill
Gdns
DrumDrum
Drum Ave.
Drum
Cres

GILMERTON ROAD

YVOTS
BANK

NEWTOFT ST.

DRUM

GILMERTON

HYVOTS
BANK ROAD

Moredun
Hyvot
Gdns
Dykes
Avenue
Hyvot
Pk
Hyvot's Bank
Haw
Place
St. Place Street

STREET

Drum
Cottages

Ravenscroft
Place
Ravenscroft
Gardens

HYVOT
DR.

Hyvot
Ct.
Hyvot
View
Hyvot
Road
Dykes
Road

Station
Road

GILMERTON

ROAD

3

ROAD

C

D

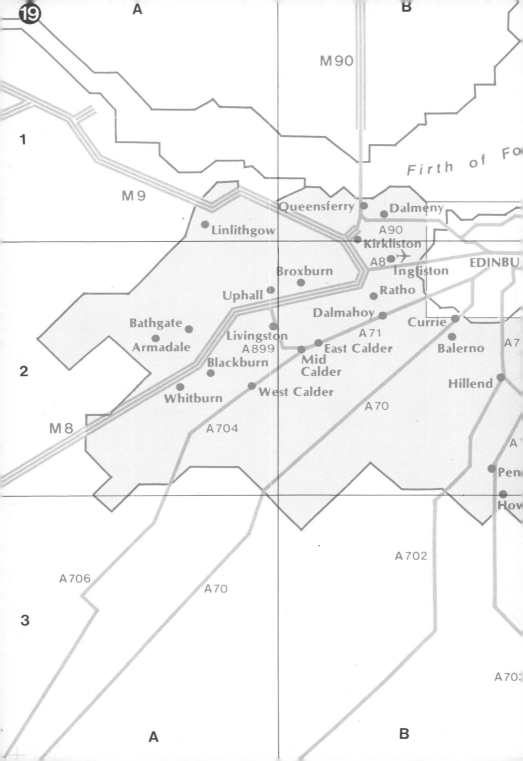

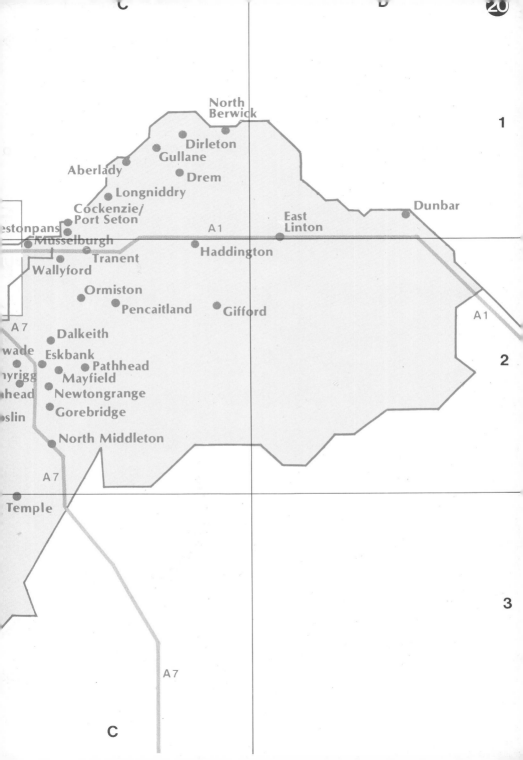

PICTURE CREDITS

By courtesy of Edinburgh City Libraries, the Edinburgh Room
pp 14, 22, 31, 38, 92-93, 95, 100-101, 168, 197
George Dalgleish p 121
The Festival Society pp 85, 189
Lady Stair's House Museum p 24
Lord Chamberlain's Office pp 74, 78-79, 80-81, 82-83
Reproduced by Gracious Permission of
Her Majesty The Queen
Photographs by courtesy of Royal Botanic Garden, Edinburgh
pp 163, 170-171
Graham Falconer, Crown copyright. Royal Commission on
Ancient Monuments, Scotland pp 44-45, 46-47, 48-49,
50-51, 94-95
Royal Scottish Museum pp 150-151, 153
Scottish Tourist Board pp 75, 190-191, 192-193, 194-195
Quarto Publishers p 228